PATTERNS OF PERSON

FRENCH FORUM MONOGRAPHS

41

Editors R.C. LA CHARITÉ and V.A. LA CHARITÉ

For complete listing, see page 179

PATTERNS OF PERSON
STUDIES IN STYLE AND FORM
FROM CORNEILLE TO LACLOS

EDWARD C. KNOX

FRENCH FORUM, PUBLISHERS
LEXINGTON, KENTUCKY

Copyright © 1983 by French Forum, Publishers, Incorporated, P.O. Box 5108, Lexington, Kentucky 40505.

All rights reserved, including the right to reproduce this book, or parts thereof, in any form, except for the inclusion of brief quotations in reviews.

Library of Congress Catalog Card Number 82-82430

ISBN 0-917058-40-2

Printed in the United States of America

To Roger M. Peel

ACKNOWLEDGEMENTS

All of the essays included here were written or revised while on a grant from the National Endowment for the Humanities, without whose moral and financial support my ideas would surely never have seen their present form. Earlier versions on La Bruyère and *Les Liaisons dangereuses* appeared in a monograph by Twayne Publishers and in *L'Esprit Créateur* respectively, and my thanks go to their editors for permission to incorporate them here in revised form.

In a more personal vein I remain deeply appreciative to Philip Berk, Georges May and especially Peter Brooks for advice and encouragement when it counted most. Jean Peytard, Philippe Lejeune, Pierre Kuentz and Philippe Hamon all shared their wisdom willingly and abundantly in what must have seemed a deplorable lack of context, and I am pleased to salute here such friendly temerity. Thanks go as well to two anonymous readers for *PMLA*.

Without long-distance logistical and intellectual *dépannage* by Carol de Dobay Rifelj and Nancy Myers O'Connor things would have proven more complicated even than they were, and I prefer simply not to envision the situation had I not had the help of Nancy Johnson and Janet Beers in preparing the manuscript.

Most of all, I am grateful for the patience and forebearance of my family: to the boys, for reminding me I could and should be about people while working on the person; and to Huguette, who knowing why not still understands why.

CONTENTS

ACKNOWLEDGEMENTS 7

INTRODUCTION 11

Syntax in the Person

I. PERSON, PERSONIFICATION AND 19
CLEOPATRE'S "GRANDEUR" IN *RODOGUNE*

II. APPOSITION AND IDENTIFICATION IN *PHEDRE* 36

III. LA BRUYERE'S *CARACTERE* AS A PATTERN 59
OF PERSON

IV. ACCUMULATION AND "DEDOMMAGEMENT" 73
IN *LES REVERIES DU PROMENEUR SOLITAIRE*

Person in Syntax

V. EPITHET, CHARACTER AND STRUCTURE 86
IN *LES LIAISONS DANGEREUSES*

VI. DISTINCTION, REPLICATION AND THE SELF 103
IN *LE JEU DE L'AMOUR ET DU HASARD*

VII. SPEECH AND AUTONOMY IN *LA PRINCESSE DE CLEVES*		120
CONCLUDING NOTE ON THE PERSON OF THE READER		132
NOTES		145
BIBLIOGRAPHY		163

INTRODUCTION

The studies in this volume proceed from what is at base a Spitzerian formalism, concerned with the relationships and interdeterminations between a *fait de style* and the literary work as a whole, and particularly with seeking out the formal and stylistic dimensions of the notion of "person" as a center of convergence in a given work.[1] It should become clear, however, that style and form have a life of their own, that at the very least the elucidation of the textual person is not simply a one-way, deductive process of verification and confirmation, be it of a conceptual intuition or of a putative external referent.[2]

"Person" as I use it here will designate a linguistic construct, the textual person in the same way we speak of grammatical persons, rather than a return to an earlier, referential type of reading.[3] While less radical than approaches predicated on the disappearance of the subject and on texts where only *ça parle*, such a focus remains heuristically appropriate and useful in dealing with literature for which person, identity and even personal essence form an integral part of the social and intellectual ethos. Moreover, the notion of textual person provides a more circumspect approach than does character to non-narrative and non-dramatic texts such as *Les Caractères* and *Les Rêveries du promeneur solitaire*, an important generic and methodological consideration for the period under study as well as for the breadth and applicability of one's results.

By "pattern" I mean to designate an arrangement of elements which is regular and recurrent, and so must be elucidated in both the temporal and spatial dimensions of a text. My use of the term is comparable to those occasions described by Michaël Riffaterre where a stylistic device occurs so frequently as to join the context, "des cas où le procédé stylistique est un *tic* de l'auteur (dans ce cas une forme donnée est facile à remarquer et surprenante parce qu'elle est récurrente dans un contexte donné—sémantique ou situationnel—contexte dans lequel son conditionnement est d'ordre psychologique)."[4] In my case as compared to both Spitzer and Riffaterre, however, it will be a question of a "tic" of the textual person rather than of the writer. (Rousseau is an exception, but even in his case we shall see how the writer and the textual person are strongly aligned.) Stated another way, the stylistic devices and effects to be examined here represent the "figure" rather than the "ground" (hence my liminary chapter on the foregrounding of "Cléopâtre"), although it bears repeating that the person as I define it is a textual design rather than a copy from life, and that however anthropomorphic the "figure" is nonetheless in the carpet.[5] Finally, I use "pattern" to underscore the fact that it is as important and valid to consider the structure or "syntax" of textual figures, as their physical description or semantic "thickness." The main theoretical contribution of what follows is thus elucidation of the person-text as an effect not only of attributive substance, but also of syntax and rhetoric as *forme-sens*, a syntactic event.

Such an approach falls under Hamon's "signifiant du personnage" category (pp. 96-97), which is notably shorter than the corresponding section on the signified. The only studies to take this approach head-on of which I was aware when I began were those of Auerbach and Starobinski on Montaigne and Spitzer on Diderot; and there are still few enough to warrant exploring the possibility that syntax may qualify or "mark" the person as fully and significantly as semic composition or actantial situation. Moreover, while most critics would continue to agree that character, at least in the classic, "readerly" canon, remains a major element of textual organization and coherence, by the same token the danger of "fetishization" of character (Cixous, p. 385), of yielding more or less uncritically to the anthropomorphic, pseudo-referential and/or ideological nature of the textual person remains even now quite real. I have attempted to examine one case of overpersonalized criticism in my final chapter, but in all I analyze the extent to which person partakes of unmotivated, primarily "impersonal" syntactic materials, and how those materials serve as moments or sites (*instances*) in the elaboration of

INTRODUCTION

the person as "something constructed by conventions as arbitrary as any other" (Price, p. 293).

At the level of the work, person or character may thus be the "fil conducteur permettant de s'orienter" (Tomachevski, p. 293), but I am equally concerned, at the level of person, with following "a linguistic thread—images, value-words, grammatical constructions"[6] and with how that thread is woven or rewoven to create a pattern. A syntactic pattern is rather different from the initially additive principle of semic characterization, depending more on recurrence and appropriation than on variation and differentiation, even though both the semic and the syntactic participate quite directly in the anaphoric, distributive existence of the person-text. Indeed, given the persistence and reverberation of certain figures or patterns, one is almost tempted to speak of *isotaxie*, by analogy with *isotopie*.[7]

What further attracted me as my work proceeded was the possibility of homologous articulation of a surface pattern onto the structure of the work as a whole, as in the case of non-description in Jacques Proust's analysis of "Manon" or Jean-Pierre Richard's exegesis of the demise of "Javert." Such an integration of one pattern into another represents a move from micro- to macro-pattern, or as I call it from syntax in the person to person in the Syntax, whether it be when creation of one character through epithet becomes in the *Liaisons dangereuses* the primary functional trait of another; when Silvia's recasting of terms becomes recasting of the dramatic structure of *Le Jeu de l'amour et du hasard*; or when the gradual disappearance of markers of uncertainty in Madame de Clèves's speech signifies acquisition of a new, authorial competence. Thus, even if attributes were merely or solely semic it would be equally relevant and important to follow what happens to and through these attributes, and to open up at the surface windows onto a deeper, "Syntactic" order in the text.

Since my approach is primarily stylistic I shall be quoting frequently and at some length but, for purposes of focus, emphasis in quotations will be my own unless otherwise indicated. Because style is the surface manifestation—and my "person" a syntactic component—of a larger, overdetermined whole, I have also been relatively generous in deciding when it was relevant or appropriate to cite work by others which sheds different but usually complementary light on a question. I have elected to present these studies in a sequence suggestive of a problematic of the person rather than chronologically, since a chronological presentation would not only banalize most theoretical possibilities, but—particularly where person is concerned—run the risk as well of implying a progression toward nineteenth-century character and a superiority of the so-called three-dimensional or "round" character over other varieties of person-text.

I take Cléopâtre in Corneille's *Rodogune* first because, while she belongs as much with the second group of "person in Syntax," she is without a name in the play (rather like Manon without a body), and because the play as a whole is rich in a criss-crossing of the animate and inanimate, the personal and personified. As such, *Rodogune* represents something of a cautionary paradigm for the essays that follow, a heightened and dramatized awareness of what's (not) in a name, but also what's in a person and what a person is in.[8] Corneille chose not to refer to Cléopâtre by name in order to avoid possible confusion with her more famous homonym and placed correspondingly greater emphasis on her role attributes, but the character herself is principally concerned with a kind of amoral personal purity. We become increasingly aware that behind or below her manipulations of those attributes is a *moi* directing the operations and indeed casting out those forces—vestigial scruples but also her confidante—which could hinder her designs. Engaging in truly self-styled rhetoric and dramaturgy she substitutes extensions of herself (*main, trône, poison*), for which she also creates a vivid presence through frequent apostrophe. And by quite literally internalizing her closest ally (the poison) she provokes finally a dénouement in which her paradoxical effacement becomes the supreme gesture of her solipsism.

Phèdre's problem is at once the same and the opposite, since her reluctance to speak the name of Hippolyte can be compared to Cléopâtre's absence of a name; but in *Phèdre* it leads to an excess of identification, as apposition becomes both the site and the symbol of an investigation of identity. Not only do numerous

INTRODUCTION   15

instances show how much personal substance is displaced from noun head to appositive, but Hippolyte ultimately replaces his father in the syntactic and psychic transference which is the root subject of the play: "Je l'aime . . . tel que je vous voi."

In the second pair of studies, the person exists for the most part outside the whole process of naming. La Bruyère's *caractère* reveals a model built up from accumulated detail and a series of predicates presented paratactically but extended iteratively as well, creating finally the image of an activity without a subject, a machine rather than a human being. The subject of a *caractère* is thus an empty grammatical slot or a mere convenience, the type-name we confer after the fact on a certain behavior. The Other in Rousseau's *Rêveries* is referred to often enough for the reader to be aware of a presence, yet here too the full importance of "them" emerges only when one realizes that the Other exists as a rhythm as well as an overt reference, that elements in series are a nagging and obsessive signifier creating for "them" a subliminal presence, and thus characterizing finally both the Other and the writer. Conversely, on the textual plane his botanical enumerations engender a stylistic "dédommagement" by parrying negative accumulations with a beneficent one. Rousseau thus represents an extreme case here: as a writer creating subconsciously the full textual presence of the Other (cf. Valmont-Merteuil's voluntary creation of Cécile); but also because accumulative rhythm in the *Rêveries* is the least anthropomorphic of the traits analyzed in this volume, and a remarkable prose example of the spatial taking precedence over the temporal and sequential, as prosody replaces action.[9]

The essays on "person in Syntax" share an obvious common element in centering around a nubile female character (Cécile, Silvia, the Princesse de Clèves), but from my perspective here it is more important to note how such a person informs the text and is informed by it, particularly and specifically with respect to speaking vs. silence. A frequent theme in discussion of character is the difficulty of distinguishing neatly or completely between verb (function) and adjective (quality and attribute). Speech and ability to speak or write thus seem a crucial aspect of person to consider and do indeed lead us from syntactic function (actually a certain dysfunction, difficulty or inadequacy in speaking/writing) to varieties of competence at the level of plot and narrative.

Cécile's case in *Les Liaisons dangereuses* partakes strongly and literally of the "empty slot" syndrome, the *personnage à faire* with whose inane babbling the epistolary network begins, but she will in fact be the creation of other characters in the work, and the latter will take their own characterial definition from that dramaturgic-narrative activity. Moreover, the failure of their enterprise will be couched in and even provoked by the very "epithetic" treatment by which they had intended to reduce and collapse the humanity of others, the final irony coming when their reduction to epistolary silence coincides with the publication of their correspondence.

Silvia in *Le Jeu de l'amour et du hasard* is both better linguistically equipped to deal with the world than Cécile and more generous in the application of her competence than the Marquise de Merteuil. Not content to rectify and extend the platitude of her servant's remarks and the resignation they express when confronting male-oriented institutions, she sets out to replicate that same activity at the level of plot, by extending the play into a third act which is not essential to the original design once Dorante has revealed his identity. Her undertaking nevertheless occurs within the permissive frame created and maintained at a higher level of the text by her father, future father-in-law and brother, who thus function as surrogates of both the playwright-director and the audience. The main character's return to silence once Dorante's promise has her, like Lisette, "raccommodée avec le reste" is thus the outcome of a highly ambiguous autonomy. *La Princesse de Clèves*, on the other hand, provides us with a more radical approach to speech and the person: from an "empty" and silent presence at the outset, the Princess moves to brief and markedly hesitant reactions, but then on to the final scene with Nemours, where thanks to her experience she arrives at the ability to speak at length and on her own initiative, and even to pronounce general truths.

Cécile and the Princess are perhaps quintessential person-texts in the sense that the novels in which they appear are both the story of, and something of a meditation on, their "creation." At the same time, both works explicitly return them to silence, since the conditions of existence of the *Liaisons* require that Valmont and Merteuil stop writing in order for the book to be published, and since the Princess' acquisition of autonomous speech turns out to be the condition and context of her (silent) retirement. By the same token, the frame perspective on Silvia's attempt at commanding male respect by going beyond the "zero degree" of a certain (linguistic) resignation also serves as a reminder of the contingency of any character's identity and existence, since as she shapes the dramatic action into her own personal creation, the creation of her person is nonetheless overseen, "contrôlée" and even controlled by the representatives of the writer and the reader-spectator.

I place *La Princesse de Clèves* last not only because it raises an issue on which I have chosen to conclude but also to complete a kind of critical circle, since as with Cléopâtre the foregrounding of the Princess' person is to some extent the product of a falling away of characters around her, a clearing-out of her surroundings, and like Cléopâtre whose suicide is a supreme affirmation rather than a retreat, the Princess' *retraite* is the preservation of a recaptured self rather than a symbolic suicide. Moreover, the Princess is an even clearer example than Cléopâtre of both syntax in the person and person in Syntax, moving as it were from subphrastic diffidence to transphrastic competence. The final autonomy achieved by the Princess in and through the form of the novel is what makes possible and indeed valorizes her detachment and return to silence at the end, and in my opinion invalidates critical references to her self-mutilation, defeat, etc. *La Princesse de Clèves* thus becomes highly emblematic of the emptiness and silence surrounding the person-text, and into which we inject our critical voices. In my conclusion I have used a survey of critical comments on the dénouement to suggest some of the problems inherent in any evaluation of the person, where the textual norms and constraints leave off and the person of the reader takes over.

Tracing shifts in various levels or registers in the other works—from presence to absence as paradoxical power in *Rodogune*, from Thésée to Hippolyte, from esthetic to ethic in *Les Caractères*, suffering to "dédommagement" in Rousseau, character to pseudo-narrator in the *Liaisons*, dialogue to plot in the *Jeu de l'amour et du hasard*—also suggests that with respect to the textual person the notion of "shift" is particularly germane in comparison with, say, the trajectory of a linear, temporal progression. To be sure, as in the *Jeu* or the *Princesse de Clèves*, such a trajectory often leads to the emergence of a new situation and/or a new person, but a pattern may also blend with another as in the *Rêveries* and *Phèdre* for example, where patterns trace a logical, even spatial shift rather than a primarily narrative path. And as I hope to have shown in the case of Cléopâtre, a "story" trajectory need not culminate in some semantic or situational "fullness" of person, but is more fundamentally here a certain ramification in the textual life of syntactical or rhetorical elements.

Rodogune, *Les Caractères* and *Les Rêveries* make it clear as well that in textual terms one need not consider the person as necessarily beginning with the subject or indeed with a name. To find in appositives both the subject of *Phèdre* and her destiny, or in epithet Cécile's primary identity, is to decenter the notion of person, to diffuse it throughout a syntactic figure as locus and to situate person finally in the tension of the process of its own creation. As such, syntax is not only an expression or implementation but a figuration of the person, and plot becomes the time it takes to assume and explore an identification figure. Person as the product of syntax and rhetoric is thus neither decorative, the ornamentation of a putative referent-norm, nor attributive in the sense of an empty space to be filled in, but a rippling and ramifying whose center is everywhere, and analogous to Barthes's text, "a construction whose body contains finally, no heart, no kernel, no secret, no irreducible principle, nothing except the infinity of its own envelopes—which envelop nothing other than the unity of its own surfaces."[10]

Chapter I

PERSON, PERSONIFICATION AND CLEOPATRE'S
"GRANDEUR" IN *RODOGUNE*

There is considerable critical awareness and agreement that something special is at work in Corneille's *Rodogune*, that in Cléopâtre the play offers a new actualization of "the idea central to Corneille throughout his life that overriding any concepts dealing with psychological realism, the characters have to be extraordinary to be dramatically viable."[1] This is of course what Corneille himself was referring to in an often-quoted observation applicable to his heroes in general and to Cléopâtre (of whom he is speaking) in particular: "Tous ses crimes sont accompagnés d'une grandeur d'âme qui a quelque chose de si haut qu'en même temps qu'on déteste ses actions on admire la source d'où elles partent."[2] Critics have further sensed that it is Cléopâtre's amorality which represents the new wrinkle, that "ethically, for the first time, we have a Cornelian 'hero' who justifies the use of dishonesty and expediency."[3]

Il nous semble que Rodogune correspond à la découverte par l'écrivain du fait que dans l'univers de son théâtre, le vice et la vertu sont en dernière instance rigoureusement équivalents et que la seule valeur structurellement fondée est la puissance de la personnalité, catégorie éminemment amorale.[4]

In developing here certain rhetorical aspects of the amoral *personnalité* to which Goldmann refers, my own point of view on the question will be that what is new is not so much the amoral side of the character—earlier heroes like Horace and Polyeucte were less moral in a limited sense than they are often made out to be—but the techniques through which the playwright develops patterns of "Cléopâtre" which set off her amorality with special and spectacular clarity of focus.

On a primitive level, *Rodogune* has about it the air of a detective story, with the fifth-act search for the murderer (Schérer, p. xx), and more generally of "a mystery story in which the question of identity is paramount" (Nelson, p. 167). Nelson is referring to the identity of the twins, and the problematic heroic status of the female characters, but he points out elsewhere that for all the complications of plot, the plays of this period are "who-is-its" more than "who-dunits" (p. 265). Such a reminder is extremely apt in the case of *Rodogune,* since the notoriously complex exposition leads in fact to a simple and symmetrical structure in the play (Cléopâtre and Rodogune on opposite sides of the fraternal Antiochus/Séleucus couple). Moreover, a first act which might have overwhelmed the spectator with information also resolves into a situation where the problem of primogeniture is increasingly superseded by our interest in learning more about this Cléopâtre who holds sway over so many destinies.

Much of what we learn in the first few scenes is particular and specific rather than extraordinary, in the sense that the situation has a familiar ring to it: consonant with Corneille's "mature" dramaturgy, today is to be *the* day.

> Enfin ce jour pompeux, cet heureux jour nous luit,
> Qui d'un trouble si long doit dissiper la nuit,
> Ce grand jour où l'hymen . . .
> . . . .
> Ce grand jour est venu, mon frère, où notre reine
> Cessant de plus tenir la couronne incertaine,
> Doit rompre aux yeux de tous son silence obstiné,
> De deux princes gémeaux nous déclarer l'aîné. (ll. 1-10)

More particular is the fact that the character who must ultimately choose between Cléopâtre and Rodogune is rather two characters, Antiochus and Séleucus, with the result that the first act, as a preparation for the debates that follow, is particularly rich in antitheses. Compared to, say, *Bajazet,* where somewhat similar elements can be found—liberation dependent on a marriage which is in turn dependent on, and the expression of, choice by a relatively weak masculine presence between two stronger female personalities—what strikes one here is that said masculine presence debates with its other self (Antiochus/Séleucus and vice versa) rather than with the object of its love (Bajazet/Atalide), and that when the time comes Rodogune will speak with both brothers together (III, 4). Once and only relatively late in the play (IV, I) is Antiochus singled out as her preferred interlocutor, and conversely Séleucus takes much of his definition precisely from the absence of a scene alone with Rodogune. In other words, the distribution of characters has a particular impact on theme here as the opposition between love and politics, a situation in which Cornelian characters typically hope and search for a solution via a synthesis in personal *dépassement* rather than election of one alternative, is enriched by a second debate between fraternal and passionate love. Moreover, that they should remain turned so resolutely toward one another and toward the subject of their passionate love, and therefore away from the throne and the mother whose power it is to bestow or withhold the crown, is all the more striking since Cléopâtre's political superiority is in fact preceded by and dependent on a family bond (see the many classroom parallels between Cléopâtre and Agrippine assigned since Voltaire, and Corneille's own reference to Cléopâtre as a "seconde Médée" in the *Avertissement*).

Yet as soon as we begin looking in the early speeches for references to that anterior bond it appears curiously absent. On the one hand, the *dramatis personae* and early *récits* stress sibling definitions: not only are Séleucus and Antiochus an unusual fraternal "doublet" in a typical Cornelian role, but Laonice and Timagène are sister and brother, and of course a great deal of the background springs from Cléopâtre's having killed Démétrius Nicanor and married... his brother. Moreover, Rodogune is a sibling royal princess, "sœur de Phraates, roi des Parthes" whereas Cléopâtre is a widowed queen. Too much should not be made of the necessarily succinct characterizations which *récits* and the unfolding plot are designed to flesh out, but when one is aware of the action to follow, it is nevertheless significant that with the minor exception of Oronte Cléopâtre should be the only non-sibling character in the list. Moreover, when in the *Discours de la tragédie et des moyens de la traiter selon le vraisem-

blable ou le nécessaire Corneille cites *Rodogune* as one of "ces actions tragiques qui se passent entre proches," but in terms of the "malheur d'Antiochus," this seems an *a contrario* confirmation that, as we shall see, a major dimension of Cléopâtre's grandiose solitude is her (voluntary) lack—despite a tightly woven set of family and marriage links—of personal "proches" as close to her as the throne, her hatred or the poisoned cup.

Cléopâtre need not of course be listed as "mère" of her sons since they are billed as "fils de Démétrius et de Cléopâtre," but the special emphasis on a particular angle of definition is nonetheless there from the start and the text rapidly develops that line of presentation. In the first 300 lines, i.e., up to Rodogune's entrance, Cléopâtre is referred to only once as a mother, by Séleucus, and in syntax which is most indicative: *"Un droit* d'aînesse obscur, sur la foi d'*une mère,* / Va combler l'un de gloire et l'autre de misère" (ll. 183-84). The antithetical *l'un*/*l'autre* is of course familiarly Cornelian, although as noted earlier it is significant that it opposes two brothers whose consensual fraternal vision is greater than the inevitable exclusion of one by the other (unlike the family resemblance between Horace and Camille which ultimately makes them mortal enemies). At the same time the nonce reference here to "une mère" and its semi-generalized antonomasia form (cf. a possible "notre mère" or any number of possible periphrases, e.g., "qui nous donna le jour") are more than "mere" style and express the brothers' preoccupation with their own situation as brothers and *amoureux*. (When Antiochus refers to a *reine* it is Rodogune, l. 160.) Furthermore, that the mother should appear in a circumstantial phrase rather than as subject is additional evidence of their perspective, an underestimation or misestimation which is decidedly not Cléopâtre's. Consequently, Corneille's decision not to refer to Cléopâtre by name for fear of confusion with her more famous homonym (see the *Avertissement*) now appears more than a curiosity; on the contrary, in terms of her person it is as significant as a change of name in the course of the action *à la* Octave/Auguste in *Cinna*. Not to accord a proper name is, if anything, all the more revealing of the character's content and situation, emphasizing Cléopâtre's role attributes and her subsequent manipulation of them.

The Queen's activity is frequently expressed as well through transfer and displacement of her authority onto the occasion of her will rather than the will itself: "ce *jour* pompeux . . . / doit dissiper la nuit" (II. 1-2); ". . . l'*hymen*, étouffant la vengeance" (I. 3); "Ce grand *jour* . . . / . . . / Affranchit la princesse, et nous fait . . ." (II. 3-5); "Un seul *mot* aujourd'hui, *maître* de ma fortune, / M'ôte ou donne à jamais le sceptre ou Rodogune" (II. 75-76); ". . . ce *secret* révélé / Me rend le plus content ou le plus désolé" (II. 77-78); "Et que ce *jour* fatal à l'heur de notre vie / Jette sur l'un de nous trop de honte ou d'envie" (II. 115-16); "Et nous mépriserons ce faible *droit* d'aînesse" (I. 127); "Qui, de la même *main* qui me cède un empire, / M'arrache un bien plus grand, et le seul où j'aspire?" (II. 131-32); "Un *droit* d'aînesse obscur, sur la foi d'une mère, / Va combler l'un de gloire, et l'autre de misère" (II. 183-84). A like figure names the object or outward sign rather than the function: *diadème, sceptre, couronne, trône*, etc., as in these examples of "to become king (or queen)" from Laonice's first speech: "Cessant de plus tenir la *couronne* incertaine" (I. 8); "Mettant au plus heureux le *sceptre* dans la main" (I. 13); "Par elle se va voir sur le *trône* montée" (I. 20). In addition to the numerous examples of this metonymic displacement in which the authority comes to reside in the instrument or the outward sign, a similar effect occurs when the feelings which animate the characters are seen as existing almost independently, personified to such a degree that they become not only source but agent, and the person simply the occasion or terrain where such activity occurs. One exchange between Séleucus and Antiochus includes a number of examples.

> . . . . . . il faut qu'en ce grand jour
> Notre *amitié* triomphe aussi bien que l'*amour*
> . . . .
> Il sème entre nous toute la *jalousie*
> Qui dépeupla la Grèce et saccagea l'Asie;
> . . . .
> Ainsi notre *amitié*, triomphante à son tour,
> Vaincra la jalousie en cédant à l'amour;
> . . . .
> Et ma *raison* sur moi gardera tant d'empire. (II. 169-203)

Such usage is of course consistent with the poetic and dramatic rhetoric of the time, but in their common effect—condensation outside or on the periphery of the person, of emotion and activity which "unpoetically" would be simply seen as the person— and in the particularly heightened degree to which they are developed in *Rodogune*, they take on special importance to the characterization of Cléopâtre.[6]

Finally, in the last scene of the first act Rodogune provides the role perspicacity which Laonice lacks:

> Laonice
> A présent que l'amour succède à la colère,
> Elle ne vous voit plus qu'avec des *yeux de mère*. (II. 343-44)
> Rodogune
> Qui que ce soit des deux qu'on couronne aujourd'hui,
> Elle sera *sa mère*, et pourra tout sur lui. (II. 349-50)

She understands best that the identity of the particular son is in fact immaterial ("qui que ce soit des deux"), that the family bond is but another instrument of Cléopâtre's approach to power. Indeed, earlier in the scene she said as much in a way which was less direct at first but which was equally attentive to the agents and emanations of queenly authority:

> La fortune me traite avec trop de respect;
> Et le trône et l'hymen, tout me devient suspect.
> . . . .
> Et je prends tous ces biens pour des maux déguisés:
> En un mot, je crains tout de l'esprit de la reine. (II. 305-11)

Nor, despite its more general approach, is her next speech any less germane to understanding the Queen's character (one notes in passing the repetition of *grand*):

> La haine entre les grands se calme rarement;
> . . . .
> Mais une grande offense est de cette nature,
> Que toujours son auteur impute à l'offensé
> Un vif ressentiment dont il se croit blessé;
> . . . .
> Telle est pour moi la reine. (II. 313-27)

What links the two speeches significantly, beyond even the subject of the Queen, is the fact that neither names her, even indirectly, until the end, but that the final word of each is *reine*, thereby building a character through a local suspense and pushing our attention and interest along toward Cléopâtre's first appearance in person. Finally, the second half of sc. 5 is given over to more direct characterization of Rodogune herself, with a very blatant, echo opposition to her definition of Cléopâtre in II. 349-50: "Quelque époux que le ciel veuille me destiner, / C'est à lui pleinement que je veux me donner" (II. 373-74); and then to a literal suspending of the action very much in keeping with the motif of naming already elucidated:

Laonice
Le prince...
Rodogune
Garde-toi de nommer mon vainqueur. (I. 385)

What does Cléopâtre bring to these various considerations? First of all, a particular distribution of characterial presence: identified in the cast of characters, she appears (like Horace and Auguste before her) only at the start of the second act, unencumbered by the necessities of the basic expository material. Moreover, her subsequent absence—remarkable in dramaturgic terms—between II, 4, and IV, 4, and her return late in the play with three monologues close together also serve to heighten the importance of the character. To this particular emphasis Corneille adds the singularity of a first scene in monologue: before we discover with Laonice the "real" Cléopâtre in II, 2, the chance to observe her alone is at least as informative. Furthermore, this is the first of four monologues by Cléopâtre (II, 1; IV, 5 and 7; V, 1), a large number in any case and particularly when compared to one for Rodogune (III, 3), two relatively short ones for Antiochus (II, 6; IV, 2), and none for Séleucus.[7]

Cutting across the symmetries between herself and Rodogune, we have then other formal and rhetorical strategies which "favor" the presence of the Queen. Broadly speaking, as the play unfolds we move from a confidant's characterization of Cléopâtre via *récit* (I, 1 and 4) to her own in monologue (II, 1) and *confidence* (II, 2); then to an exchange with her sons (II, 3); skip then to a confrontation with each son followed each time by a monologue (IV, 3-5; IV, 6-7); and then to a last monologue followed by the extended final scene with Rodogune and the others (V, 1, 3-4). Her character is thus established before her confrontations with her sons, reconfirmed thereafter and further completed after poisoning Séleucus and before the final confrontation—the only one—between the two female characters (V, 3-4). Consequently, the plot establishes a pendular rhythm not only among specific characters but among types of scene, in a structured variety which lessens somewhat the rather rigid symmetry of situation and action.

Before taking up Cléopâtre's monologues in detail, we need to look at the role of *confidences* in character creation. Her words to Laonice shortly after the first monologue are almost didactically typical of the protagonist-confidant relationship:

> *Cléopâtre*
> *Sais-tu* que mon secret n'est pas ce que l'on pense?
> . . . .
> Pour un esprit de cour, et nourri chez les grands,
> Tes yeux dans leurs secrets sont bien *peu pénétrants*.
> *Apprends, ma confidente, apprends à me connaître.* (II. 439-43)

The discovery plot which in a sense represented the brothers' point of view—"who is the elder?"—becomes increasingly, then, the full revelation of who—and what—Cléopâtre is, and as the play proceeds Laonice will in fact serve less as a sounding-board than as a measuring-stick for the evolution of her mistress.

We learned earlier that Laonice was singularly close to the Queen in terms of her authority yet distant with respect to its application:

> La reine, à la gêner prenant mille délices,
> Ne commettait *qu'à moi* l'ordre de ses supplices;
> Mais, quoi que m'ordonnât cette âme toute en feu,
> Je promettais beaucoup, et j'exécutais peu. (II. 267-70)

In a notable case of characterial self-distribution, Laonice will now proceed to draw still further away as the plot progresses. Her other lines in the rest of II, 2, are equally brief and functionally "confidantial": "*J'ai cru* qu'Antiochus les tenait éloignés / Pour jouir des Etats qu'il avait regagnés" (II. 453-54); "*Je vous connaissais mal*" (I. 503); and her two and a half lines compared to Cléopâtre's forty-five or so make of that scene a quasi-monologue. Laonice is present in II, 3, but does not speak, and when next we see her (III, 1) a major shift has occurred: the scene now takes place in Rodogune's apartment (a change Corneille was at pains to justify in his *Examen*) and the Princess' first words ("Voilà comme l'amour succède à la colère," l. 759) provide not only a sarcastic echo of her earlier lucidity concerning Cléopâtre's aims, but indicate as well that Laonice has informed her between Acts II and III of what Cléopâtre told her in the scene just discussed.[8] Laonice will not return until Cléopâtre does (IV, 3) and here again her role is mechanically informative, as her account of the wedding party's approach includes the dramatically necessary announcement of the customary wedding cup (ll. 1542-46) and the account of popular reaction (ll. 1548-52). Moreover, since the previous scene was a long monologue by Cléopâtre, Laonice's twenty lines also represent a respite for the Queen and our interest in her, albeit justified and integrated into her machinations by her "Mais voici Laonice; il faut dissimuler" (l. 1537); not to speak is, for the audience, to hide even more palpably. And in closing, Laonice underscores even further the irony of the situation and Cléopâtre's dominant position: "Mais je les vois déjà; Madame, c'est à vous / A commencer ici des spectacles si doux" (ll. 1557-58). The former agent of Cléopâtre's authority thus comes to function at the level of dialogic prop for her, and thereafter (V, 4) as a figurative and then quite literal crutch, her textual presence reduced to stage directions (in italics in the text): "Antiochus, *rendant la coupe à Laonice ou à quelque autre*" (ll. 1809-10); "*Elle s'en va, et Laonice lui aide à marcher*" (ll. 1830-31).

The role of confidant to Cléopâtre began as the typical maieutic one, drawing out of the main character what the playwright chose not to place in the monologues and—in the case of the plot here—what must theoretically not be revealed too soon, although as already noted Rodogune is also unusual in that the Queen's antagonist does learn much of what is afoot relatively early and from that very confidant. With respect to Cléopâtre's "grandeur" the confidant is a foil not just in the typically classical fashion, but in her increasing, horrified distance as well. In that sense it is dramatically more significant for us to watch the Queen's proximity lose its last faithful inhabitant than for the portrayal of her final hours to have begun in the splendid isolation which will in fact be the outcome of the plot.

The play's action can thus be construed on at least one level as a depiction of Cléopâtre's increasing propensity to talk to herself. At the same time, the confidant role does not remain vacant; a Cornelian tragedy could hardly be expected to end in a solitary monologue, and so that propensity is not altogether literal; yet perhaps the most striking particularity of *Rodogune*—and most distinctive aspect in Cléopâtre's "grandeur"—is this evacuation of the space around her and its repopulation by other elements. We have already seen how, through the distribution of characters and scenes, Cléopâtre's presence onstage is all the more remarkable for its particular intermittence: it remains now to examine what she has to say when onstage and to whom she says it.

It is quickly clear, in her first two scenes of self-presentation (II, 1-2), that Cléopâtre is both very Cornelian and a noticeable departure from earlier models: "Je hais, je règne encor. Laissons d'illustres marques / En quittant, s'il le faut, ce haut rang des monarques; / Faisons-en avec gloire un départ éclatant" (II. 411-14). We have the same quasi-theatrical desire to make a dazzling exit, to leave one's mark on history and thereby to command admiration that was the hallmark of Rodrigue, Horace, Cinna, Polyeucte. At the same time, however, the temporal situation ("je règne encor") and the desire to maintain or at least prolong that situation is rather different from that of the younger heroes eager to prove their ability to *prendre la relève* of illustrious parents or in the sight of a father-like king. More important and relevant still since Cléopâtre belongs to the outgoing generation, her juxtaposition in "Je hais, je règne encor" reads like a debased version of Auguste's dilemma in *Cinna* II, 1: where he yearns restively for a way "out" of an earlier self, she looks only for an extraordinary expression of the same self in a (final) illustrious application of her hate.

> Je fis beaucoup alors, et ferais encor plus
> S'il était quelque voie, infâme ou légitime,
> Que m'enseignât la gloire, ou que m'ouvrît le crime,
> Qui me pût conserver un bien que j'ai chéri
> Jusqu'à verser pour lui tout le sang d'un mari. (II. 470-74)

Here we have not only a sinister echo of more *généreux* exchanges between persons and things ("Pour le trône cédé, cédez-moi Rodogune," l. 123), but Cléopâtre's version of the typical Cornelian "Je le ferais encor si c'était à refaire" and even an openly amoral pastiche (*voie, ouvrît, jusqu'à*) of Horace's theorizing on the hero's career (*Horace* II, 3). Cléopâtre's amorality resides most fundamentally in her egocentrism, her desire to act solely for her own ends and indeed for herself as the only end worthy of her efforts: "Aucun des deux ne règne, et *je règne pour eux*" (l. 446); ". . . si je nomme un roi, / C'est pour le commander, et combattre *pour moi*?" (ll. 493-94); "Et je ferai régner *qui me voudra servir*" (l. 502). Rid of the various alibis of which earlier heroes availed themselves in the forging of the Cornelian self, Cléopâtre is both sender and beneficiary, initiator and recipient, source and destination.

I differ here rather basically with Serge Doubrovsky, who sees Cléopâtre's nature as sexually defined and impossible to divest oneself of ("se dénaturer"), and her *drame* as that of a woman whose position on the throne is exceptional in the sense of accidental, necessarily destined to be shared by a man:

> Dire qu'au moment où Cléopâtre vise au pouvoir *absolu*, elle ne peut l'obtenir que par la *médiation* d'autrui, c'est une autre façon de dire qu'elle veut, en fait, régner comme homme, mais qu'elle ne peut y parvenir que comme femme... il s'agit de supprimer *tous les intermédiaires masculins*, mari ou fils, qui la séparent du pouvoir absolu. (p. 295, italics in the original)

But if she is woman before being Queen she is self before woman. Even deeper than her motherhood, which functions as instrument and mask, and her femininity—which is finally, like politics, contextual here—there lies at the base of her (in)humanity a *moi* to be affirmed; moreover, such affirmation can be traced in both her language and the structure of the play and characterized precisely by her own particular approach to the question of mediated expression of the self. Thus, in a number of pertinent quotations adduced by Doubrovsky to demonstrate Cléopâtre's "feminine" nature, we find an even earlier, more intimate pronominal definition of her:

> Sans violence aucune
> J'aurais vu Nicanor épouser Rodogune,
> SI, content de lui plaire et de *me* dédaigner,
> Il eût vécu chez elle en *me* laissant régner. (ll. 463-66)

> *Je* ne veux point pour fils l'époux de Rodogune. (I. 1512)
> Héritier d'une flamme envers *moi* criminelle,
> Aime *mon* ennemi, et péris comme lui. (II. 1516-17)

While I agree that "le parricide, chez Horace ou Auguste, est récupérable par l'ordre social" (p. 295), the formulation in the next sentence ("le personnage principal de *Rodogune*, d'abord invisible, puis visible sur la scène, c'est le *trône*") seems useful and germane only if considered loosely figurative, since a strict application of the notion runs counter to the developing action as I am tracing it here and may lead one to overemphasize the political register in the play.

Doubrovsky's formulation is recast slightly three pages later (". . . au lieu de *transcender* sa féminité, elle cherche à l'*escamoter* . . . La passion de Cléopâtre est une passion politique impure, qui entend simplement utiliser le trône comme *moyen* de nier la condition féminine," p. 298; italics in the original), but in terms of the play as it evolves more light seems to me shed by Goldmann's approach: "le procès qui clôt chacun de ces [premiers] drames . . . met en lumière la nécessité d'une médiation, incarnée par le personnage du roi, entre le héros et la société" (p. 131). Cléopâtre occupies in fact the position of both mediator and "mediatee," with consequences not only for her existential *projet* but for her personal (dramatic) destiny as well.

Her first monologue shows, even beyond the choice of rhetorical mode, that she is alone and aloof in a very special way. Not only does she finish in a threatening apostrophe to her "imprudente rivale" (l. 419), but in fact here as later she is continually apostrophizing. She begins by clearing the terrain, almost in anticipation of the analogous removal on Laonice's part: "Serments fallacieux . . . / Heureux déguisements . . . / Vains fantômes d'Etat, évanouissez-vous!" (II. 395-98). She then turns to address her hatred in lines which reveal fully that if "today is the day" there is still more than one possible resolution for the suspense all the characters feel.

> Recours des impuissants, *haine* dissimulée,
> Digne vertu des rois, noble secret de cour,
> Eclatez, il est temps, et voici notre jour.
> Montrons-nous toutes deux, non plus comme sujettes,
> Mais telle que je suis et telle que vous êtes. (II. 404-08)

RODOGUNE   31

Because her speech is thus constructed totally of three successive apostrophes, it is already abundantly clear before the dialogue with Laonice that she prefers her own choice of interlocutor (and ally: note the first person plurals), and that they are apt to be personifications, internal creations rather than persons. Seen in that light, Laonice's removal, however voluntary, is only a matter of time and there is further evidence of the same in sc. 2, where Cléopâtre "lapses" into an apostrophe to the throne which completes the speech: "Délices de mon cœur...," ll. 476-82). Her preference for personification over person thus applies even to her confidant, replaced by the objects and instruments of Cléopâtre's position.[9]

Thanks to her exposition of self, when she returns in Act IV, sc. 4, her insistence on all she has done and is doing for her sons (*"J'avais su prévenir... Sans moi, sans mon courage... Je* fais plus maintenant," ll. 1310-19) is thus susceptible of an even more ego-based understanding on the audience's part, as will be her (last) unequivocal words to Séleucus.

> *Je puis, come je veux,* tourner le droit d'aînesse. (l. 1423)
>
> *J'en prends* à la connaître, et la faire avorter;
> *J'en prends* à conserver malgré toi *mon ouvrage.* (ll. 1454-55)
>
> Comme reine, *à mon choix* je fais justice ou grâce,
> Et je m'étonne fort d'où vous vient cette audace,
> D'où vient qu'un fils, *vers moi* noirci de trahison,
> Ose de mes faveurs me demander raison. (ll. 1463-66)

And to the extent that one of the main dramatic dimensions of self-definition is choice of interlocutor, certain other lines provide further and equally significant confirmation of her orientation.

> (to Antiochus)
> Avez-vous oublié que vous parlez *à moi?* (l. 1285)
> (to Laonice)
> Ne lui témoignez rien; il lui sera plus doux
> D'apprendre tout *de moi,* qu'il ne serait de vous. (ll. 1385-86)
> (to herself)
> Je ne veux plus *que moi dedans ma confidence.* (l. 1391)

After an unsuccessful attempt to impose that *moi* on Séleucus (IV, 6), Cléopâtre hesitates briefly before killing him, in a binary "against/for" monologue which includes the "Sors de mon cœur, nature" apostrophe (l. 1491 ff.) which some critics have compared to Lady Macbeth's injunction:

> Come, come, you spirits
> That tend on mortal thoughts, unsex me here;
> And fill me, from the crown to the toe, top-full
> Of direst cruelty! Make thick my blood,
> Stop up th'access and passage to remorse;
> That no compunctious visitings of Nature
> Shake my fell purpose .... (*Macbeth* I, 5)[10]

Doubrovsky classes *Rodogune* in his section on "La liberté contre la nature" but sees "Sors de mon cœur, nature" as "une parodie de l'effort héroïque, car la 'nature' est déjà sortie" (p. 296). He is perhaps right that this *stance* perspective is not fully prepared for, and even that it appears to contradict her previous attitude; but when one considers the second hemistich of that line as well ("... ou fais qu'ils m'obéissent") it is clear that Cléopâtre is also ridding herself of the inoperative elements of her personality and that in terms of a rhetorical analysis the moment is consistent with the overall disengagement of her surroundings. In that light the monologue thus appears more "sincere," a penultimate hesitation—"Leur amour m'offensait, leur amitié m'accable" (l. 1476)—where Cléopâtre is frustrated as *both* mother and Queen by Rodogune:

> Et contre mes fureurs je trouve en mes deux fils
> Deux enfants révoltés et deux rivaux unis.
> Quoi! sans émotion perdre trône et maîtresse!
> Quel est ici ton charme, odieuse princesse? (ll. 1477-80)

But if her jealousy may appear "feminine," her choice of verb significantly conflates the two planes of love and politics ("Pour régner sur deux cœurs, tu n'es pas encor reine," l. 1484) and, by necessitating a common subject for the two, will lead to a deeper, typically and literally *self*-styled resolution: "*J*'ai commencé par lui, *j*'achèverai par eux" (l. 1490). Cléopâtre is thus casting out the remaining sentimental encumbrance in a kind of solipsistic purification; the apostrophe is reminiscent of the opening lines of II, 1, and the monologue as a whole culminates in a renewed affirmation of herself as sole beneficiary of her criminal activity: "Et de me rendre heureuse à force de grands crimes" (l. 1496).

The monologue after the death of Séleucus (V, 1) is once again constructed around several apostrophes. Four lines of exposition are followed almost imperceptibly by two addressing the dead son "Ils le suivront de près..." (ll. 1501-02), then immediately by several whose meaning remains suspended until she at last names her interlocutor:

> O toi, qui n'attends plus que la cérémonie
> . . . .
> Poison, me sauras-tu rendre mon diadème?
> Le fer m'a bien servie, en feras-tu de même?
> Me seras-tu fidèle? (ll. 1503-09)

The poison is to pick up where the sword left off, but what is particularly new here is the promotion of the instrument of vengeance to a privileged dialogic status, in analogous fashion to her addressing her emotions and the throne. In the second half of the last line quoted, she turns her scornful wrath on the last vestigial scruples ("Et toi, que me veux-tu, / Ridicule retour d'une sotte vertu," ll. 1509-14) and thence shows no hesitation in her attitude toward Antiochus ("Reste du sang ingrat d'un époux infidèle...," ll. 1515-22). And finally the "come what may" philosophy of the Cornelian hero reappears in lines so typical they could almost have been lifted from several other contexts, but which culminate in an apostrophe peculiarly characteristic of Cléopâtre:

> Qui se venge à demi court lui-même à sa peine:
> Il faut ou condamner ou couronner sa haine.
> Dût le peuple en fureur...
> . . . .
> Dût le Parthe vengeur...
> Dût le ciel égaler...
> Trône, à t'abondonner je ne puis consentir;
> Par un coup de tonnerre il vaut mieux en sortir;
> Il vaut mieux mériter le sort le plus étrange.
> Tombe sur moi le ciel, pourvu que je me venge! (ll. 1523-32)

We have then a monologue which is typical of Cléopâtre in its apostrophic construction, and apostrophes which are themselves characteristic in their mixing of persons and personification on an equal footing. What is further noteworthy is that all five apostrophes demonstrate the character's single-mindedness and so propel us toward a dénouement which Cléopâtre already sees as a "do or die" (or "do *and* die") attempt at personal vengeance: "Je perds moins à mourir qu'à vivre leur sujette" (l. 1536).

For all the melodrama involved in the manipulation of the wedding cup, it is also much more: not simply the concentration in a visible object of what is at stake in the plot, but the objectification as well of Cléopâtre's most intimate desire and the extension of her self. (Cf. the poison which is referred to but never seen in *Britannicus*, or Phèdre's metaphorically poisonous passion overcome by real poison at the end, ll. 1637 ff.) This is further underscored by Cléopâtre's deceptively simple and apparently decorous "Recevez de ma main la coupe nuptiale, / Pour être après unis sous la foi conjugale" (ll. 1591-92). The irony of "unis" is obvious and recalls other ironic references such as Cléopâtre's "Pour réunir bientôt ce que j'ai séparé" (l. 1502), but in terms of the rhetorical modes analyzed here "ma main" is hardly less essential to the status and stature of Cléopâtre. It is not only the physical link between the cup and herself, but an echo and a resuscitation of earlier instances: "Qui, de *la même main* qui me cède un empire, / M'arrache un bien plus grand, et le seul où j'aspire?" (ll. 131-32); "Le roi meurt . . . *par la main* de la reine" (l. 263); "Rodogune, mes fils, le tua *par ma main*" (l. 630); ". . . *mes mains* sur le père enhardies" (l. 1487). Thus another staple of poetic diction takes on new significance in a new context, and is of course developed further in the melodramatic *"Une main* qui nous fut bien chère / Venge ainsi le refus . . ." (ll. 1643-44).[11] The debate that follows is a lengthy one but the reference to "une main" has focused attention through its suspenseful anonymity, and it is only poetically appropriate that Cléopâtre should be the one to relieve the suspense, and should do so in a typically pronominal self-affirmation, the more effective for its simplicity: "Je le ferai moi-même" (l. 1793).

Nor is her "explanation" any less personalized, quite the contrary: in this final moment even the rhetorical gap between herself and her emotions narrows ("Ma haine est trop fidèle, et m'a trop bien servie," l. 1812), and by swallowing the poison she literally internalizes her closest ally. (From our point of view here, this is surely one of the most significant "embellissements de l'invention" referred to by Corneille in the *Avertissement*, since according to his sources Antiochus forced his mother to drink the poison she had prepared for him.)

Acting for oneself implies, finally, not only acting by oneself but ultimately even on oneself. When she takes her *moi* as the most worthy object of her act, we follow Cléopâtre to a kind of paradoxical vanishing point of the person where doing away with herself is the crowning achievement of . . . her self: "*Je* t'ai défait d'un père, et d'un frère, et *de moi*" (l. 1818). Earlier heroes had demonstrated that in Cornelian terms death is hardly the worst of fates, that to leave one's mark on history and achieve one's *gloire* by fully realizing and transcending oneself is to become larger than life by living on in the memory of one's "audience." Yet Cléopâtre carries even that outlook further. Our rapport with her is direct since in the final tableau there is no representative audience of characters to inspire or mediate an admiring reaction on our part. And in an action which is stripped as well of the family, social and religious codes which were the ethical context—and pretext—of earlier heroic actions, death by her own hand has a singular personal purity to it which leaves death in combat or battle or even political or religious martyrdom, tainted with hypocrisy. In grammatical, dramatic, and ethical terms, Cléopâtre becomes her own destiny, and that is her *grandeur*.

Chapter II

APPOSITION AND IDENTIFICATION IN *PHEDRE*

Rodogune as a "who-is-it" led to an investigation of syntax, rhetoric and plot, tracing first a gradual withdrawal into the *moi*, and then the withdrawal of the *moi* from the scene of the play's apparent action. A more restrictedly syntactic approach should now show that apposition in *Phèdre* is not simply an aspect of tragic diction or of the rhetoric of the person, but an emblem of a similar "who-is-it" dimension in the play.

"Apposition" will refer here to a particular mode of juxtaposing to a character information which furthers or deepens the character's situation or "thickness," and /or our understanding of that character. For reasons which will become clear, I class in the appositive category not only typical noun appositives but also participial constructions and those adjectives which are set off noticeably from their head noun, or whose copula or relative pronoun (unlike the case of predicate attributes and relatives) has been deleted. In other words, elements that differ from the usual elements of characterization in that their placement is not a simple case of description or attribution. On the one hand, appositives are dependent on the syntactic function of their referent which, in the case of noun appositives, they share. At the same time, however, they are "detached" from their referent in the sense that in Racine noun appositives are usually (and participials and adjective appositives almost always) set off from their head-noun referent by commas and are thus most often accompanied by a pause, in diction but also in comprehension. Furthermore, they may be placed before or after that referent, with great importance for characterization. The relationship between appositive and referent is thus primarily logical and even spatial, as subsidiary information is ap-posed and "secondary" to the main statement rather than basic. In his use of appositives in *Phèdre*, however, Racine not only "poises" much character substance outside and even prior to the direct story line but, insofar as that substance is not completely juxtaposed to a character in the way of usual qualifiers, he draws us as well into a reflection on the space that separates referent and appositive, and on what it means to go from one to the other.[1]

Perhaps the most striking appositional use of participial constructions comes in Racine's *récits*, where they provide a maximum of economy and grace, transmitting moreover the necessary information in a highly patterned and rhetorical form. (Both Spitzer and France have commented on this aspect, with particular reference to *Bajazet*, ll. 473-80; and *Phèdre*, ll. 75-92 and 539-46.) One of the purest examples comes from *Athalie*:

> Faut-il, Abner, faut-il vous rappeler le cours
> Des prodiges fameux accomplis en nos jours?
> Des tyrans d'Israël les célèbres disgraces,
> Et Dieu trouvé fidèle en toutes ses menaces;
> L'impie Achad détruit, et de son sang trempé
> Le champ que par le meurtre il avait usurpé;
> Près de ce champ fatal Jézabel immolée,
> Sous les pieds des chevaux cette reine foulée,
> Dans son sang inhumain les chiens désaltérés,
> Et de son corps hideux les membres déchirés;
> Des prophètes menteurs la troupe confondue,
> Et la flamme du ciel sur l'autel descendue;
> Elie aux éléments parlant en souverain,
> Les cieux par lui fermés et devenus d'airain,
> Et la terre trois ans sans pluie et sans rosée,
> Les morts se ranimant à la voix d'Elisée?
> Reconnaissez, Abner, à ces traits éclatants,
> Un Dieu tel aujourd'hui qu'il fut dans tous les temps. (*Athalie*, ll. 109-26)

This is perhaps also an extreme example, but I quote it at length to underscore the amplitude the construction can achieve, and to demonstrate as well how unified it remains here in terms of reference and meaning. Some fourteen full-line entries all follow appositively from "Prodiges" in an expressive elaboration rather than a narrative development. Moreover, all of the entries are preparing at the same time the appearance of "Dieu" which functions retroactively as their source as well as the rhetorical goal toward which they are tending. They thus become—quite literally—features (*traits*) in the characterization of "Dieu."[2]

A few lines earlier we have an equally extreme example, although this time in a much more heavily noun-oriented apposition:

> Mathan, d'ailleurs, Mathan, ce prêtre sacrilège
> Plus méchant qu'Athalie, à toute heure l'assiège;
> Mathan, de nos autels infâme déserteur,
> Et de toute vertu zélé persécuteur. (II. 35-38)

Here the verb is almost lost in the appositive characterization, and coming early on, these lines serve in a way as a reminder that the *dramatis personae* are in fact a list of appositives, i.e., that all characterization is in a sense adduction of traits to a functional site in the text: *JOAS, roi de Juda, fils d'Okosias; ATHALIE, veuve de Joram, aïeule de Joas; MATHAN, prêtre apostat, sacrificateur de Baal.*

A more typical example occurs in the first scene of *Iphigénie*:

> *Agamemnon*
> Heureux qui, satisfait de son humble fortune,
> Libre du joug superbe où je suis attaché,
> Vit dans l'état obscur où les dieux l'ont caché! (II. 10-12)

What is characteristic here is the mixture of nominal, adjectival and participial appositives (and a Latinate reminiscence in "Heureux qui . . ."). But perhaps more striking from our point of view is the fact that where Agamemnon's confidant evokes a vision of his master, the latter devotes in large measure his appositives to himself. Thus a few lines later, a passage within a long speech begins with participial references to Ulysse but quickly shifts toward himself and lamentation on his plight:

> Ulysse, en apparence, approuvant mes discours,
> De ce premier torrent laissa passer le cours.
> Mais bientôt, rappelant sa cruelle industrie,
> Il me représenta l'honneur et la patrie,
> Tout ce peuple, ces rois, à mes ordres soumis,

PHEDRE

> Et l'empire d'Asie à la Grèce promis;
> De quel front, immolant tout l'Etat à ma fille,
> Roi sans gloire, j'irais vieillir dans ma famille.
> Moi-même, je l'avoue avec quelque pudeur,
> Charmé de son pouvoir, et plein de ma grandeur,
> Ce nom de roi des rois et de chef de la Grèce
> Chatouillait de mon cœur l'orgueilleuse faiblesse. (II. 71-82)

The verb "représenta" underscores the tableau aspect of the scene, and "Charmé" further indicates a distanced self-awareness on Agamemnon's part. The speech also includes a line which is in a sense a separate, lamentatory appositive to the account which preceded it—"Quel funeste artifice il me fallut chercher!" (I. 92)—a function used to effect in *Phèdre* as well. For the moment what seems crucial is the extent to which the various appositives create a sense of a character looking inward (and backward, toward the past), of a dialogue which thus remains always to some degree a confrontation of two monologues rather than an exchange.

> *Andromaque*
> Captive, toujours triste, importune à moi-même,
> Pouvez-vous souhaiter qu'Andromaque vous aime?
> *Pyrrhus*
> Je souffre tous les maux que j'ai faits devant Troie.
> Vaincu, chargé de fers, de regrets consumé,
> Brûlé de plus de feux que je n'en allumai.
> (*Andromaque*, II. 301-02, 318-20)

The highly developed sense of prior self expressed in these appositives leads then to a kind of characterial essentialism. Furthermore, in Andromaque's case the appositives not only precede their noun-head, emphasizing her self and internalizing her situation, they are "dangling," mixed references as well. If the grammatical subject of her question is Pyrrhus ("vous"), the appositives indicate that the real subject is clearly Andromaque, and we shall find in *Phèdre* other examples of the rich effects Racine derived from this more flexible classical usage.

Néron's *récit* of Junie's appearance (*Britannicus* II, 2) is well-known as an example of the Racinian *clair/obscur* tableau, and of the importance of visualized scenes and seeing in general in Racine:

> Cette nuit je l'ai vue arriver en ces lieux,
> Triste, levant au ciel ses yeux mouillés de larmes,
> Qui brillaient au travers des flambeaux et des armes,
> Belle, sans ornement, dans le simple appareil
> D'une beauté qu'on vient d'arracher au sommeil. (II. 386-90)

Appositives clearly have their role to play in this kind of remembered vision (see the striking placement of "Triste" and "Belle"), but what is further remarkable is the way in which Néron also frames this scene with participial and adjectival appositives that enable us to see him seeing:

> Excité d'un désir curieux,
> . . . .
> J'ai voulu lui parler, et ma voix s'est perdue:
> Immobile, saisi d'un long étonnement,
> Je l'ai laissé passer dans son appartement.
> J'ai passé dans le mien. C'est là que, solitaire,
> De son image en vain j'ai voulu me distraire.
> Trop présente à mes yeux je croyais lui parler;
> J'aimais jusqu'à ses pleurs que je faisais couler. (II. 385-402)

As with Agamemnon, we have in a *récit* passage the Racinian character contemplating his past self as explanation of the present predicament, and another example of a mixed appositive ("Trop présente . . . je croyais . . .") illustrating syntactically how one character becomes an obsessive attribute of another, as in the Thésée/Hippolyte relation analyzed below. Later in the same scene Néron will provide a further and analogous frame on his own situation, as a similar participial construction underscores the importance of Agrippine: "Eloigné de ses yeux, j'ordonne, je menace" (I. 496). Ultimately, as Pierre Kuentz has shown, Néron is not only actor, *metteur en scène* and spectator of his story, but—in his use of syntax, period and rhyme—its poet as well. His case is therefore an excellent example of the difficulty and illadvisedness of seeking to oppose too strictly in Racine the expressive and narrative functions, and/or implicitly choosing between them.[3] To a degree remarkable even in a dialogic genre like theater, the characters *are* their language, in a tragic situation where "being" as a linguistic and speech function is pursued to its limit. "La tragédie est seulement un échec qui se parle" (Barthes, p. 67). Perhaps no other Racinian play presents

PHEDRE 41

this coincidence of saying, being and doing, or "song" and "action," so clearly and so deeply as *Phèdre*, and I turn now to the role of apposition in that particular linguistic complex.

Hippolyte makes lengthy use of participials early on in a *récit* of the type referred to earlier in *Athalie*:

> Tu sais combien mon âme, attentive à ta voix,
> S'échauffait au récit de ses nobles exploits,
> Quand tu me peignais ce héros intrépide
> Consolant les mortels de l'absence d'Alcide
> Les monstres étouffés et les brigands punis,
> Procruste, Cercyon, et Scirron, et Sinnis,
> Et les os dispersés du géant d'Epidaure,
> Et la Crête fumant du sang du Minotaure. (II. 75-82)

It is thus both the biographical account of his father's exploits and the record of their effect on Hippolyte. Ariane and Phèdre are mentioned only briefly, seen medallion-like via participial constructions which are virtually free-standing since the main verb ("tu récitais") occurs some six lines earlier. "Ariane aux rochers contant ses injustices, / Phèdre enlevée enfin sous de meilleurs auspices" (II. 89-90). Moreover, while they are characterized by the appositives "contant" and "enlevée" they are in fact themselves appositives of the earlier "Tant d'autres" (I. 87), itself a (negative) avatar, like "faits moins glorieux" (I. 83), of "ses nobles exploits" (I. 76). As such they occur on an equal grammatical and syntactical footing with the other proper names and like them are attributes of "mon père." At the same time, however, the spectator or reader familiar with the mythological background is aware that these names will take on greater importance than the others as the plot develops, a fact stressed rhetorically and thematically as well since reference to them appears as the turning point in the speech. Having mentioned the sisters, and particularly Phèdre, Hippolyte turns promptly to his own reactions and evokes the theme of silence, of not speaking and suppressing what one should not—or does not want to hear:[4] "Tu sais comme à regret écoutant ce discours, / Je te pressais souvent d'en abréger le cours" (II. 91-92). Stylistiquement, rhetorically and thematically the mention here of Ariane and Phèdre is thus particularly significant.

As in *Athalie*, however, this is not the first occurrence of appositives. Hippolyte's decision to leave, on which the play opens and which hindsight tells us is a theme analogous and even equivalent to that of not speaking, is justified when he identifies himself through his situation: "Depuis plus de six mois éloigné de mon père, / J'ignore . . ." (ll. 5-6). At the outset then we have an appositive functioning as so many others do: applied by the character to himself, and inserted in its sentence context ahead of the pronoun to which it refers. Appositives do not of course always function in this way, since they may refer to other characters, but in that case it is often a confidant who does so (even if his comprehension of the situation leaves something to be desired): "Phèdre ici vous chagrine, et blesse votre vue. / Dangereuse marâtre, à peine elle vous vit . . ." (ll. 38-39). In almost all cases the appositive draws attention to itself and even carries more weight than its referent, since it usually adumbrates a pronoun subject and most often in a head or end position rather than a medial one. (On these two types see Spitzer, p. 325). A further shift of emphasis is of course the dangling or mixed appositive, which occurs here in more ironic (because ambiguous) fashion than those already quoted:

> De ses jeunes erreurs désormais revenu,
> Par un indigne obstacle il n'est point retenu,
> Et fixant de ses vœux l'inconstance fatale,
> Phèdre depuis longtemps ne craint plus de rivale. (ll. 23-26)

And as the next lines indicate ("Enfin en le cherchant je suivrai mon devoir, / Et je fuirai ces lieux que je n'ose plus voir"), this is an early and like incidence where mention of Phèdre's name seems instantly to trigger Hippolyte's turning away, toward himself and his desire to flee. (See also the earlier "Ce héros n'attend point qu'une amante abusée . . . / Cher Théramène, arrête, et respecte Thésée," ll. 21-22.) Moreover, in his next remark he seemingly cannot bring himself to name her: "Tout a changé de face, / Depuis que sur ces bords les Dieux ont envoyé / La fille de Minos et de Pasiphaé" (ll. 34-36).

In his analysis of periphrasis in Racine, R.A. Sayce concluded that, contrary to what one might expect, periphrasis and direct statement are only theoretical opposites, that in fact the former often prepares for the latter, which is all the more effective for such foregrounding.[5] His primary examples of this relationship are taken from the early scenes of *Phèdre* but, whereas he was concerned with the local effect of a shift from indirect to direct statement, periphrasis can also be integrated into the larger, reciprocal relationship of language and person in *Phèdre* (which Barthes developed on a mythic and primal level but with relatively little reference to style or syntax as such).

Where periphrasis and the Racinian appositive come together in effect is in this shifting of attention away from a "merely" grammatical subject, moving from the matrix to the constituent substance contained in the adjacent phrase or circumlocution. Sayce rightly stresses, for example, the extent to which periphrasis (and this one in particular) "suggests wider horizons" (p. 86) and is a rich source of useful information rather than idle decoration; and no classroom edition fails to point out the rich phonetic and mythic content of this line. What has gone somewhat unnoticed is that "La fille de Minos et de Pasiphaé" is not only a full alexandrine, but that the line as a whole functions as the direct object noun phrase. In other words, like the original referent "Phèdre," the sentence is also oriented, even somewhat distended, toward both mythic and rhythmic ends.

A similar example of the conjoining of the dramatic and the poetic occurs a few lines later, where this time Phèdre is evoked through an antonomasia:

> Et d'ailleurs quels périls vous peut faire courir
> Une femme mourante et qui cherche à mourir?
> Phèdre atteinte d'un mal qu'elle s'obstine à taire,
> Lasse enfin d'elle-même et du jour qui l'éclaire,
> Peut-elle contre vous former quelques desseins? (II. 43-47)

The antonomasia ("une femme mourante") not only confirms her morbid condition, but also provides a semi-general backdrop against which the proper name will stand out even more. Moreover, like the "Lasse . . ." appositive and the earlier periphrasis, the antonomasia provides phonetic information ("mourante/

mourir") as well as rhythmic; and, because it occupies the entire line, it represents a further "distortion" since it is now the inverted subject of the sentence in which it appears. Furthermore, "Phèdre" occurs here at the center of a concentric and quasi-palindromic characterization sequence: question—antonomasia ("une femme mourante")—referent ("Phèdre")—appositive ("atteinte ... Lasse ...")—question. One can of course object to isolating these five lines from the six that precede, but it is nonetheless justifiable and even revealing to do so since thematically they are a furtherance of the (faulty) information Théramène has already begun to provide about Phèdre; and more importantly they point up structurally the fact that appositives, periphrasis and antonomasia are basically devices which identify rather than narrate, casting new light on the character in an attributive rather than a "story" way (often because they encapsulate earlier events). Moreover, in their rhythmic dimension and the pause they occasion, apposition and periphrasis are almost physical proof as well that they represent amplification rather than advancement in plot terms. The same is true of the other like characterizations in the lines leading up to Hippolyte's long *récit*:

Hippolyte
Je fuis, je l'avouerai, cette jeune Aricie,
Reste d'un sang fatal conjuré contre nous. (ll. 50-51)

Théramène
Pourriez-vous n'être plus ce superbe Hippolyte,
Implacable ennemi des amoureuses lois,
Et d'un joug que Thésée a subi tant de fois?
Vénus, par votre orgueil si longtemps méprisée,
Voudrait-elle à la fin justifier Thésée? (ll. 58-62)

And finally, after Hippolyte's long account and toward the end of the first scene, Théramène's assessment of the changes in Hippolyte's outlook uses appositives to evoke both the former and the present self, and reminds us that the play as a whole is more devoted to portraying and assessing the results of the changes than in detailing the evolution of the process itself:

Avouez-le, tout change: et depuis quelques jours
On vous voit moins souvent, orgueilleux et sauvage,
Tantôt faire voler un char sur le rivage,
Tantôt, savant dans l'art par Neptune inventé,

PHEDRE 45

> Rendre docile au frein un coursier indompté.
> Les forêts de nos cris moins souvent retentissent;
> Chargés d'un feu secret, vos yeux s'appesantissent. (II. 128-35)

Immediately Théramène mentions Aricie, Hippolyte reiterates his intention to leave (II. 137-38), and exits when Oenone announces the arrival of Phèdre (I. 150). At the same time, one is struck by the fact that the weight of passion which Théramène conveyed in Hippolyte's case with a preposed participial ("Chargé d'un feu secret") bears down on Phèdre as well and in an accumulation which is in fact a juxtaposition of virtually synonymous elements (emphasized by anaphora, alliteration and assonance) leading to a recapitulative "tout," a construction Racine has frequent recourse to, whether the "tout" precedes or follows:

> Que ces vains ornements, que ces voiles me pèsent!
> Quelle importune main, en formant tous ces nœuds,
> A pris soin sur mon front d'assembler mes cheveux?
> Tout m'afflige, et me nuit, et conspire à me nuire. (II. 158-61)

(See also Spitzer, pp. 325-26.) Her next words are an apostrophe to her mother's father, the Sun, and directly reminiscent of "La fille de Minos et de Pasiphaé" in their mythological content, periphrastic first two lines, basic appositive orientation ("auteur/ toi/qui") preceding the referent "Soleil," and suspension of story content until the last:

> Noble et brillant auteur d'une triste famille,
> Toi, dont ma mère osait se vanter d'être fille,
> Qui peut-être rougis du trouble où tu me vois,
> Soleil, je te viens voir pour la dernière fois. (II. 169-72)

A major dimension of the play thus concerns *identification*. Not only are characters continually and voluminously evoked in apposition as well as in their primary grammatical function, but on a broader level an analogous trend seeks in *Phèdre* to establish just who is an attribute of whom: who it is that characters have on their minds or in their hearts and specifically whom they are in fact (not) talking about. As the mixed appositives indicate particularly well, grammatical subject is to real subject as referent is to appositive, and apposition and periphrasis will be closely and frequently linked to the saying vs. silence dilemma. Hippolyte flees at the sound of a (female) proper name, and now even Phèdre's vague metonymic reference to Hippolyte ("un char fuyant dans la carrière," l. 178) is cause for immediate and alarmed second thoughts on her part:

> Insensée! où suis-je? et qu'ai-je dit?
> Où laissé-je égarer mes vœux et mon esprit?
> Je l'ai perdu: les dieux m'en ont ravi l'usage.
> Oenone, la rougeur me couvre le visage:
> Je te laisse trop voir mes honteuses douleurs;
> Et mes yeux, malgré moi, se remplissent de pleurs. (II. 179-84)

One notes in "Insensée" the highly unusual self-referential epithet poised between two speeches and whose judgmental appositive function is thus an appraisal of both the self already involved and the one whose shame continues to emerge into the light of day. This is also one of the most characteristic examples of the concern for the tell-tale signs—in fact motifs running throughout the play—of her condition: the flushed face, the revealing eyes, and above all the words and names which betray. The focus sharpens considerably when Oenone, having misunderstood in typical confidant fashion ("rougissez d'un silence," l. 185), rambles on in ignorance until Phèdre cuts her off at the mention of Hippolyte's name:

> *Oenone*
> Rebelle à tous nos soins, sourde à tous nos discours,
> Voulez-vous, sans pitié, laisser finir vos jours?
> . . . .
> Songez qu'un même jour leur ravira leur mère,
> Et rendra l'espérance au fils de l'étrangère,
> A ce fier ennemi de vous, de votre sang,
> Ce fils qu'une Amazone a poré dans son flanc,
> Cet Hippolyte . . .
> *Phèdre*
>   Ah, Dieux!
> *Oenone*
>   Ce reproche vous touche?
> *Phèdre*
> Malheureuse! quel nom est sorti de ta bouche? (II. 187-206)

Far from a mere lofty patterning, periphrasis, antonomasia and preposed appositives become the center of the character's preoccupations and the symbol of what is at stake.

PHEDRE 47

A few lines later Oenone has brought Phèdre round to where she is willing to speak, albeit assigning responsibility for it to her confidant ("Tu le veux," l. 246), approaching it with extreme diffidence and hesitation (ll. 247-59), and still without daring to give a name to the object of her passion:

> *Phèdre*
>   Tu connais ce fils de l'Amazone,
> Ce prince si longtemps par moi-même opprimé?
> *Oenone*
> Hippolyte? Grands dieux!
> *Phèdre*
> C'est toi qui l'as nommé! (ll. 262-64)

We should note as well another use of apposition: after she has agreed to "talk," one of Phèdre's hesitations takes the form of a lament which like the "Insensée" just discussed is in fact a judgment cast syntactically as an apposition, on her scandalous conduct (which she thus avoids detailing or even in fact naming, as she will again in the first scenes of confrontation with Thésée): "O haine de Vénus! O fatale colère! / Dans quels égarements l'amour jeta ma mère!" (ll. 249-50). We are thus left with the emotional residue in the character who remembers, as once again appositional material is used to reverberate rather than to recount. Oenone emits a similar lament when she realizes the horror of Phèdre's love: "O désespoir! ô crime! ô déplorable race! / Voyage infortuné!" (ll. 266-67). One dimension of the action in *Phèdre* thus consists of a tendency to compress at key points situation and character, attribute and referent, into a single entity, generating a lamenting, apposed consensus rather than a way out of the impasse.

Such is in a sense the subject of Phèdre's "Mon mal vient de plus loin" *récit*-monologue, and is evident in terms of rhetorical analysis. In terms of the plot of course, she finishes the speech with a desire to die which will be postponed because Panope arrives to report Thésée's death; and when it comes, Phèdre's suicide will be an obliteration of the problem rather than a solution to it. One need not insist once again on the frequent use of apposition in such a *récit*, nor on the apparent initial hesitation on Phèdre's part to name the "fils d'Egée" (l. 269) and "mon superbe ennemi" (l. 272). What is more crucial to the movement of identification at work in the play is that here for the first time the process is reversed. Until now, characters were "expanded" and set off, poised by apposition and periphrasis. Here, on the other hand, identification becomes a fitting together, and even equating, an identifying *with*, as Phèdre undertakes to show that the forces of destiny have refused to remain at a distance, that they have invaded the story at hand in the personalized form of Vénus: "Je reconnus Vénus et ses feux redoutables" (l. 277). At the same time, however, "Vénus" is the first, last and most telling evocation of her plight: "D'un sang qu'elle poursuit, tourments inévitables" (l. 278); "Vaines précautions! Cruelle destinée!" (l. 301); "C'est Vénus tout entière à sa proie attachée" (l. 306). The "C'est" of this last line represents, in its undeleted presentative dimension, the last syntactical phase before a "true," detached appositive, but its function is completely analogous in ramifying the tragic dilemma, in this case furthering as well the mythological presence which will erupt literally with the monster at the dénouement.

Phèdre is identified with Vénus, as Hippolyte will be with the monster and Thésée already is with Neptune, but a second major element emerges now in the confusion between Thésée and Hippolyte. Phèdre prays to Vénus adoring in fact Hippolyte all the while (l. 285); worse yet, as a new "dieu" (l. 288) Hippolyte implicitly replaces Vénus and more obviously his own father: "Mes yeux le retrouvaient dans les traits de son père" (l. 290). Where Vénus, as the personification of passion, partakes of both apposition and "intraposition" with respect to Phèdre as character, through the reverberant family resemblance Hippolyte achieves—quite despite himself—a superimposition, as Thésée fades beneath the new identification.

The first act thus not only poses a situation but establishes identity and the process of identification as fundamental to the meaning of *Phèdre* since persistent apposition is not simply a case of pattern rhetoric at the surface of the text, but a basic mode of existence for the characters and—to the extent that identification implies or solicits an inquiry into the relationship between that figure and its referent—even a kind of discovery plot.

Aricie's appearance in Act II underscores not only thematically but stylistically her resemblance to the other tragic characters. Ismène characterizes Hippolyte to her much as Théramène had in line 134, emphasizing the importance of outward signs and of the corollary theme of speaking and naming:

> Dès vos premiers regards je l'ai vu se confondre;
> Ses yeux, qui vainement voulaient vous éviter,
> Déjà pleins de langueur, ne pouvaient vous quitter.
> Le nom d'amant peut-être offense son courage;
> Mais il en a les yeux, s'il n'en a le langage. (II. 409-14)

And in a long narrative explanation of her feelings, Aricie begins by identifying herself in typical appositive syntax:

> O toi qui me connais, te semblait-il croyable
> Que le triste jouet d'un sort impitoyable,
> Un cœur toujours nourri d'amertume et de pleurs,
> Dût connaître l'amour et ses folles douleurs?
> Reste du sang d'un roi noble fils de la terre,
> Je suis seule échappée aux fureurs de la guerre. (II. 417-22)

She then goes on, in an articulation of her speech fully reminiscent of Phèdre's in I, 3, to stress in further appositives and highly rhetorical fashion the impression Hippolyte has made on her. Her speech and her situation are thus symmetrical to Phèdre's in style and outlook, with the poignant and crucial difference that where Phèdre is overwhelmed by the realization of Vénus' vengeful interference, Aricie's pride acknowledges no obstacle or foreign presence other than Hippolyte's own timidity. Indeed, in a significant reversal she treasures the father's best traits identified in the son: "J'aime, je prise en lui de plus nobles richesses, / Les vertus de son père, et non point les faiblesses" (II. 441-42; cf. I. 290 and Phèdre's "Je l'aime . . . tel que je vous voi," II. 635-40). One notes a highly oratorical, almost Cornelian development in the anaphoric appositives evoking one's *gloire*, and the "C'est là" which in Phèdre's case identified Vénus but which indicates here the goal Aricie has set for herself, rather than divine interference from without:

> Pour moi, je suis plus fière et fuis la gloire aisée
> D'arracher un hommage à mille autres offert,
> Et d'entrer dans un cœur de toutes parts ouvert.
> Mais de faire fléchir un courage inflexible,
> De porter la douleur dans une âme insensible,
> D'enchaîner un captif de ses fers étonné,
> Contre un joug qui lui plaît vainement mutiné;
> C'est là ce que je veux; c'est là ce qui m'irrite. (II. 446-53)

The "irritation" leads her to end on a hesitant note, however, proud but hardly daring to hope and even recalling the "triste jouet..." with which she began: "Tu m'entendras peut-être, humble dans mon ennui, / Gémir du même orgueil que j'admire aujourd'hui" (II. 458-59).

What follows in Act II is two essential and similar confrontations. In sc. 2 Hippolyte goes further than he expected, partly because Aricie is too surprised to engage in a real dialogue, but partly as well because he cannot resist coming to tell her he is leaving. Conversely, when he is told Phèdre is coming he has little to say—"Phèdre! Que lui dirai-je? Et que peut-elle attendre..." (l. 565)—and his cold, curt answers in sc. 4 serve as a foil and even a seeming inspiration for Phèdre's excessive declaration.

Hippolyte's main speech thus contains echoes of the "saying too much" motif: "Je me suis engagé trop avant" (l. 524): "Puisque j'ai commencé de rompre le silence" (l. 526). But when he elaborates, his remarks are a treasure trove of already familiar rhetorical devices leading to the portrait of a passive victim contemplating and lamenting, like other characters, his own plight:

> Vous voyez devant vous un prince déplorable,
> D'un téméraire orgueil exemple mémorable.
> Moi qui, contre l'amour fièrement révolté,
> Aux fers de ses captifs ai longtemps insulté;
> Qui, des faibles mortels déplorant les naufrages,
> Pensais toujours du bord contempler les orages;
> Asservi maintenant sous la commune loi,
> Par quel trouble me vois-je emporté loin de moi. (II. 529-36)

As real subject he is nonetheless and first of all the grammatical object ("Vous voyez devant vous..."), and the antonomasia "un prince" heightens both the contemplative distance and the fallen pride of an Hippolyte unable to refer directly to himself at first. Moreover, "Moi" is almost lost among appositives and relatives,

PHEDRE 51

and expression of his former volition (ll. 531-34) is caught between noun and participial appositives (ll. 530, 535) stressing his present, lamentable passivity. Indeed, to trace the span from "vous voyez" to "me vois-je emporté" is to perceive and overtly to specify how appositives create a character medallion, even for the character himself.

In the next three lines the same movement begins again as the pronoun "je" is preceded by virtually all the characterial substance ("honteux, désespéré . . . déchiré . . . vainement") and followed only by the verb ("je m'éprouve"), whose scant, almost secondary importance, is thus conveyed. The speech then pivots on the reason for all this: "Présente, je vous fuis; absente, je vous trouve" (l. 542). One notes the theme of the haunting mental image of the Other which Phèdre has already introduced (and will develop again shortly) with respect to Hippolyte, but syntactically we have once again significant mixed appositives in "présente" and "absente," the more significant for their doubly elliptical nature: they refer not only elsewhere, i.e., not to the subject of the main clause, but indeed their referent has thus far been only implicit in Hippolyte's speech. (At the same time the gender markers stress audibly the invasion of Hippolyte's masculine world by a foreign, female element.) Once again then a subject is introduced in its ramification before it is named or inserted into the basic grammatical matrix.

As Hippolyte continues we note in the style how ironically identical is his situation to Phèdre's: in two accumulations involving "tout" (ll. 545-46, 459), and in the fundamental formulation of a self which the context indicates is, like Phèdre's, not only lost ("Maintenant je me cherche, et ne me trouve plus") but overwhelmed, "full" of the Other. Finally, the speech concludes with other links to both plot and modes of expression in the foreshadowing "Je ne me souviens plus des leçons de Neptune" (l. 550); in the rueful appositive appraisal ". . . quel farouche entretien! / Quel étrange captif pour un si beau lien!" (ll. 555-56); and in an echo of the reference to speech with which Hippolyte began his declaration: "Songez que je vous parle une langue étrangère" (l. 558). Here his summation is both right and wrong and therefore poetically apt. He belongs to another world and is unable to express himself other than in "des vœux mal exprimés" (I. 559); but those wishes are in fact all the more eloquent for it, and Aricie has already told us this is the Hippolyte she loves.

Two scenes later the exchange which Hippolyte anticipates as "un fâcheux entretien" (l. 580) is profoundly and physically disturbing for Phèdre: "Le voici: vers mon cœur tout mon sang se retire. / J'oublie, en le voyant, ce que je viens lui dire" (ll. 581-82). She recovers her composure sufficiently to cite politics and her son's future as her reason for coming to see him, but for all his incomprehension—perhaps because of it—the conversation moves inexorably toward the real subject, as Phèdre notes with several references to verbs of seeing and saying:

> Que dis-je? Il n'est point mort, puisqu'il respire en vous.
> Toujours devant mes yeux je crois voir mon époux:
> Je le vois, je lui parle; et mon cœur ... je m'égare,
> Seigneur; ma folle ardeur malgré moi se déclare. (II. 627-30)

Phèdre's "Oui, prince, je languis" speech (ll. 634-62) has been widely commented upon. What interests us most here is first of all a certain syntactic mode of characterization, where appositives and a relative expand on "Thésée":

> Oui, prince, je languis, je brûle pour Thésée!
> Je l'aime, non point tel que l'ont vu les enfers,
> Volage adorateur de mille objets divers,
> Qui va du dieu des morts déshonorer la couche;
> Mais fidèle, mais fier, et même un peu farouche,
> Charmant, jeune, traînant tous les cœurs après soi. (II. 634-39)

That is, the enumerative lines 638-39 represent not only examples of alliteration and rhythmic *coupes*, but at a higher, syntactic level the five adjectives and the participle are a continuance of the ramifying "tel," "adorateur," and "qui." Moreover, these appositional references to "Thésée," apparently post-posed for once, are (like the appositive attributes of "Dieu" in *Athalie*) preposed at the same time since almost all refer as well to the Hippolyte who appears in the next line, as he has already been characterized and indeed rather as he has already characterized himself. Phèdre says as much quite explicitly in the next line, which is therefore the first pivot in the speech: "Tel qu'on dépeint nos dieux, ou tel que je vous voi" (l. 640). But this is obviously far more than a search for an adequate, equivalent evocation of Thésée: appositive material shows once again its ascendancy over the head noun, with Hippolyte an alternate to "dieux" as a pole of comparison, and the final appositive for the "Thésée" referent. What had previously appeared as a superimposition of one face on another which resembled it closely occurs here as an apposition, in a graduated effort designed not to shock Hippolyte and a culmination of apposition in its intimate link to saying vs. silence.[6] Moreover, that identification is itself further ramified in the lines that follow, where "votre" and "cette" make manifest the resemblance (with Hippolyte now the referent) which is also implicit in the renewed use of marked *coupes*: "Il avait votre port, vos yeux, votre langage" (l. 641).

This first third of her speech closes on a new appositive—"Digne sujet des vœux des filles de Minos" (l. 644)—but only superficially repeats the earlier "Volage adorateur de mille objets divers" since the paths of Thésée and Hippolyte crossed as it were in the middle of the passage, and that chiasmic movement is further confirmed by the initial "Adorateur" having become "sujet" and "objets" having become "filles de Minos." Likewise, this latter periphrasis only apparently refers to both Phèdre and her sister, since as we already know Phèdre as "La fille de Minos et de Pasiphaé," and since the "sujet" is of course as much Hippolyte as Thésée. We have then something of a new (but defective) palindrome on the apparent noun-head "Thésée": appositive ... "tel"/"vous" ... appositive, where "vous" serves in fact as an anaphora of "tel." And even as the "tel"/"vous" transfer is the archapposition commanding all the others and moving Phèdre and us away from "Thésée," so her speech, pursuing that basic urge, will now go on to elaborate and even establish new ones.

The middle third of the speech ("Que faisiez-vous alors? ... ," ll. 645-52) develops Hippolyte as the conditional hero replacing his father ("Par vous aurait péri le monstre de la Crète," l. 649—an ironic mention as well, considering Hippolyte's ultimate fate). And the final third completes the transfers as Phèdre replaces her sister ("Mais non: dans ce dessein je l'aurais devancée," l. 653), and culminates in appositives ("Compagne"/"descendue") which serve as background surrounding "Phèdre." Her role is thus doubly foregrounded, as referent now rather than appositive, and in the striking use of her own name. Moreover, she actualizes in that reference and in mention of their union ("avec vous") what in the *bienséant* grammar of her remarks is still only in the conditional mood, thus bringing to light as well the full sexual sense of "labyrinthe," and the moral resonance of "perdue":

> Compagne du péril qu'il vous fallait chercher,
> Moi-même devant vous j'aurais voulu marcher;
> Et Phèdre au labyrinthe avec vous descendue
> Se serait avec vous retrouvée ou perdue. (II. 659-62)

In her next long speech, she extends the union of herself and Hippolyte by extending her reproach to his understanding as well as to her having said too much ("Ah! cruel! tu m'as trop entendue!" l. 670), an ironic reference insofar as Hippolyte in fact understands only for the first time, but accurate in that they are now on an equal footing in contemplation of the horror of it all. The speech is slightly less appositive and more pronominal in its structure, although as Barthes has noted "J'aime" (l. 693) remains problematical in terms of the opposition between "real" and grammatical structure ("L'amour est un état grammaticalement sans objet... comme si l'acte s'épuisait hors de tout terme," p. 58). And this isolation is further underscored through appositives which now apply to her and to her victimizers, developing anew through several ample and full-time constructions the earlier tone of lyrical, self-referential lament.

> ... Ne pense pas qu'...
> Innocente à mes yeux, je m'approuve moi-même,
> . . . .
> Objet infortuné des vengeances célestes,
> . . . .
> Les dieux m'en sont témoins, ces dieux qui dans mon flanc
>
> Ces dieux qui se sont fait une gloire cruelle
> . . . .
> Tremblante pour un fils que je n'osais trahir,
> . . . .
> Faibles projets d'un cœur trop plein de ce qu'il aime! (II. 673-97)

As the speech and the scene move toward a close Hippolyte reemerges as subject, although significantly her periphrastic and appositive references seem designed to rehabilitate him as "Digne fils du héros qui t'a donné le jour" (l. 700), rejuvenate his courage and kindle his disgust (with another ironic reference to delivering the world from a monster, ll. 700-02). Even in her suicidal "solution" she and her intended lover remain united, symbolically in the sexual sword ("Au défaut de ton bras prête-moi ton épée," l. 710) and syntactically in the mixed appositive construction of "Impatient déjà d'expier son offense, / Au-devant de ton bras je le sens qui s'avance" (ll. 705-06).

The final scene of Act II thus represents a summing-up, an enrichment and a continuation of thematic and stylistic elements, and as the third act opens Phèdre is recalling ruefully the effects of having said too much: "J'ai dit ce que jamais on ne devait entendre," l. 742). There are now a number of differences, however: she appears to regret equally the fact that she shocked and horrified Hippolyte and that her confession failed to win him over. Furthermore, now that her love is out in the open, she begins to hope for a somehow more satisfactory outcome: "J'ai déclaré ma honte aux yeux de mon vainqueur, / Et l'espoir malgré moi s'est glissé dans mon cœur" (ll. 767-68). Most of all it means that she will refuse to flee, will rely more on Oenone, and will now be more concerned with triumphing jealously over a possible rival than with resisting the influence of Vénus: "Toi-même, rappelant ma force défaillante, / Et mon âme déjà sur mes lèvres errante, / Par tes conseils flatteurs tu m'as su ranimer" (ll. 769-71); "Je ne me verrai point préférer de rivale" (l. 790).

At the end of this first scene Oenone is dispatched to implement Phèdre's new designs in the hope that in another assimilation of characters Hippolyte, tempté by the crown, will become father to her son . . . and husband to her: "Peut-être il voudra bien lui tenir lieu de père! / Je mets sous son pouvoir et le fils et la mère" (ll. 805-06). "Je n'espère qu'en toi," she says to Oenone (l. 811), but as though to ensure further the desired outcome, in sc. 2 Phèdre incites Vénus to achieve another kind of union of herself and her lover, bringing the latter to join her in submission to the goddess of love: "Cruelle, si tu veux une gloire nouvelle, / Attaque un ennemi qui te soit plus rebelle," ll. 817-18). Phèdre is thus at a crucial turning point: with will enough only to delegate since she is totally Vénus' victim, and with only the hope that she be united, "identified" with her son under Hippolyte's sway, or with Hippolyte under Vénus' domination. Her only action to date had been to *say*; and with the news that Thésée is alive (sc. 3) all that remains for her at best is to hear the incriminations of others, to attempt feebly to defend herself, in any case to lament. In terms of overt action the center of the play thus represents a stasis for a character whose definition as a victim of Vénus was passive to begin with. She is Vénus' plaything and will in a way become the same for an Oenone who unwittingly goes beyond her mistress' wishes. In the meantime, her role is to seek refuge in flight or in death, or failing that to remain silent: "Mon zèle n'a besoin que de votre silence" (Oenone, l. 894).

That silence will be a function of an extreme reticence born of her shame in Thésée's presence, and after a half-dozen lines in sc. 4 she will leave the stage to the others until sc. 4 of the following act. At the same time, the other characters make significant use of appositive constructions. Hippolyte attempts to set his father up as the conquering hero returned, and in contrast to himself:

> Déjà plus d'un tyran, plus d'un monstre farouche,
> Avait de votre bras senti la pesanteur;
> Déjà de l'insolence heureux persécuteur,
> . . . .
> Hercule, respirant sur le bruit de vos coups,
> Déjà de son travail se reposait sur vous.
> Et moi, fils inconnu d'un si glorieux père,
> Je suis même encor loin des traces de ma mère! (II. 938-46)

Caught between his knowledge of Phèdre's passion and his own love for Aricie, Hippolyte is unable to answer his father's calls for him to speak and deplores "Phèdre, toujours en proie à sa fureur extrême, / . . . / Moi-même, plein d'un feu que sa haine réprouve, / Quel il m'a vu jadis, et quel il me retrouve!" (II. 989-94).

But in the next scene Oenone cleverly begins her interpretation of Phèdre's silence with typical (but ambiguous) appositive insistence on her condition: "Honteuse du dessein d'un amant furieux / Et du feu criminel qu'il a pris dans ses yeux, / Phèdre mourait, seigneur, . . ." (II. 1014-16). Her strategy works, and

PHEDRE 57

in answer to Hippolyte's diffident reaction in the next scene, Thésée quickly thunders against his son with appositive and with epithet, the appellative variant of apposition: "Perfide! oses-tu bien te montrer devant moi? / Monstre, qu'a trop longtemps épargné le tonnerre, / Reste impur des brigands dont j'ai purgé la terre" (II. 1044-46). From there it is but a step to turn his "monstrous" son over to Neptune (II. 1065 ff.) and the monster who will be his avenging delegate. Even specifying that it is Aricie he loves is not enough to shake Thésée's peremptory identification of his son with the lowly and the wicked:

>*Hippolyte*
>Chargé du crime affreux dont vous me soupçonnez,
>Quels amis me plaindront, quand vous m'abandonnez?
>*Thésée*
>Va chercher des amis dont l'estime funeste
>Honore l'adultère, applaudisse à l'inceste,
>Des traîtres, des ingrats sans honneur et sans loi,
>Dignes de protéger un méchant tel que toi. (II. 1143-48)

From Phèdre's return on (IV, 4), one can find other examples of the kinds of appositive already outlined. In Hippolyte's rather too patterned diction in V, 1, and of course in Théramène's account of the latter's death (V, 6), but perhaps most notably in Phèdre's bitter and raving scenes of jealousy.

>Et moi, triste rebut de la nature entière,
>. . . . .
>Me nourrissant de fiel, de larmes abreuvée,
>Encor, dans mon malheur de trop près observée,
>Je n'osais dans mes pleurs me noyer à loisir.
>Je goûtais en tremblant ce funeste plaisir;
>Et, sous un front serein déguisant mes alarmes,
>Il fallait bien souvent me priver de mes larmes. (II. 1240-50)

Yet this very example, as an inflection of Phèdre's recent "Je suis le seul objet qu'il ne saurait souffrir" (I. 1212), and—when one is attuned to the appositive dimension—as an ironic and magnifying echo of Aricie's "triste objet d'un sort impitoyable," points up that what is more significant about appositives in *Phèdre*, beyond a certain elegance of diction and economy in supplying background (neither a negligible quantity), is the way they highlight the relationship between a referent and its ramification, and elaborate resemblances, mergings, and separations among characters.[7]

Be they quasi-narrative or attributive or both, belong to the past, evoke the present or anticipate future events, close attention to the appositives focuses our interest and curiosity on identification. The basic process of assigning (and detaching) attributes, qualities and/or a situation to a character takes on quite special importance here in the sense that characters are called on as well to align themselves (or be aligned), and even identify (or be identified), *with* one another.[8] Phèdre is an actualization of Vénus and Hippolyte an incarnation of his father, and in a sense the question at stake in the plot is whether, how, and by whom such identification will admit of effective and complete transfer, thus bridging the space between referent and appositive: whether Phèdre can act on her own, Vénus through her or she through Oenone; whether the son will agree to replace the father; whether the monster will claim his own or merely an innocent in whom Thésée has mistakenly identified monstrous qualities.

Stylistically specific to, and symbolic of, this inquiry, apposition in *Phèdre* represents then not only a major rhythmic, semantic and thematic locus for the meaning of the play but a crucial element as well in the elaboration of that meaning. Racine's diction and style give a sense of homogeneity to his universe, and appositives in particular create within that universe a kind of family resembance, fully as much as do certain thematic or structural constants. What is striking about *Phèdre*, however, is how that family resemblance is actualized in literal and mythic senses as well.[9] Apposition in *Phèdre* is, finally, the point where syntax, person and myth converge, and it is because the play thus resonates on so many levels around the question of identification that the tragic web seems woven so tightly and the effect of it all so great.

Chapter III

LA BRUYERE'S *CARACTERE* AS A PATTERN OF PERSON

One of the major models of patterning of the person in the generation preceding La Bruyère was the portrait. Putatively based on an individual and presenting a series of traits or qualities juxtaposed in parallel fashion, the portrait proceeded from the physical to the psychological, and depending on the genre in which it appeared (novel, memoirs, sermon, satire, or in isolation) it ran the gamut from description to moral exemplum, and from convention and idealization to caricature.[1]

Latin rhetoric had already distinguished between *portrait* and *character*: "Portrayal consists in representing and depicting in words clearly enough for recognition the bodily form of some person. Character delineation consists in describing a person's character by the definite signs which, like distinctive marks, are attributes of the character. . ."[2] On the one hand, an individual in his physical appearance, to which seventeenth-century writers will add psychological, "moral" analysis; on the other, emphasis on the signs which distinguish and typify. Formally and generically, La Bruyère's sketches belong to the Theophrastan *caractère* mode, bolstered by translations from the English tradition and adapted to the literary climate of his time. The word *caractère* in his title is far more ambiguous than its twentieth-century equivalent and even its English cognate, referring in its various contexts to personal psychology, force of character, moral fiber, characteristics, character-types or social role.[3]

By *caractère* I refer to those remarks which some critics call portraits or anecdotes, vignettes featuring individuals or types, as distinct from the fragments which could be called *maximes*, *sentences* or *pensées*. Distinct from the portrait as well, they represent the intersection of the psychological, social, esthetic and moral dimensions of the work, and are moreover its most original aspect and the pieces for which La Bruyère is best remembered. My intent here is to elucidate the various stylistic and formal elements which go into the construction of *caractère* as a pattern of person (hence my spelling of "caracterial"), and to strike a balance between the exceptional or nonce device on the one hand and the strict invariant or lowest common denominator on the other. The elements isolated here are therefore virtual but probable with respect to a given *caractère*. I have tried to construct a continuous, logical model, moving from syntactical detail to larger considerations at the level of mode and metaphor. In a work whose overall structure of organization remains highly problematic, this fundamental coherence of *caractère* pattern, whatever its degree of actualization in a given case, remains a basic reference point and locus of meaning, one which generates not only the "air de famille" among the *caractères* but the sense as well of a unified vision of man in society.[4]

Even a reader familiar with the literature of La Bruyère's time is struck by the numerous specific references to clothing (*MP*, 28; *F*, 29; *C*, 48). There are those who make a point of their finery and choice of elegant material (*V*, 3; *H*, 71; *QU*, 16, 24); others seem more interested in jewelry (*BF*, 21), to the point of envying the trappings of a prince of the Church (*MP*, 26). The wise man eschews ridiculous affectation (*M*, 11) whereas Philémon cuts a magnificent but hollow figure (*MP*, 27).

Un homme à la cour, et souvent à la ville, qui a un long manteau de soie ou de drap de Hollande, une ceinture large et placée haut sur l'estomac, le soulier de maroquin, la calotte de même, d'un beau grain, un collet bien fait et bien empesé, les cheveux arrangés et le teint vermeil, ... cela s'appelle un docteur. (*MP*, 28)

Clothes do not make the man, but they are a convenient means for identifying him and especially for discovering what he is not. As we shall see, La Bruyère effects a reversal of values whereby overt manifestation of a desire to impress and deceive becomes

LA BRUYERE 61

part of an indictment against those who parade about like peacocks. Moreover, clothes can be classed with other elements of what we now call conspicuous consumption: one's retinue (*BF*, 1), a fine carriage (*BF*, 16; *V*, 15), palatial surroundings (*BF*, 23, 78, 79; *G*, 29). La Bruyère's reference to food and drink (*BF*, 1, 47, 63; *V*, 4; *G*, 28) and particularly to digestion as evidence of self-satisfaction (*BF*, 18; *H*, 122; *J*, 82; *QU*, 24) are all the more striking for their rarity outside the novels and satirical poetry considered vulgar by his contemporaries.

Even more than clothes, cosmetics and makeup is the locus where the personal and the material, the dissimulator and the means of dissimulation come together (*F*, 5; *M*, 12). But perhaps the most telltale sign of all is the almost total absence in *Les Caractères* of corporeal description as such, and the immediate leap to the point at which one's physique is debased into an attitude, an expression of what one would like to appear: "Il y a dans quelques femmes une grandeur artificielle, attachée au mouvement des yeux, à un air de tête, aux façons de marcher, et qui ne va pas plus loin" (*F*, 2). Natural simplicity is lost as men and women seek out socially determined ways of being or seeming to be.

N**, avec un portier rustre, farouche, tirant sur le Suisse, avec un vestibule et une antichambre, pour peu qu'il y fasse languir quelqu'un et se morfondre, qu'il paraisse enfin avec une mine grave et une démarche mesurée, qu'il écoute un peu et ne reconduise point: quelque subalterne qu'il soit d'ailleurs, il fera sentir de lui-même quelque chose qui approche de la considération. (*BF*, 11)

La Bruyère devotes two chapters to the art and importance of speaking (*SC, CH*), and abundant other references confirm its position in social activity. Speaking is action, and just as it is worthwhile cultivating one's voice (*M*, 14) one can reap prestige by having the ear of a great noble (*Cœur*, 71; *C*, 16). Name-dropping is a prominent activity, and failing the inspiration of illustrious names one can always try to bluff via self-inflation ("un homme de ma qualité," *BF*, 21), extravagant use of the language, or even like Théodecte sheer sound production (*SC*, 12). The only problem of course is that one may be found out. Some condemn themselves through their own momentum (*SC*, 14), others by their incompetence (*H*, 83).

La Bruyère's use of *style indirect libre* provides much more subtle irony. He sometimes chooses to italicize lest the point be missed (*F*, 29; *SR*, 11). Elsewhere italics, like quotation marks, are simply missing: expressions like "que ce soit l'intérêt seul" (*MP*, 10) belong first to the character, verbally or mentally, but are half appropriated, "liberated," by the observer. In certain cases the author even expands the device from one detail among many to a major element in the development, as in the long passage imitating the charlatan's spiel (*QU*, 68), or to the whole remark. "C'est déjà trop d'avoir avec le peuple une même religion et un même Dieu: quel moyen encore de s'appeler *Pierre, Jean, Jacques*, comme le marchand ou le laboureur? Evitons d'avoir rien de commun avec la multitude; affectons au contraire toutes les distinctions qui nous en séparent" (*G*, 23). The religious skeptic (*EE*, 22) and the name-dropper (*G*, 23) are at opposite poles of presentation from the "dialogue" with Acis (*SC*, 7), whose speech is in fact indicated by the author without actually being transcribed. The point to be made here, however, is precisely that there is a continuum, however spotty, of speech and speakers (see Garapon, pp. 139-41). It is not a question of opposing direct and indirect discourse, but of noting the variety of ways in which speech appears.

Moreover, there are many remarks which combine more than one trait, leading the reader to conclude that a detail of speech, for example, should be considered suggestive and associative rather than exclusive or definitive, limited to the instance where it appears. And if various details and examples make up the category of speech, that category in turn is one of many which are juxtaposed by La Bruyère. The accumulated details (clothes, speech, attitude, etc.) are subsumed into a higher syntactic level in a series of verb phrases, juxtaposed in a grouping of elements which often partake of different categories or orders of observation but which through their unarticulated *rapprochement* are implicitly considered similar or even identical manifestations emanating from a common source. "On ne tient guère plus d'un moment contre une écharpe d'or et une plume blanche, contre un homme qui *parle au Roi et voit les ministres*" (*F*, 29; italics in the original). The individual thus heaps up things, hoping that extension from one detail to another will create the impression of a character all of a piece: "il porte une perruque, l'habit serré, le bas uni, et il est dévot: tout se règle par la mode" (*M*, 16).[5]

Like their Theophrastan predecessors, La Bruyère's *caractères* can thus be depended on: "un sot ni n'entre, ni ne sort, ni ne s'assied, ni se lève, ni ne se tait, ni n'est sur ses jambes, comme un homme d'esprit" (*MP*, 37); but the *moraliste* also turns that dependability around to show not only deductively that type T will do t_1, t_2, t_3, etc., but conversely that if someone does t_1, t_2, t_3, etc., we can begin to speculate on what type he represents (*M*, 11, 21). And for all their frantic scurrying about they have no follow-through: *caractère* as a significant arrangement of details and observation is at base a question of attitudes, in the sense of both striking a pose and as outlook or mental set.

... Cydias, après avoir toussé, relevé sa manchette, étendu la main et ouvert les doigts, débite gravement .... (*SC*, 75)

Rien ne découvre mieux dans quelle *disposition* sont les hommes à l'égard des sciences et des belles-lettres ... Le comédien, couché dans son carrosse, jette de la boue au visage de CORNEILLE, qui est à pied. (*J*, 17)

Ces mêmes modes que les hommes suivent si volontiers pour leurs personnes, ils affectent de les négliger dans leurs portraits ... ils leur préfèrent une parure arbitraire, une draperie indifférente, fantaisies du peintre qui ne sont prises ni sur l'air ni sur le visage, qui ne rappellent, ni les mœurs ni la personne. Ils aiment des *attitudes* forcées ou immodestes, une manière dure, sauvage, étrangère, qui font un capitan d'un jeune abbé, et un matamore d'un homme de robe; une Diane d'une femme de ville; comme d'une femme simple et timide une amazone ou une Pallas; une Laïs d'une honnête fille; un Scythe, un Attila, d'un prince qui est bon et magnanime. (*M*, 15)

Moreover, it is also a fact that the *caractères* contain very few "pure" anecdotes, events (e.g., *H*, 35) told from beginning to end without some kind of overt authorial intervention. In that sense, the *caractère* is faithful to the tradition of portraiture in which the present tense cites constant attributes or expresses a general truth, although the portrait was basically a series of static notations using *être* or *avoir*. Like Theophrastus, La Bruyère frequently places his characters in a kind of typical time, describing a number of activities in the present tense but in juxtaposition rather than sequence, thereby creating an effect of range and generality. The story of Arrias' discomfiture, for example, is apparently based on a real event. A closer look, however, shows that the anecdote is one manifestation among many.

Arrias a tout lu, a tout vu, il veut le persuader ainsi; c'est un homme universel, et il se donne pour tel: il aime mieux mentir que de se taire ou de paraître ignorer quelque chose. On parle à la table d'un grand d'une cour du Nord: il prend la parole.... Quelqu'un se hasarde de le contredire... "C'est Sethon à qui vous parlez, lui-même ...." (SC, 9)

The talk at the noble's table is an example, a subcategory, of his general character trait, and the contradiction in turn a particular instance within that example. The fact that the most dramatic and juiciest morsel (Arrias' comeuppance) comes last is only confirmation that sooner or later the character's negative potential was bound to create a scene.

A number of *caractères* even extend outside the realm of immediate observation, so that the catalogue of what they do includes what they might do as well. At least five constructions introduce or express this kind of hypothetical activity: the *si*-clause (i.e., "if and when"), inversion of subject and verb, "experimental" imperatives, the future and the conditional. Curiously, the paratactic composition which seems ultimately to impel this extension in time also reduces the conditional, conjectural aspect of this possible behavior, so that it flows naturally and unobtrusively from the observed activities. As such it underscores the excessive consistency which is a major feature of the type.[6]

Si on lui demande quelle heure il est, il tire une montre qui est un chef-d'œuvre; la garde de son épée est un onyx... (*MP*, 27)

Laissez faire Ergaste, et il exigera un droit de tous ceux qui boivent de l'eau de la rivière, ou qui marchent sur la terre ferme... (*BF*, 28)

Vient-on de placer quelqu'un dans un nouveau poste, c'est un débordement de louanges en sa faveur, qui inonde les cours et la chapelle, qui gagne l'escalier, les salles, la galerie, tout l'appartement... *Commence-t-il* à chanceler dans ce poste où on l'avait mis, tout le monde passe facilement à un autre avis... (*C*, 32)

Despite then a certain number of *caractères* whose names are didactically significant (Cydias, Periandre, Tryphon, Gnathon, etc.), *caractère* is a pattern based on predication: although our reading begins at the grammatical subject, that subject is in a sense the last step in the process of juxtaposing paratactically objects, traits, actions; verb phrases; moments; cases—a prime example of Todorov's "forme vide que viennent remplir les différents prédicats."[7] Pamphile (*G*, 50) shows traces of the process, moving successfully from *Pamphile*-Dangeau to *un Pamphile*, then *les Pamphiles*, and Ménalque is so colossal an accumulation that La Bruyère felt obliged to note: "Ceci est moins un caractère particulier qu'un recueil de faits de distractions" (*H*, 7).

Theophrastus had used both typical time and hypothetical extension, but La Bruyère's variety of presentation makes for an intellectual operation which is considerably different. As already noted, in addition to the deductive mode, there are many *caractères* whom we first discover in their behavior because the explanation of their conduct comes in the middle or at the end of the passage, if at all. Pamphile (*G*, 50) combines all of the possibilities, but *caractères* like Hermagoras (*SC*, 74) or Théognis (*G*, 48) are simple descriptions. As with free indirect discourse, it is up to the reader to induce from the evidence what makes so-and-so "tick." "Il ne faut pas juger des hommes comme d'un tableau ou d'une figure, sur une seule et première vue: il y a un intérieur et un cœur qu'il faut approfondir. Le voile de la modestie couvre le mérite, et le masque de l'hypocrisie cache la malignité" (*J*, 27).

Generally, however, the *moraliste* leads the way and, if induction is one of La Bruyère's main innovations to the *caractère* tradition, the implied author and "je" are its major practitioners, rather than the reader: "On ne les a jamais vus assis, jamais fixes et arrêtés . . . Ils ne viennent d'aucun endroit, ils ne vont nulle part: ils passent et ils repassent. Ne les retardez pas dans leur course précipitée, vous démonteriez leur machine . . ." (*C*, 19). La Bruyère juxtaposes a series of present tenses to express frenetic social activity, and consequently his characters—despite their own attempts at extension or because of them—find themselves on a sterile, repetitive treadmill: "Il fera demain ce qu'il fait aujourd'hui et ce qu'il fit hier; et il meurt ainsi après avoir vécu" (*V*, 12). Although few of the *caractères* which do go somewhere are as explicitly enigmatic as *F*, 36 ("Qu'est-ce qu'une femme que l'on dirige?"), as many as 125 remarks in all have a conclusion which is more than a natural outcome. The most striking example of juxtaposition followed by interpretive conclusion is of course *BF*, 83: "Il est riche . . . il est pauvre." The *moraliste*'s explanation casts a harsh spotlight, throwing everything into sharper focus. A larger number, for example, refer to time running out or out of control, and even to death, as counterweights to the extension of which La Bruyère so disapproves.

> Je suppose qu'il n'y ait que deux hommes sur la terre, qui la possèdent seuls, et qui la partagent toute entre eux deux: je suis persuadé qu'il leur naîtra bientôt quelque sujet de rupture, quand ce ne serait que pour les limites. (*SC*, 47)
>
> Il faut avoir trente ans pour songer à sa fortune; elle n'est pas faite à cinquante; l'on bâtit dans la vieillesse, et l'on meurt quand on en est aux peintres et aux vitriers. (*BF*, 40)
>
> Titius assiste à la lecture d'un testament avec des yeux rouges et humides ... Il y a un codicile, il faut le lire: il fait Maevius légataire universel, et il renvoie Titius dans son faubourg, sans rentes, sans titres, et le met à pied. Il essuie ses larmes: c'est à Maevius à s'affliger. (*QU*, 59)

The rationale for the disapproval is that extension inevitably becomes overextension. La Bruyère says as much when he refers to Cydias' overrefined thoughts and overwrought logic (*SC*, 75) or social climbers in the clergy (*MP*, 26), but he discerns it on a more fundamental level as well: "une chose folle ... c'est l'assujettissement aux modes quand on l'*étend* à ce qui concerne le goût, le vivre, la santé et la conscience" (*M*, 1).

In their extensive mania, individuals give away whatever source of their own definition once existed: Théodecte cannot be distinguished from his host (*SC*, 12); Pamphile is not a Great but an imitation (*G*, 50); the financiers are not men, they *have* money (*BF*, 58); "... affectant ainsi un caractère éloigné de celui qu'ils ont à soutenir, ils deviennent enfin, selon leurs souhaits, des copies fidèles de très méchants originaux" (*V*, 7).

In the caracterial model, overextension thus culminates in hyperbole: Théognis exacerbates his own proliferation in order to take no chances: "Marche-t-il dans les salles, il se tourne à droite, où il y a un grand monde, et à gauche, où il n'y a personne" (*G*, 48). Likewise, the bourgeois swallow food for a hundred families in one gulp (*BF*, 47); eating is Cliton's life and perhaps his resurrection (*H*, 122); impertinent jokesters teem like insects (*SC*, 3), and whole families are born in a single night (*C*, 57). One's presence and identity no longer have meaning, but yield for their definition to the means of extension: a musician gets back into the case with his lute (*J*, 56), Antagoras is an old piece of furniture (*H*, 125), Diphile a bird (*M*, 2). And as with the interpretive conclusions which "block" the completion of possible narrations, so at a critical point the metonymic principle of composition—identification and definition by contiguity, extension of detail—pulls up short, absorbed and appraised by metaphor as another, and major, mode of interpretation and judgment.

The mechanical metaphors in the *Caractères* suggest that "what makes a *caractère* tick" is more than idle colloquialism, although it would be at least as accurate in a sense to say that ticking makes a *caractère*. Furthermore, the metaphorical function in general is remarkably consistent in the work. The main sources of metaphor (machinery, commerce, theater, animals, sickness, enslavement) all refer in context to the process or result of depersonalization. Society is a world where behavior is regulated like a machine rather than spontaneous, and interpersonal contact is comparable to financial exchange. Willing slaves or stricken with a sickness, men so lose their human dignity that they are taken for monkeys, birds, insects, etc.

L'homme du meilleur esprit est inégal ... Le sot est automate, il est machine, il est ressort ... qui l'a vu une fois, l'a vu dans tous les instants et dans toutes les périodes de sa vie; c'est tout au plus le bœuf qui meugle, ou le merle qui siffle: il est fixé et déterminé par sa nature, et j'ose dire par son espèce. (*H*, 142)[8]

One could hardly find a better example of stylistic convergence. The various devices—types, hyperbole, metaphor, juxtaposition, the generalizing present tense—come together to show how a new typology results necessarily from the loss of self and human dignity (*J*, 103).[9]

The consistent observation of concrete and specific details is extremely important in the *Caractères* and a major innovation in the seventeenth-century *moraliste* context, but as we have seen La Bruyère maintains the *moraliste*'s external point of view, above fashion and convention so that detail is perceived as the locus of a personal "code" (my word), in the sense of both a system of signs and an ethos, a stylized presentation of self to society. In a few instances he acknowledges the importance of manners (*SC*, 31, 32; *J*, 85), but he spends most of his time castigating personal eccentricities and more generally a whole era which has gone awry.

The most literal examples of such a code are titles: "... à force de beaux noms, de disputes sur le rang et les préséances, de nouvelles armes, et d'une généalogie que D'HOZIER ne lui a pas faite, il devient enfin un petit prince" (*QU*, 7). Self-inflation runs not only into the past but also into the higher reaches of society (*V*, 20) and even extends abroad: "Certaines gens... allongent leurs noms français d'une terminaison étrangère, et croient que venir de bon lieu c'est venir de loin" (*QU*, 9). Moreover, Kirsch aptly points out the use of the same verb (*allonger*) applied to names and to a team of horses (*SC*, 9; *QU*, 9).[10]

Another obvious code in need of interpretation is the "newspeak" which many parvenus affect. La Bruyère is as attentive to the hypocrisy of jargon and neologisms as he is to name-droppers and usurped titles: "'propre à tout'... ce qui signifie toujours ... propre à rien" (*MP*, 10); "Epouser une veuve, en bon français, signifie faire sa fortune" (*BF*, 61); "sa tannerie, qu'il appelle bibliothèque" (*M*, 2). The verbs of definition (*signifier, appeler*) emphasize the fact that we are dealing with signs which must be given special scrutiny where things are no longer called by their right names (*C*, 62; *QU*, 6, 73; see also Stegmann on *décryptage*, pp. 146-50, 190-92).

Finally, in a few instances La Bruyère points out explicitly what is transpiring: "qui avec cela se souvient de quelques distinctions métaphysiques" (*MP*, 28): "ils accompagnent un langage si extravagant d'un geste affecté et d'une prononciation qui est contrefaite" (*SC*, 6); "sa voix, sa démarche, son geste, son attitude accompagnent son visage" (*C*, 61). In the last case, the author has already compared Théodote to an actor arriving on stage, and it becomes apparent that a character's system of self-expression is in fact a series of clues on two levels. The desire to distinguish oneself may or may not lead to social prestige, but in the context of the *Caractères* it necessarily results in self-incrimination. The code exists, so to speak, solely to be broken. "Drance veut passer pour gouverner son maître, qui n'en croit rien... [his efforts] marquent mieux un fat qu'un favori" (*Cœur*, 71).

LA BRUYERE 69

The point is that if one's code is to succeed it must seem to be a continuation, a simple expression of one's person rather than a borrowing. The first and most direct step in breaking it is therefore to show it up as a code, a representation rather than a reality, and at the most general level of assessment this is the function of figurative references to mask and theater. Theater was of course a conventional expression for social function and drama: what distinguishes La Bruyère's use of the device is the sense of a continuity, which he establishes at one pole by references to makeup but which runs through all aspects of his "presentation." The people he observes are perceived as actors who arrive on the social scene with schemes resembling stage machinery or masks, and who hope to play a more important role than the one in which they were originally cast. The field of the theatrical motif is thus literal, conventional and figurative, sustaining countless references to seeming and appearances, enriching and complicating the notion of "character."

In a few rare but extremely significant remarks the theatrical image is taken one step further, and we find ourselves in a foreign land whose conventions we no longer share and which consequently have become opaque. Some references express an ironic ethnocentrism whereby customs which seem perfectly natural appear barbaric to other eyes: gambling (*BF*, 71, 72), abuse of alcohol (*J*, 24), apparent worship of the king at Versailles (*V*, 74), the obligation of a bride to entertain on the day after her wedding night (*V*, 19). All are negative proofs that one should find rationality everywhere (*J*, 22), ironic indictments of "our" elegance (*J*, 23). Still more significant are the remarks which see "our" world as not only strange but systematically so, a country where joy is a mask and suffering hidden (*C*, 63). The court is a new world (*C*, 9) and the town is divided into so many little republics, each with "its own laws, customs, jargon and amusements." (*V*, 4). Extension and self-inflation thus have culminated in the establishment of coteries preoccupied only with self and the exclusion of the unwelcome or uninitiated. "L'homme du monde d'un meilleur esprit, que le hasard a porté au milieu d'eux, leur est étranger: il se trouve là comme dans un pays lointain, dont il ne connaît ni les routes, ni la langue, ni les mœurs, ni la coutume . . ." (ibid.).[11]

This man of the world embodies the *moraliste* undertaking to get at the meaning of the signs, and in the last example his very failure is an indictment, the positive foil to social exaggeration and abuse. This "representative" does not always fail, however, and a number of remarks deal explicitly and even theoretically with successful observation.

Celui qui a pénétré la cour connaît ce que c'est que vertu et ce que c'est que dévotion; il ne peut plus s'y tromper. (*M*, 20)

Un homme de mérite se donne, je crois, un joli spectacle, lorsque la même place à une assemblée, ou à un spectacle, dont il est refusé, il la voit accorder à un homme qui n'a point d'yeux pour voir, ni d'oreilles pour entendre, ni d'esprit pour connaître et pour juger... (*C*, 60)

The lucidity of the successful observer is in direct opposition to the blindness, conceit and/or favorable predisposition which La Bruyère defines as the miserable state of *prévention* (*J*, 41; *G*, 1). "L'homme, qui est esprit, se mène par les yeux et les oreilles" (*H*, 154); "j'ouvre de fort grands yeux sur eux, je les contemple: ils parlent, je prête l'oreille; je m'informe, on me dit des faits, je les recueille" (*F*, 42; *G*, 20). Thus while one can agree with Jean Mouton's emphasis on the importance in the *Caractères* of objects and a vision of them, he seems to use objectification as something of an ethical *pis-aller* on the writer's part, which I think is to approach things from the wrong direction.[12]

Vision in the *Caractères* is rather an elucidation of the "extensive" nature of *caractère*, playing over the range of human activity, the variety and interaction of social types, highlighting certain aspects and imposing finally its own ethic. The observation of significant detail and its extension rather than emphasis on its explanation, "masquer le concept sous le percept" in Roland Barthes's formulation,[13] creates finally a *caractère* which is empty at the center—"les grands n'ont point d'âme" (*G*, 25); "les hommes n'ont point de caractère" (*H*, 147)—but which is at the same time in a kind of perpetual generation, expressed by a syntax of predication and potential. The code is broken almost immediately, however, by the *moraliste*'s arrangement and presentation of the results of his observation, and through hyperbolic and metaphoric figures of dehumanization, the caracterial process is shown and judged to be in fact degenerative. Borrowing its basic structure—paratactic juxtaposition of predicates—from the Theophrastan and portrait traditions, La Bruyère's *caractère* represents a loosening and apparent individualizing of the ancient genre, but is nonetheless antithetical to the presuppositions of the portrait insofar as the latter posits an "essence" to be described. The emphasis on predication and the equivalence among predicates imply on the contrary a subject which is empty, absent, a grammatical minimum and at best a second thought or the type-name one gives to a certain behavior. The person of *Les Caractères* is thus the creation of a writer whose positive ethical ideal expresses itself for the most part as an esthetic of the negative. Even La Bruyère's positive models are, in their primary definition, reversed images of human failings: the opposite of negative *caractères*, moral rather than behavioral, simple and modest rather than "extended" and self-important. In a word, examples of integrity in the congruence they embody between self and representation, and in their resistance to loss of self through the passage of time and social decline.

L'honnêteté, les égards et la politesse des personnes avancées en âge de l'un et l'autre sexe me donnent bonne opinion de ce qu'on appelle le vieux temps. (*J*, 83)

L'on contemple dans les cours de certaines gens, et l'on voit bien à leurs discours et à toute leur conduite qu'ils ne songent ni à leurs grands-pères ni à leurs petits-fils: le présent est pour eux; ils n'en jouissent pas, ils abusent. (*C*, 95)

Il faut l'avouer, le présent est pour les riches, et l'avenir pour les vertueux et les habiles. HOMERE est encore et sera toujours; les receveurs de droits, les publicains ne sont plus... Que sont devenus ces importants personnages qui méprisaient Homère ... Que deviendront les *Fauconnets*? (*BF*, 56)

Whether it be in regard to women's affectation (*F*, 6), overnight prestige (*C*, 32, 57; *J*, 59), a courtier turned pious (*M*, 18), a commoner rehabilitated (*QU*, 3), or sacred eloquence as entertainment (*CH*, 1), the passage of time is the context and symbol of a general degradation, most often expressed by the notion of *becoming*. Hopeful references to the future derive more from rhetoric than from a neutral sense of history, and La Bruyère's frequent use of the present perfect in *BF* to depict money as a major source of the disruptive and pernicious process of change —"l'étrange disproportion que le plus ou le moins de pièces de monnaie est entre les hommes" (*BF*, 5)—contrasts strikingly with the "eternal" present of *moraliste* writing and perhaps represents, together with the emphasis on external, concrete detail, his major contribution to seventeenth-century writing on the person.

Onuphre (*M*, 24) is a spectacular and unique example of a *caractère* who has mastered the system, thanks to a "parfaite, quoique fausse imitation de la piété," and whose *caractère* is a juxtaposition of successes. Ménalque (*H*, 7) is at the other extreme, hopelessly but spectacularly awash in a sea of signs. In an oblique relationship to the Ménalque/Onuphre continuum of social presence, indeed in a different realm, is the man whose honorable qualities are summed up in his unfamiliarity with the Court (*C*, 1). All three obviously belong to the writer's world, but as I am using the terms the first two belong primarily to *esthetic*, the third to *ethic*. The eccentrics are an ironic tribute to the center (ex-centrics), and that mankind should seek happiness "hors de nous-mêmes" (*H*, 76), having therefore "quelque chose à se reprocher" (*H*, 136), is mankind's misfortune but the reader's gain. Virtue as its own excuse is more important perhaps, but less colorful and less dramatically "patterned" than the significant disproportion of a coquette who dresses up as she passes away (*F*, 7), Sannion the hunter if only he could shoot straight (*V*, 10), or Iphis whose foot keeps him home (*M*, 14).[14] In La Bruyère's hands, that misdirected consistency, the logical and seemingly inevitable result of a certain human weakness or negative potential, culminates in a disproportion which is not only a "sign" of the times but one which still signifies—precisely because of its schematic pattern—in a very modern way: "... les embrassements et les caresses des grands ... achèvent de lui nuire, il se déconcerte, il s'étourdit: c'est une courte aliénation" (*C*, 50). I turn now to a case where accumulative rhythm is an equally determinant signifier of the person, but is situated deep in the psyche of the written self rather than in an empty, outer shell.

Chapter IV

ACCUMULATION AND "DEDOMMAGEMENT" IN
LES REVERIES DU PROMENEUR SOLITAIRE

Jean Starobinski has described a recurrent sentence type in Rousseau's *Rêveries du promeneur solitaire* as "une sorte de litanie, qui commence en général par l'adjectif *seul*, et qui se continue par une succession de termes négativement détérminées par la préposition *sans*. Cette séquence obsédée, où la virgule intervient comme un soupir, donne concrètement l'impression du manque d'appui, de l'absence de prise positive sur les choses ...,"[1] and Marcel Raymond in the Pléiade edition (pp. 1765-66) cites an example as early as the second page of the *Rêveries*: "Sans adresse, sans art, sans dissimulation, franc, ouvert, impatient, emporté...."[2]

Yet the very fact that *seul* is missing but implicit in the example seems an indication that the rhythm itself may bear some of the same connotations, and indeed if we focus more consistently on the rhythmic aspect of such a sentence type its importance in the *Rêveries* emerges even more dramatically. That is, although as Leo Spitzer remarked in his study of rhythm in Diderot, "whenever one deals with the problem of expressivity of language, 'expression' can be stated only when meaning and linguistic form converge,"[3] close attention here will show—as did Spitzer—that the meaning of the lexical elements found in the rhythmic pattern has in a sense been anticipated by the syntax, and they are no more "meaningful" than this deeper, almost subliminal source. Specifically, accumulative rhythm in the *Rêveries* appears to carry consistently and throughout the work a very particular and noticeable emotional charge.

As I will be using the term, "accumulation" designates a phenomenon which is somewhat less organized and precise than "enumeration," which it includes, and is concerned with elements—words, phrases, clauses—in like grammatical and syntactical situations, often presented asyndetically. In other words, I shall not be looking here at metric syllable counts, or periodic sentence structure, although either may also be at work in some of my examples. Nor shall I develop at length here the semantic relationship among the accumulated elements: generally speaking, they are synonymous and provide slight rather than significant variations, referring back—as in the examples mentioned by Starobinski and Raymond—to such archlexemes as *injury* and *nature*, or archsememes like *solitude* and *the* (maleficent) *Other*. And finally, it goes without saying that because "accumulation" is at base syntactic, there is no logical contradiction in speaking of negative accumulations, as in the case of Starobinski's description.

Among other advantages, tracing primarily the rhythm shows how very early this source of meaning occurs in the work, and so helps elucidate the impact of the extremely effective opening sentence: "Me voici donc seul sur la terre, n'ayant plus de frère, de prochain, d'ami, de société que moi-même" (p. 995). Earlier critics have dealt with the significance to the *Rêveries* of *donc* and *seul*,[4] and in a recent thesis Jenny H. Batlay has shown in an analysis of the first paragraph and its ramifications how the grammatical subject/object dichotomy and especially the *moi/ les autres* opposition constitute "the matrix which expands to form the underlying semantic network of the text."[5] Her study includes much stylistic analysis, since her intention is to demonstrate the binary nature of the form of the work, and at every level. Thus, when comparing openings of *Les Confessions* and *Les Rêveries*, i.e., "Moi seul" vs. "Me voici donc seul," she enunciates a principle which recalls Spitzer's remark: "In order to confirm similarity between two statements, one must analyze the structure in which these elements of discourse are embedded" (p. 131). While my perspective is similar, it is stylistic and subphrastic only, and while the results do not attenuate the fundamental opposition between Rousseau and "les autres" at the

LES REVERIES DU PROMENEUR SOLITAIRE 75

roots of the text it will become clear as well that at the syntactic level, accumulation—which is in a sense the opposite of binary structure—nonetheless plays a crucial role in the work.[6]

One obvious function of accumulation is to connote a weight or burden, a notion most palpable where the enumeration presents a *bilan*, often introduced by words referring specifically to a quantity or totality:

Je tombai dans les pieges qu'on creusa sous mes pas, l'indignation, la fureur, le délire s'emparerent de moi, je perdis la tramontane, ma tête se bouleversa, et dans les ténébres horribles ou l'on *n'a cessé* de me tenir plongé je n'apperçus plus ni lueur pour me conduire, ni appui, ni prise où je pusse me tenir ferme . . . (p. 1076)

Je vois *toute* une generation se precipiter *tout* entiére dans cette etrange opinion, sans explication, sans doute, et sans que je puisse . . . (p. 1076)

Other such *bilans* include a specific indication, a key word which alerts the reader to the writer's perspective, to the burden but also to how he assesses the phenomenon:

Je la relus après le depart de Mad^e d'Ormay, j'en examinai la tournure, j'y crus trouver *le motif* de ses visites, de ses cajoleries, des grosses louanges de sa préface . . . (p. 1008)

. . . un tel *labyrinthe* d'embarras, de difficultés, d'objections, de tortuosités, de ténébres . . . (p. 1017)

. . . tristes momens que je passe encore au milieu des hommes, *jouet* de leurs caresses traitresses, de leurs complimens ampoulés et derisoires, de leur mielleuse malignité. (p. 1081)

The tone of these examples brings us close to the psychic wound at the work's point of departure, the writer's feeling and conviction that he is the victim of willful and aggressive malfeasance. Furthermore, in other sentences we find that the *bilans* which were in a sense didactically illustrative, naming the phenomenon as well as expressing it, now give us a more concrete portrayal through the style itself, as though the writer were reliving those feelings as he set them down on paper, and as though the reader were to participate in them at each reading.[7] In some cases the intensity centers around the physical. "Les yeux etincellans, le feu du visage, le tremblement des membres, les suffocantes palpitations tout cela tient au seul physique et le raisonnement n'y peut rien..." (p. 1083); "Un signe, un geste, un coup d'œil d'un inconnu suffit pour troubler mes plaisirs ou calmer mes peines..." (p. 1094); "Seul, malade et delaissé dans mon lit, j'y peux mourir d'indifference, de froid et de faim..." (p. 1080). More frequently, as is partly the case in this last example, the intensity is psychological:

> ... je compris que les causes, les instrumens, les moyens de tout cela m'étant inconnus et inexplicables devoient être nuls pour moi. Que je devois regarder tous les détails de ma destinée comme autant d'actes d'une pure fatalité où je ne devois supposer ni direction, ni intention, ni cause morale, qu'il fallait m'y soumettre sans raisonner et sans regimber parce que cela serait inutile, que tout ce que j'avois à faire encore sur la terre étant de m'y regarder comme un être purement passif... (p. 1079)

> Les offenses, les vengeances, les passedroits, les outrages, les injustices, ne sont rien pour celui qui ne voit dans les maux qu'il endure que le mal meme et non pas l'intention... (p. 1080)

In the first example, accumulation—of clauses as well as single words—evokes the desperate resignation signified by the verb *devoir*, and in both a whole dimension of the *Rêveries* emerges, in the poignant contradiction of enumerating those things which reputedly no longer matter to a writer who declared early on that "tout ce qui m'est extérieur m'est étranger desormais" (p. 999).[8] The effect is analogous to the accumulation of *sans* commented on by Starobinski, and it becomes more and more clear that in the context of the *Rêveries* accumulative rhythm is associated with a threat—past or future, real or imagined. The syntax is a sign of psychic disarray, the stylistic manifestation of a recurrent disposition toward suffering.

Thus the opening sentence, which posits the distinction between *moi* and *les autres* and sets the *moi* at the center of a series of widening circles, is at the same time establishing the pertinence of a syntactic rhythm which recurs throughout the work, and significantly a few lines later we have a sentence of the same rhythmic type but where the *moi* is no longer the (grammatical) subject: "Les voila étrangers, inconnus, nuls enfin pour moi puisqu'ils l'ont voulu" (p. 995). The syntax here, in its close reflection of the opening sentence, is evidence that the rhythm has its own referent, simultaneously in the Others and in the pain Rousseau has suffered because of them; in that sense the rhythm can be said to express both terms of the fundamental

LES REVERIES DU PROMENEUR SOLITAIRE 77

moi/les autres polarity, and to confer on the Other, at a subconscious level, the textual presence which in *Les Liaisons dangereuses*, for example, will occur in a lucid, voluntary manipulation of the Other via epithet. The presence of the anguished *moi* in the *Rêveries* is thus overdetermined, occurring not only in the pronoun and the theme of the Other but also in a rhythm which slows the assimilation of the sentence and causes the reader to dwell, however briefly, on what thereby becomes an obsession and—because the elements are synonymous—nothing but the obsession. The sentence is briefly stalled, marking time and blocked by the Other as an obstacle to a smoother reading: in a quite literal sense, Rousseau "can't get over them." Numerous other examples occur in the first two pages:

> Je m'imagine toujours qu'une indigestion me tourmente, que je dors d'un mauvais sommeil, et que je vais me réveiller bien soulagé ... ; Eh! comment aurois-je pu ... comment le puis-je concevoir ... Pouvois-je ... , moi, le même homme que j'étois, le même que je suis encore, je passerois, je serois tenu sans le moindre doute pour un monstre, un empoisonneur, un assassin, que je deviendrois ... que toute la salutation ... qu'une generation toute entiére ... , tombé d'erreur en erreur, de faute en faute, de sotise en sotise ... , Sans adresse, sans art, sans dissimulation, sans prudence, franc, ouvert, impatient, emporté ... ; La diffamation, la depression, la dérision, l'opprobre ... (pp. 995-96)

This dense clustering at the outset of the work is a key to its reading, inducing the reader to associate from the start a particular rhythm with its nervous resonance in the writer, whatever the apparent or manifest subject of the sentence.

The variety of the work allows of several possible functions. Disculpation or accusation of past actions (examples 1 and 2), stigmatizing of others (example 3), *bilan* of a current painful situation (example 4), extrapolation from painful experience (examples 5 and 6):

> Enfant encore et livré à moi-même, alléché par des caresses, séduit par la vanité, leurré par l'espérance, forcé par la necessité, je me fis catholique ... (p. 1013)

> ... par quelle bizarre inconséquence mentois-je ainsi de gaité de cœur, sans nécessité, sans profit. (p. 1025)

> ... dès lors je devins le bureau général d'adresse de tous les souffreteux ou soidisans tels, de tous les avanturiers qui cherchoient des dupes, de tous ceux qui sous prétexte du grand crédit qu'ils feignoient de m'attribuer vouloient s'emparer de moi de manière ou d'autre. (p. 1052)

Aujourd'hui que mon cœur serré de détresse, mon ame affaissée par les ennuis, mon imagination effarouchée, ma tête troublée par tant d'affreux mistéres dont je suis environné, aujourd'hui que toutes mes facultés affoiblies par la vieillesse . . . (p. 1021)

Mais les Oratoriens que j'aimois, que j'estimois, en qui j'avois toute confiance et que je n'offensai jamais, les Oratoriens, gens d'Eglise et demi-moines, seront à jamais implacables, leur propre iniquité fait mon crime que leur amour-propre ne me pardonnera jamais, et le public dont ils auront soin d'entretenir et ranimer l'animosité sans cesse, ne s'appaisera pas plus qu'eux. (p. 999)

J'ai vu ces gens qu'on appelle vrais dans le monde. Toute leur véracité s'épuise dans les conversations oiseuses à citer fidellement les lieux, les tems les personnes, à ne se permettre aucune fiction, à ne broder aucune circonstance, à ne rien exagérer. (p. 1031)

The unity, however, is in the common denominator of a rhythm sufficient in itself to transmit the impression of a psychic vulnerability with which it is consistently associated, and which is never far away nor far below the surface. The text thus engenders an impression of fragility and precarious instability, as the rhythm is seemingly set off by a variety of provocations: "Mon imagination effarouchée, les combine, les étend, et les augmente" (p. 997); "j'y crus trouver le motif de ses visites, de ses cajoleries, des grosses louanges de sa préface . . ." (p. 1008); "Un signe, un geste, un coup d'œil inconnu suffit pour troubler mes plaisirs ou calmer mes peines" (p. 1094). This last example is typical of Rousseau's manic-depressive hypersensitivity to outside influences. Moreover, one is struck at the stylistic level by the "carry-over" power of the accumulative rhythm. Even when his emotions and reactions appear calmed, or should be so, rhythmic traces remain to indicate that all is not so serene as it appears. This will be of particular importance in my discussion of Rousseau's botanizing, but it is clear elsewhere as well:

Qu'on épie ce que je fais, qu'on s'inquiete de ces feuilles, qu'on s'en empare, qu'on les supprime, qu'on les falsifie, tout cela m'est égal desormais. (p. 1001)

Cette idée, loin de m'être cruelle et déchirante me console, me tranquillise, et m'aide à me résigner. (p. 1010, following several lines of negative enumerations)

Les jours où je ne vois personne, je ne pense plus à ma destinée, je ne la sens plus, je ne souffre plus, je suis heureux et content sans diversion, sans obstacle. Mais j'échape rarement à quelque atteinte sensible, et lorsque j'y pense le moins un regard sinistre que j'apperçois, un mot envenimé que j'entends, un malveillant que je rencontre, suffit pour me bouleverser. (p. 1082)

LES REVERIES DU PROMENEUR SOLITAIRE 79

In other cases where a certain sense of healthy well-being and happiness emerge, such feelings are nonetheless linked closely in time and space to accumulations in the negative mode:

> Une grande révolution qui venait de se faire en moi, un autre monde moral qui se devoiloit à mes regards, les insensés jugemens des hommes ... le besoin toujours croissant ... le desir enfin ... tout m'obligeoit à cette grande revue ... (p. 1015)
>
> Il n'est pas possible qu'une solitude aussi complette, aussi permanente, aussi triste en elle-même, l'animosité toujours sensible ... les indignités ... ne me jettent quelques fois dans l'abbatement; l'espérance ébranlée, les doutes decourageans reviennent encor de tems à autre ... C'est alors que ... j'ai besoin de me rappeler mes anciennes résolutions, les soins, l'attention, la sincérité de cœur que j'ai mise à les prendre reviennent alors à mon souvenir et rendent toute ma confiance. (p. 1023)

In other words, Rousseau's resolutions are not to be expressed gratuitously nor in complete and detached autonomy, and we return to the paradoxical functioning of memory in the *Rêveries*: how to relate once and for all the end of an obsession without relating—and reconstituting in memory and in text—the object of that obsession? Stated another way, what does it mean psychically and stylistically to write, as part of one's avowed intentions: "Je fixerai par l'écriture [the 'contemplations charmantes'] ... J'oublierai mes malheurs, mes persecuteurs, mes opprobres ..." (pp. 999-1000)?

A major and recurring notion in the *Rêveries* is that of *dédommagement*, the need for a refuge from suffering and/or compensation for it; consideration of some compensatory figures in the text will allow us now to see at least one other way accumulative rhythm functions in the work.[9]

One of the dominants in the thematic structure of his writing is a concentric perception of things, with a concomitant oscillation between expansion and withdrawal, and great value assigned to the necessity and ability to circumscribe the self: the opening sentence—beginning and ending with Rousseau's *moi*—is one of the most striking syntactic examples. On another level, the island represents a refuge which is literal, psychological and symbolic (see the two etymological faces in French: *isolement/ isolation*).[10] Spatially, the lac de Bienne as described in the Cinquième Promenade is at once the literal and associational example of a circular refuge far from the Others, as are *a fortiori* the île de Saint Pierre, its smaller sister, a boat on the lake. Temporally, the search for a refuge seems to replicate the idea of the *âge d'or* as a special moment in time, and the *Rêveries* are full of special moments from the writer's life, havens which he is now trying to set down in a certain permanence if not recoup altogether in his writing. His stay on the île Saint Pierre is the prime temporal and geographical refuge, and critics have perhaps not insisted enough on the textual position of that Promenade, which not only recounts and unites the themes of refuge, but which is itself an island almost at dead-center in the work as it exists, and in which the famous lakeside passage ("Quand le lac agité . . . ," pp. 1044-45) occupies the mid-point.

This is all by way of underscoring the importance of writing as *dédommagement*, as the plane on which but also through which a compensation takes place. Starobinski, in his masterly explication of a complicated state of affairs reminds us, following Marcel Raymond, that reveries are in fact quite rare in the text, or rather that Rousseau is in fact creating a "deferred echo" of his earlier daydreams, a "reviviscence" the writing of which, in its loose and disparate structure, will create a kind of second *rêverie*, which in turn will offer a "transmutation clarifiante," a unifying and retrospective vision of Rousseau's life and experience, and whose common denominator is the passage from suffering and conflict to a state of limpid simplicity, "convertir la douleur en volupté."[11] What I shall be looking at here is not so much the fact of writing as *dédommagement*, but the compensatory nature of the form of the writing itself.

In their discussions of psychology and rhythm, Osmont and Galliot call attention to the crucial role in the lakeside passage of binary rhythms and phonic structures, re-creating at the stylistic level the oscillation which is an ordered, mastered fluctuation leading to the semi-hypnotic state essential to the ecstasy Rousseau is recalling. Binary couplets, however, appear throughout the work to be less salient than the accumulative rhythm, confirming the finding of other stylistic studies of Rousseau. They are at once more numerous and less surprising or striking, and perhaps for that very reason have a balancing, stabilizing effect, one of reinforcement leading to consolidation—or at least striving toward such a situation—rather than the recurrent nagging effect of triadic and/or asyndetic combinations. Of course, as with accumulative rhythm, the mimetic value of binary structures is not perfectly and completely consistent, and one could list a number of counterexamples. What seems more important, however, is to note that not only is the mimetic correlation very high, but the distribution of both such rhythms correlates in a significant way with the variations of tone, outlook and meaning in the work. (It bears repeating that the value assigned here to rhythms in the work is but one source of the text's effects and, in a sentence like "Moi le même homme que j'étois, le même que je suis encor, je passerois, je serois tenu sans le moindre doute pour un monstre, un empoisonneur, un assassin, que je deviendrois l'horreur de la race humaine, le jouet de la canaille . . . " [p. 996], hyperbole and metaphor are as determinant of meaning as is the syntactic structure. At the same time, as I pointed out earlier, such a sentence placed as it is on the second page of the work alerts the reader to both the stylistic effects, and sets up a correlative expectation which will be maintained with a very high degree of consistency.)

The values are established then at the outset, and each will color to a great extent the subsequent contexts in which it appears. One major instance is the Dixième Promenade, and the fact that it is incomplete in no way affects the function of the stylistic devices clustered within the fragment, nor the pertinence of my hypothesis concerning the antithetical effect of the two rhythms in the work as a whole. On the contrary, binary structures occur here with a density similar to that of accumulative structures in the first few pages of the work and, as readers have so often noted, the *Rêveries* which had begun on a tormented (and tortuous) note of half-imposed, half-assumed "insularity" resulting from earlier persecutions now attain a serenity of which the Cinquième Promenade (again with its binary rhythm) was the principal antecedent.

un jeune homme vif mais doux et modeste . . . une femme charmante, pleine d'esprit et de graces . . . ; ce premier moment decida . . . et produisit . . . ; cet état delicieux mais rapide ou l'amour et l'innocence . . . ; je ne vivois plus qu'en elle et pour elle . . . ;

> Quels paisibles et délicieux jours . . . ; ils ont été courts et rapides; pas de jour où je ne me rappelle avec joye et attendrissement cet unique et court tems de ma vie où je fus moi pleinement sans mélange et sans obstacle . . . (pp. 1098-99)
>
> J'ai passé soixante et dix ans sur la terre, et j'en ai vécu sept. Sans ce court mais precieux espace . . . car tout le reste de ma vie, foible et sans resistance, j'ai été tellement agité, ballotté, tiraillé par les passions d'autri . . . (p. 1099)
>
> aimé d'une femme pleine de complaisance et de douceur . . . aidé de ses leçons et de son exemple . . . ; le gout de la solitude et de la contemplation . . . avec les sentimens expansifs et tendres . . . ; Le tumulte et le bruit les resserrent et les etouffent, le calme et la paix les raniment et les exaltent; j'ai joui d'un siécle de vie et d'un bonheur pur et plein . . . ; rempli par des soins affectueux ou par des occupations champêtres; des diversions sur cette inquietude et des ressources pour en prévenir l'effet. (p. 1099)

The examples are given in the order they occur, but are separated to set off the single accumulation in the Promenade ("agité, ballotté, tiraillé") and to show as well that the three binary structures which immediately precede it are not true counterexamples but take on much of their negative coloring from the immediate context.

One other instance of mimetic rhythm is the Septième Promenade, where this time binary structures are comparatively few and accumulations quite numerous. This is, of course, the Promenade where Rousseau evokes at length his botanizing, enumerating and cataloguing, and at first glance it may seem obvious or at least logical that in such a context the writer have recourse to a syntax of accumulation and enumeration. But stylistic analysis, where we are analyzing the linguistic form through which meaning is generated, reminds us that this "obvious" procedure in fact works the other way round, i.e., we did not know he was botanizing until he told us so, and in that telling (our reading) we absorb other important information along with, and at the same time as, the discovery of his activity.[12]

At a conscious level, Rousseau presents his botanic avocation as just that, an amateur's absorption and as such a useful and healthy—indeed, healing—middle term between sterile and painful remembering with nothing but his own problems as its objects, and the ultimately manipulative and destructive work of the professional. It is a pastime in which an old man can still indulge, a contemplative and inexpensive activity, the opposite of the reductive, abusive and exploitative work of others, and a welcome compensation for his declining imagination. Moreover, through a "chaine d'idées accessoires" (p. 1073) botany takes Rousseau beyond the feeling for nature which is only a first stage to the joy of remembered moments, into his past and even into a whole greater than himself but from which "they" are absent. It is thus an amusement but also a crucial mode of both expansion and introversion, an activity which is not so much transitive as reflexive, the action being turned back onto the subject and therefore ultimately therapeutic, a compensation not only for the infirmities of old age but for the pain as well with which memory and active reflection would otherwise fill his mind.

A number of formulations evoke the role and the importance of such an activity, to which he consents but which also takes hold of him, reshaping a banal or ordinary perspective and distinguishing Rousseau once again in the midst of his adversity, his difficulties—once they are turned around—becoming for him solutions.

Plus un contemplateur a l'ame sensible plus il se livre aux extases qu'excite en lui cet accord. Une rêverie douce et profonde s'empare alors de ses sens, et il se perd avec une délicieuse ivresse dans l'immensité de ce beau sistême avec lequel il se sent identifié. (pp. 1062-63)

Je me sens là-dessus tout à rebours des autres hommes. (p. 1065)

Je sens des extases, des ravissements inexprimables à me fondre pour ainsi dire dans le système des êtres, à m'identifier avec la nature entiére. (pp. 1065-66)[13]

As early as the second sentence, we are told that the written record of his daydreams has been supplanted: "un autre amusement lui succede, m'absorbe, et m'ote meme le temps de rever" (p. 1060). But it is not a simple exchange of one activity for another: one can develop as critics have the similarities and differences between the two, but in the light of a stylistic analysis it is clear that at least this first series of three is a positive one (as will be many others).[14] In biographical and chronological terms these positive accumulations almost certainly have their roots or their beginnings in the pleasure Rousseau takes in *herborisation*, but the pleasure continues to ramify throughout the Promenade even when it is not localized in the specific taxonomic function. This rhythmic pattern is so pervasive in the Septième Promenade as to create a lyrical tone not only in keeping with the optimism expressed through other devices—a rare self-deprecating humor, for example—but able as well to overcome the kind of negative "litany" with which the *Rêveries* began.

> privé ... des forces qui me restoient pour couvrir la campagne, sans guide, sans livres, sans jardin, sans herbier, me voila repris de cette folie ... ; Je commence toujours a bon compte par le mouron, le cerfeuil, la bourache et le seneçon. (p. 1061)
>
> ... vous demanderont des herbes pour guérir la rogne des enfants, la galle des hommes ou la morve des chevaux ... ; Ces idées medicinales ... fletrissent l'email des pres, l'eclat des fleurs, dessechent la fraicheur des boccages, rendent la verdure et les ombrages insipides et dégoutants; J'ai souvent pensé en regardant de près les champs, les vergers, les bois et leurs nombreux habitans ... (p. 1064)
>
> le plaisir ... seroit empoisonné par le sentiment des infirmités humaines s'il me laissoit penser à la fiévre, à la pierre, à la goute et au mal caduc; ... des medecins que j'estimois, que j'aimois, et à qui je laissois gouverner ma carcasse ... (p. 1065)[15]

Rousseau now records the grafting onto an apparently unshakeable nervous rhythm, of a new and therapeutic content.

> Je pris gout à cette recreation des yeux, qui dans l'infortune repose, amuse, distrait l'esprit et suspend le sentiment des peines.... Les odeurs suaves, les vives couleurs, les plus elegantes formes semblent se disputer à l'envi le droit de fixer nôtre attention. (p. 1063)
>
> Brillantes fleurs, email des près, ombrages frais, ruisseaux, bosquets, verdures, venez purifier mon imagination salie par tous ces hideux objets. (p. 1068)
>
> Je ne reverrai plus ces beaux paysages, ces forets, ces lacs, ces bosquets, ces rochers, ces montagnes ... je n'ai qu'à ouvrir mon herbier et bientot il m'y transporte.... C'est la chaine des idées accessoires qui m'attache à la botanique. Elle rassemble et rappelle à mon imagination toutes les idées qui la flatent davantage. Les près, les eaux, les bois, la solitude, la paix surtout et le repos qu'on trouve au milieu de tout cela sont retracés par elle incessamment à ma mémoire. Elle me fait oublier les persecutions des hommes, leur haine, leur mépris, leurs outrages et leurs maux ... (p. 1073)
>
> ... au lieu de desespoir qui sembloit devoir être enfin mon partage j'ai retrouvé la sérénité, la tranquillité, la paix, le bonheur même ... (p. 1077)

Botany thus not only gives a certain poise to Rousseau's instability by allowing him to focus on friendly objects, thereby "fixing" and crystallizing his problems in concrete terms outside himself: at the level of style it also assuages a certain psychic impulse, feeding a nagging and gnawing rhythm which would otherwise take his heart and soul for nourishment. Rousseau is of course not unaware of this process of displacement and transmutation,[16] but the reader attentive to style finds that the compensation is even more pervasive than the author himself perhaps realized, affecting not only the psyche but the writing which is our introduction to it. Writing is not a complete or permanent *dédommagement*, since Rousseau must recall painful memories and in setting them down must to some extent relive them. Conversely, however, to reconstitute in his writing a semblance of the botanical activity is to reverse the emotional charge borne by accumulative rhythm elsewhere in the text. Where binary structures play a crucial role in the tone of the Cinquième and Dixième Promenades, putting as it were fluctuation to a good and therapeutic use, in the Septième it is the accumulative rhythms which signify the precarious triumph, as uncontrolled recurrence is mastered and a new content infuses the rhythmic mold. To that extent and for the brief duration of that Promenade Rousseau is, stylistically as well as psychologically, intellectually, socially, *dédommagé*.

Chapter V

EPITHET, CHARACTER AND STRUCTURE IN
LES LIAISONS DANGEREUSES

The first letters of the *Liaisons dangereuses* are replete with information characterizing their authors. Cécile (I) writes from her convent (it is rare to see this underscored in the letterhead, and it will contrast markedly with the second letter, written by the Marquise de Merteuil *au Château de . . .*); she writes about frivolous "bonnets et pompons," but when she states overtly that she is putting them aside in order to write to Sophie the new subject matter is hardly more substantial; and she writes in a tone of innocent and bubbling insouciance which will long remain her hallmark in the work. Critics have dealt at length with Laclos's success at characterizing the major figures via noticeably individualized tones and styles, and I shall not dwell here on that particular dimension of characterization.[1]

At the same time, the first letter also introduces a theme which contributes not only to characterization, but also to our perception of the very process of characterization, how characters are created, and in the very special case of the *Liaisons* how they create one another. Thus Cécile is aware that "Maman . . . me traite beaucoup moins en pensionnaire que par le passé" but she could scarcely be expected to understand the importance to the ensuing action of such a role-oriented remark. Indeed, emergence from the convent will not in fact change Cécile's basic status since she remains almost literally a *personnage à faire*: "J'ai ma harpe, mon dessin et des livres comme au Couvent . . . et il ne tiendrait qu'à moi d'être toujours à rien faire." So virtual a status at the outset of the novel is perhaps not startling but is nonetheless a crucial element because she is there to be molded and because that status is emphasized so explicitly. Her character is not a "given" (except insofar as lack of a character is what characterizes her), and due to the plurality of narrative levels in the epistolary form that character will in fact be imposed by others, quite obviously and overtly replacing Madame de Volanges.

Moreover, the first anecdotal sequence—the arrival of a carriage—shows Cécile is no better at characterizing others, as she wrongly infers the identity of *le Monsieur*: "on me m'a encore parlé de rien . . . Maman m'a dit si souvent qu'une Demoiselle devait rester au Couvent jusqu'à ce qu'elle se mariât . . . Tu juges combien je l'examinais! . . . le Monsieur était un Cordonnier." Nor is this prototypical misapprehension of social and sexual role merely a rubric to be filled gradually by the plot, since in her spontaneity and the excess of her reaction to a banal event Cécile has begun to demonstrate the hypersensitive *émotivité* which will make her a subject of great interest to Merteuil.

Letter II immediately and explicitly proposes quite a different point of view on the same question: "si une fois vous formez cette petite fille . . . Au reste, l'Héroïne de ce nouveau Roman . . . un certain regard langoureux qui promet beaucoup en vérité." Cécile as we know her from the first letter is recognizable, but her potential is now not only extended but subsumed, put to use in a new scheme of things which in its lucid and cynical self-consciousness is at the opposite extreme from Cécile's mistaken attribution of role. Where both are in a sense looking for a proper mate for her, Cécile fit the role of intended to the first male she saw, whereas Merteuil has settled on her candidate only after a careful process of selection, one that takes into account both Cécile's nascent sensuality and Merteuil's own relation to Gercourt, and that chooses in Valmont a uniquely appropriate instrument of vengeance, since he too has a score to settle with Gercourt and since through Cécile he will be attacking Madame de Volanges for her advice to Madame de Tourvel. Moreover, if one traces the appellative dimension of the character who calls herself in unwitting prescience "ta pauvre Cécile" (I), it is striking to find that no one calls her "merely" Cécile. For Danceny she is "Mademoiselle" (XVII) and will become "ma Cécile, mon aimable amie, ma charmante Cécile" (XXXI). For Merteuil and Valmont, on the other hand, she is "la petite Volanges" (II), "cet enfant" (XX), "mon élève" (LXIII), "votre pupille" (LXX). Epithet—a term I shall use here to designate a class including certain adjectives, noun equivalents and metaphors—is thus used to mark a certain superior or ironic distance from other characters, and identifies as much or more its user as the character who is theoretically its object.

The *géométrie passionnée* is thus established very early in the text as the elements fall clearly and explicitly into place: a character is waiting to be created, socially and sexually, and two other characters are not only delighted to oblige but through the epistolary form will be "writing" the character to each other. Epithet thus functions as part of the "double-speak" which Valmont and Merteuil affect, is univocal only to them and thus proof of their highly developed complicity. The first anecdotal example, developed at great length by Merteuil (in order to goad Valmont but also of course by way of demonstration for the reader), is her account in letter X of her elaborate preparations for compensating Belleroche, and specifically her delineation of the theatrical and play-acting dimension of the whole affair. Roles (*laquais, femme de chambre, Sultan, Sultane*, etc.) are assigned and assumed easily, styles selected carefully (in *le Sopha, Héloïse*, La Fontaine), special directions added to their rendezvous, etc., all in the knowledge of their effect: "Toute cette marche romanesque lui échauffait la tête d'autant." Merteuil's control is exercised on three planes—sexual, dramaturgic, stylistic—all in the name of her own pleasure: "je modérai ses transports, et l'aimable conquetterie vint remplacer la tendresse. Je ne crois pas avoir jamais mis tant de soin à plaire, ni avoir été jamais aussi contente de moi." Whatever immediate pleasure she experiences, it is clear that the fullest pleasure comes only with intellectualization of the whole process, in both the *mise en scène* in which pleasure occurs ("je me plaisais à le considérer comme un Sultan au milieu de son sérail"), and the further pleasure of recounting it, with appropriate *double-entendre* euphemisms and delineations of role, to Valmont: "ses hommages réitérés, quoique toujours reçus par la même femme, le furent toujours par une Maîtresse nouvelle." Hence not only her underscoring what the Chevalier does not know about the house, but Valmont's intimate familiarity with the *ottomane* as well. "Il ne sait pas cela, lui; mais, pour son bonheur, je le sais pour deux."

Valmont's analogous performance is the equally spectacular letter XLVIII, written to Tourvel using Emilie's anatomy as a writing desk and full of *double-entendre*:

> une nuit orageuse ... un calme dont j'ai besoin, et dont je n'espère pas jouir encore ... assez d'empire sur moi ... dans ce moment, je suis plus heureux que vous ... la table sacrée sur laquelle je vous écris, consacrée pour la première fois à cet usage, devient pour moi l'autel sacré de l'amour ... vous quitter un moment pour dissiper une ivresse qui s'augmente à chaque instant ...

Here too the pleasure is in sharing—can the eye wink lasciviously if there is no one to see it?—and doubly so since Emilie reads it before it is sent on to Merteuil and thence to la Présidente.[2]

Of course, the various types of metaphor have not escaped the attention of the critics.[3] Martin Turnell dwells at length on the importance of military metaphors, and Versini appears to have drawn up the most complete inventory of motifs: theater and dramaturgy, pedagogy, gambling, jurisprudence, medicine, orientalism, medievalism, religion, music, the journey. Roger Mercier chooses to move from the theatrical metaphor back to reality, and traces to what extent "chacun est tour à tour regardé et regardant" (p. 675). Christine Belcikowski on the other hand elucidates the process in the other direction, showing how one moves from the metonymic to the metaphoric, from the presence of the Château or gambling as a pastime to their mythic significance. Versini's approach belongs more to literary history and philology, discerning what is "Laclos's" and what was conventional at the time the novel was written.[4] What I hope to show here is how character and structure are both reflected and determined by a double actualization of epithet. That is, Laclos unquestionably reactivates in his novel what were dormant figures, the new formal context rejuvenating the stylistic conventions. As the story evolves, however, it becomes clear that where Valmont and Merteuil are elaborating as it were a common *parole* from the *langue* of literary tradition, Merteuil will increasingly have recourse to what amounts to an idiolect in order to distinguish herself from Valmont as well as from the others.[5]

The world of interpersonal activity as portrayed in the *Liaisons* has thus shrunk drastically, as Valmont and Merteuil voluntarily limit their interest to *la chose*, but in setting to paper their preparations and their conquests, the scope again widens at a figurative level to include the textual activities just mentioned. The venue has changed and narrowed—from battlefield to salon, and from there to the alcove and even to the *ottomane*—but as Michel Butor points out "le véritable champ de bataille est dans les lettres."[6] Sexual pleasure is but a pretext: true eroticism, as Valmont and Merteuil practice it, lies in delectation of sensuality, and sharing one's cleverness in a second-order delectation, a kind of "value-added," which is a main function of figurative language in the *Liaisons* (and is destined to become the norm which Valmont will violate). Epithet is thus both the means to an end and a kind of internal publication, a signal to one's correspondent (and of course, to the reader) as to how well the system is working. Valmont's and Merteuil's "epithetic" treatment of other characters, by reducing them to two and even one dimension, serves to enhance their own characterial aegis. When one notes as well that in fact the epithets and metaphors function in networks and how often they evolve around "the supervising polarization *victim/victimizer*,"[7] it is clear that the ability to put a new name on things and especially on persons is the sign of a very particular "authorial" competence. The *nouveau Roman* Merteuil proposes to Valmont is thus a crucial link in the chain of fictional illusion established by the "publisher's" foreword and the "editor's" preface, and we have a frame situation where the social and sexual enterprise of the characters is in perfect symbiosis, i.e., both suited to and determined by the epistolary form. In its dramatic aspect the novel is made up of one character responding to another, but the narrative dimension necessarily relates what is "said" with a time-lag which is in turn the prime terrain and opportunity for the expression of an irony taking, at the level of character and person, a privileged form in the epithet.[8]

Furthermore, as Georges May demonstrated (pp. 182, 187), the *double-entendre* structure situates the reader willy-nilly as a party to the conspiracy, a silent but knowing witness to the process of distinguishing the characters who know and understand from those who do not, and leads necessarily to the perception of a hierarchy of characters in the work. At the highest level, initiating and sharing communication, are Valmont and Merteuil; at a second level come the characters of the stories they are writing: Cécile, Danceny, la Présidente. The characters in the interpolated stories—Gercourt, Belleroche, Prévan, Emilie— represent a third level, whose primary formal attribute is of course that they do not write letters. One could even sketch in a fourth level, of characters who not only do not write but who have no other name but a generic or epithetic one: *le Cordonnier*, Emilie's *buveur hollandais* (XLVIII), Prévan's *Trois Inséparables* (LXXIX). Moreover, it is in the nature of Merteuil's and Valmont's plan to make a character change level according to their whim and will: the case of Emilie is a notable example, but Cécile is to be sent back to Gercourt's level after very special training, and indeed by definition Merteuil and Valmont are situated at a higher level precisely by, and because of, the way they evoke via epithet their dabblings in other levels. Especially where Tourvel is concerned, Valmont takes particular pleasure in assuming the role most appropriate to his intended victim's religious outlook: "la folâtre Dévote ... j'oserai la ravir au Dieu même qu'elle adore ... Je serai le Dieu qu'elle aura préféré" (VI). It is hardly, however, a status Merteuil is likely to relinquish gladly ("Me voilà comme la Divinité," LXIII), and the intended hierarchy contains from the outset the ironic germ of its own failure since one character at least (Tourvel) will not be contained at her assigned level, and will by her abundant humanity interject herself into a higher level of the scheme. The project of collapsing other characters into epithetic types will fail, and that failure will entail a realignment of hierarchical values which is itself expressed by epithets, now transferred by Merteuil to Valmont.[9]

Turning again to the early letters, we find Valmont (IV) confirming that he shares the metaphoric wave-length with Merteuil, italicizing even the epithet she used: "je regrette de ne plus être votre esclave, et tout *monstre* que vous dites que je suis ...." Moreover, he develops two figurative networks of his own. The first refers to seduction as a pseudo-Cornelian grand design, recalling Merteuil's *Chevalier, aventure, Héros* (II) and blending ultimately with the military metaphors: "conquérir est notre destin ... au bout de la carrière ... le plus grand projet que j'ai jamais formé ... son succès m'assure autant de gloire que de plaisir ... Voilà ce que j'attaque; voilà l'ennemi digne de moi." The problem of course is that while *conquérir* referred to the seducing male in general, the *ennemi* (Tourvel) is cited by name in the letter. Worse yet, the second series, more resolutely epithetic and therefore even closer to the persons implicated, has as we have seen its source in Tourvel's *dévotion*: "vous seriez un jour la Patronne de quelque grande ville, tandis que votre ami serait au plus un Saint de Village ... Mon bon Ange m'a conduit ici pour son bonheur et pour le mien ... la Divinité que j'y adore ...." Where Valmont had intended to prove that Tourvel was more worthy of his efforts than Cécile—"une jeune fille qui n'a rien vu, ne connaît rien ... me serait livrée sans défense"—in fact his tropes unwittingly but eloquently demonstrate as well her superiority to Merteuil in his eyes (*Patronne/Divinité*); nor in the long run will the "adoration" sememe prove well chosen to express ironic distance. Finally, the structure of the letter also betrays in its articulations the degree of Valmont's involvement —"donner, avec vous, un exemple de constance au monde. Mais de plus grands intérêts nous appellent ..."; "c'est pour m'y perfectionner que je me vois forcée de vous désobéir"— and a final pirouette presumably intended to bring attention back to his correspondent only compounds the offense: "Me voilà donc depuis quatre jours livré à une passion forte ... J'ai bien besoin d'avoir cette femme ... un sentiment de reconnaissance pour les femmes faciles, qui m'amène naturellement à vos pieds."

As the plot progresses, Valmont will continue to believe that there is no qualitative difference in his prolonged attentions to Tourvel—"entre la conduite de Danceny avec la petite Volanges, et la mienne avec la prude Madame de Tourvel, il n'y a que la différence du plus au moins" (LVII)—and in letter CX a cavalier reference to the intermixing of two character levels ("l'écolière est devenue presque aussi savante que le maître") serves as an involuntary and ironic comment on his lack of success with Tourvel and her increasingly large place in his feelings. Letter CX is full of epithetic formulations, but they now prove Valmont is incapable of measuring the differing degree of difficulty involved in each project and the implications for his relationship with Merteuil (one notes the difference in orientation between *reprendre* and *à l'usage*): "J'occupe mon loisir en rêvant aux moyens de reprendre sur mon ingrate les avantages que j'ai perdus, et aussi à composer une espèce de catéchisme de débauche, à l'usage de mon écolière." His quoting Saint-Preux ("j'avais une âme pour la douleur: donnez-m'en une pour la félicité"), intended as apposite irony, in fact only points up the higher irony of Valmont's continuing to believe that Cécile and Tourvel are elements of one story—"Mieux partagé que lui, je possède à la fois les deux existences . . . je vous dois le double récit de mes peines et de mes plaisirs"—rather than irreconcilable plots which militate against the Valmont-Merteuil solidarity.

A few letters later the two are more clearly dissociated: "Je prévois que la vengeance ira plus vite que l'amour. La petite Volanges est rendue . . . Mais il n'en est pas de même de Madame de Tourvel: cette femme est désolante, je ne la conçois pas . . . et en vérité je crains qu'elle ne m'échappe . . ." (LXXVI). Valmont is unaware how aptly *amour* refers to his own case, and the absence of epithet in the reference to Tourvel is in its way prior proof of his inability to *la concevoir*. Nowhere more than in his "triumphant" letter CXXV is the dislocation, the uncontrolled mixing of levels, more obvious. A moment of doubt is brushed quickly aside in favor of an account of her seduction, yet remains eloquent testimony to the real import of his situation: "Serai-je donc à mon âge, maîtrisé comme un écolier, par un sentiment involontaire et inconnu? Non: il faut avant tout le combattre et l'approfondir." And failure to shed tears on cue is this seducer's *fiasco*, especially incriminating when we recall those he did shed earlier (XXI). Finally, no proof of insufficient hypocrisy could be more direct or literal—a notable lapse—than his own assessment: "L'ivresse fut complète et réciproque: et, pour la première fois, la mienne survécut au plaisir . . . et, il faut tout avouer, je pensais ce que je disais." What were separate orders (person and persons) are now one, and specific momentary pleasure deriving from a different source is now continuous (*survécut*). His ecstasy is thus shared (*réciproque*) with Tourvel but ironically with Merteuil as well, for he also says what he thinks (or feels): "et cependant le charme subsiste." He has thus been drawn beyond his selfish pose and led to doubt his libertine self-sufficiency ("que je n'aie pas en moi seul la plénitude de mon bonheur"). It is in fact Tourvel who has seduced Valmont, converted the character and brought him over to her level, although it would be more accurate to speak of her moral plane or register, since she clearly represents a world of a different order from that of Merteuil.[10]

Merteuil's outrage (V) at the "insolence rare" of Valmont's initial letter (IV) led her to attempt several approaches and to voice several objections. The danger of losing to an unworthy adversary: "Quel rival avez-vous à combattre? un mari!"; the Président's lack of interesting potential: "votre prude est dévote, et de cette dévotion de bonne femme qui condamne à une éternelle enfance . . . ce ne sera jamais qu'une espèce"; and Tourvel as an unacceptable addition to her correspondent's aegis: "Je ne m'accoutumerai jamais à dire mes secrets à l'amant de Madame de Tourvel." And finally she points out that by not attending to Cécile he allows Gercourt to maintain his superiority and will miss a promising opportunity which she evokes in a series of epithets and suggestive metaphors, as though to remind him of the pleasure to be had and lest he forget what it is like.

la petite Volanges a déjà fait tourner une tête. Le jeune Danceny en raffole . . . elle chante mieux qu'à une Pensionnaire n'appartient. Ils doivent répéter beaucoup de Duos, et je crois qu'elle se mettrait volontiers à l'unisson: mais ce Danceny est un enfant . . . Il m'appellerait perfide, et ce mot de perfide m'a toujours fait plaisir; c'est, après celui de cruelle, les plus doux à l'oreille d'une femme.

And indeed the word *revenir*, her first word to Valmont and now repeated in letter V, becomes a prime expression of a previous identity which is degenerating. "Revenez, mon cher Vicomte, revenez: que faites-vous, que pouvez-vous faire chez une vieille tante dont tous les biens vous sont substitués? Partez sur-le-champ; j'ai besoin de vous . . ." (II); "Je reconnais bien là votre mauvaise tête qui ne sait désirer que ce qu'elle ne croit pas pouvoir obtenir . . . revenez à vous" (V).

As in the case of epithet we have here a particularly dense statement of character, action and form. The geographical distance which separates the characters is justification for their letter writing, but there has already arisen a distance at a less literal level, between the former hypocrite and his present self. Moreover, the one is the cause of the other: something mysterious is keeping Valmont from coming back; he is already overdue and will of course remain so in Merteuil's view of things even when he turns to Cécile ("Mais vous, qui n'êtes plus vous . . . Savez-vous que voilà plus de quinze jours que cette ridicule aventure vous occupe, et que vous négligez tout le monde?" X; "on commence à s'occuper de vous à Paris . . . il y fut dit positivement que vous étiez retenu au Village par un amour romanesque et malheureux," CXIII). As with the work as a whole, Merteuil's first word thus expresses both the germ of their project's failure, and the *sine qua non* for the correspondence which is the record of that failure and whose "publication" is indeed an act of vengeance as well as the book we are reading. Epithetic and metaphoric characterization are thus at the heart of each story, of the correspondence, and of the book, as the touchstone of success becomes the slate on which failure is written and publicized.[11]

Merteuil understands far better than Valmont that his two projects of seduction are not destined to be of equal length, much less destined to coalesce into one homogeneous epistolary narrative with him as author and herself as reader; that because their narrative energies are of unequal force and even different in orientation and nature, symmetry is impossible and one of the stories must take precedence over the other. At the same time, however, Valmont and Merteuil are by choice committed inextricably to—and by—the epistolary bond, and this complicity which began as banter and then competition will become ultimately a fatal struggle for hegemony.

> songeons, pour animer notre zèle, vous, qu'il s'agit de la fille de Madame de Volanges, et moi, qu'elle doit devenir la femme de Gercourt. (LI)
>
> de ces deux aventures, l'une est entreprise contre mon gré, et je ne m'en mêle point; pour l'autre, comme vous y avez mis quelque complaisance pour moi, j'en fais mon affaire ... donnez quelques soins à cet enfant, et faisons-en, de concert, le désespoir de sa mère et de Gercourt. (CVI)
>
> Parlez-moi vrai, vous faites-vous illusion ou cherchez-vous à me tromper? la différence entre vos discours et vos actions ne me laisse de choix qu'entre ces deux sentiments ... (CXLI)
>
> je serai ou votre amant ou votre ennemi ... Hé bien! la guerre. (CLIII)

From cold war to hot war: the military metaphor, which previously evoked conquest by seduction at a lower level, is used now to characterize the Valmont/Merteuil relationship and designates a major and irrevocable shift of the primary action onto the highest level of character.

Similarly, after advising Cécile on epistolary style (CV), the Marquise will take Valmont to task in much the same terms (CVI) and will later cite his use of epithets as specific proof he has lost control and is too favorable in his characterization of Madame de Tourvel: "ce n'est plus l'adorable, la céleste Madame de Tourvel, mais c'est *une femme étonnante, une femme délicate et sensible*, et cela, à l'exclusion de toutes les autres, *une femme rare enfin*, et telle *qu'on n'en rencontrerait pas une seconde*" (CXXXIV, emphasis in the text). But not content with picking his style apart and throwing his epithets back in his face, over the course of the narrative she has also taken a more radical stylistic approach, applying to him epithets which were to have been reserved for secondary characters: "la véritable école est de vous être laissé aller à écrire ... relisez votre Lettre: il y règne un ordre qui vous décèle à chaque phrase" (XXXIII); "votre Présidente vous mène comme un enfant" (LXXXI); "dès que les circonstances ne se prêtent plus à vos formules d'usage, et qu'il vous faut sortir de la route ordinaire, vous restez court comme un Ecolier" (CVI); "ne sacrifiez pas votre réputation à un caprice puéril" (CXIII); "En vérité, Vicomte, vous êtes bien comme les enfants ..." (CXXXIV).

LES LIAISONS DANGEREUSES 97

We have come a long way from the complicitous *monstre que vous êtes* of the second letter and have reached the heart of the matter. The various projects concocted during the course of the narrative have borne epithets and metaphors like signals of their orientation, but this game of ulterior meaning is doomed from the start since what was to be symmetrical exchange of epithets between Valmont and Merteuil reveals immediately an imbalance in the respective positions of the intended objects, Cécile and the Présidente. Valmont uses epithet as much as does Merteuil but tends toward a single source (adoration of a divinity) applied to Tourvel in particular. Merteuil attacks Valmont in the same epithetic way, hoping at first to goad him into returning to the original plan but realizing finally that epithets must serve to distinguish herself rather than reintegrate Valmont, that she must attempt to salvage a new hierarchy from the collapse of the old one.

Nor is Merteuil's distinction as affirmed in her style limited to playing the epithet game better than the others, since she has recourse to other stylistic devices and formulations which seem almost *a priori* rejections of possible characterizations of herself by others. In her famous letter LXXXI, for example, we discover a person who allows of no external formative influences, claiming all such initiatives for herself and attributing her superiority to that autonomous creation of her self. The letter is of course a tying together at the center of the work of a great many themes and motifs: will, intelligence, observation, deceit, eroticism, etc., as well as of many familiar epithets and metaphors, but equally striking is her insistence on manipulations and metamorphosis: sensitivity is transformed into an erotic instrument, and strength derived paradoxically from her vulnerable and passive status as a woman.

Her creation is thus doubly original. As critics have noted, her "ancestors" are more socio-historical and less clearly literary than Valmont's.[12] And unlike any other character, she is the result of self-knowledge rather than of stylistic manipulation by another, emerging from a process of will and through a unique blend of activity and passivity which makes her mode of existence *reflexive*: "j'avais su me créer des moyens inconnus jusqu'à moi

... je suis mon ouvrage." Self-created, self-centered, self-styled; and like Cléopâtre self-sufficient, were it not for her crucial need for an appreciative audience of at least one.

Moreover, she is the only character for whom such a blend of active and passive appears possible. Her superiority thus proceeds from a self-analysis and circumspection which allow her to play a variety of roles, including—because she is both actress and director—apparently submissive ones ("le considérer comme un Sultan ... dont j'étais tour à tour les Favorites différentes," X), thus keeping the male from "fixing" her. In that sense the victim/victimizer opposition is in fact the result of a fluid, dynamic and multiform process. (Within the time-span of the correspondence, her revenge on Prévan, LXXXV, which she is rehearsing here, is the most notable example of strength-in-apparent-passivity.)

Little wonder then that she should be the only character whose past is recounted in such detail (men come to strength more easily, through a simple and linear development of their social position), but if she considers herself a noteworthy synthesis of active and passive, where men are concerned she seeks to impose a one-way trajectory from autonomy and strength to a state of submission: "Ces tyrans détrônés devenus mes esclaves." We have once again the sense of levels of role and character, representing the theoretical formulation of the structure Merteuil would impose on all her plots. And, like the only too appropriate choice of "Nouvelle Dalila" (the symmetrical equivalent of Valmont's ill-chosen series on divinity), reference to those levels foreshadows a crucial moment in the long process of characterization and distintegration which forms the plot of the novel.

vous n'en avez pas moins de l'amour pour votre Présidente ... tel enfin que je conçois qu'un Sultan peut le ressentir pour sa Sultane favorite, ce qui n'empêche pas de lui préférer souvent une simple Odalisque. Ma comparaison me paraît d'autant plus juste que, comme lui, jamais vous n'êtes ni l'Amant ni l'ami d'une femme; mais toujours son tyran ou son esclave. (CXLI)

This brings us full circle, and Valmont is now relegated to the status of victim, one of those characters whose primary vocation is to bear the epithets and metaphors which express the ironic vision of the "superior" characters.

Cécile as pupil and schoolgirl under the watchful eye of Valmont-Merteuil will be replaced by Valmont reduced by Merteuil to the status of schoolboy, and because he was bewildered by the *fatalité* which bound him to Tourvel (C) rather than the "Dieu qu'elle aura préféré" (IV); Merteuil as a new Delilah goes down with her Valmont-Samson; and the divine epithets applied insistently to Tourvel by Valmont signal the eviction of the master characters from their position of demiurges presiding over all characterial activity. Characterization by epithet is of course only one of the textual dimensions that express this coalescence of levels as a textual destiny: Cécile is not the only one to kiss a letter since Valmont will do the same (XLIV); Danceny will precede Valmont in Merteuil's bed and Valmont's anger is ample proof of the importance of such a confusion of prerogative (CLI); and the cavalier "ce n'est pas ma faute" in Valmont's letter of separation (CXLI-CXLII) takes on quite a different resonance for the reader who recalls not only how voluntaristic the plan was theoretically to have been but also the fact that Merteuil had already used the same phrase to postpone her reunion with Valmont (CVII), and that Valmont himself had used it (unconvincingly) a few letters earlier: "Non, je ne suis point amoureux; et ce n'est pas ma faute si les circonstances me forcent d'en jouer le rôle" (CXXXVIII). And finally, as we have already seen, the military metaphors which were to have characterized intelligent, successful, in a word orthodox seductions will in fact find their most exclusive application in the Valmont-Merteuil antagonism: "Hé bien! la guerre" (CIII), even as Merteuil, who had decided to apply her theatrical skills in the figurative "grand Théâtre du monde" (LXXXI), gets her comeuppance at the Comédie Italienne (CLXXIII). The transfer of a metaphor to the main character level is thus the localized but crucial expression of a whole series of levelings and conflations of elements which should have remained distinct. The final irony, then, is that irony, as the protagonists were of a mind to practice it, by escaping them ultimately applies to them.

J'ai pu avoir quelquefois la prétention de remplacer à moi seule tout en sérail; mais il ne m'a jamais convenue d'en faire partie... *l'écolier, le douceureux* Danceny, uniquement occupé de moi... travailler plus efficacement que vous à mon bonheur et à mes plaisirs ... autrefois, ce me semble, vous faisiez un peu plus de cas de moi; vous ne m'aviez pas destinée tout à fait aux troisièmes rôles ... Votre servante, Monsieur le Vicomte. (CXVII)

Whereas in La Bruyère *caractères* empty of humanity and hyperbolically extended culminate necessarily in metaphor, with the *moraliste* there to record and judge what he sees, in the *Liaisons* fullness of character depends on a willful depersonalization, a prior reduction of others into type and even *caractère*, as the main characters strive for self-aggrandizement through a narrative and authorial function. Epithet as I have defined and traced its function here is thus a salient pattern of person and a primary linkage point between characterization and narrative, but it bears repeating, before going on to examine two works whose main character is also a woman, that while the Marquise attempts to show her superiority in the manipulation of epithets she is also at pains to be the sole source of her own characterization and in ways not available to other characters. Valmont cannot of course be relegated with complete impunity to the inferior status of the others, since he alone knows her secret and possesses the evidence to make it public. Yet even as she sets out on the course which can only lead to her Delilah-like downfall, she remains somehow larger and more "heroic" than the others.

As the tension mounts between herself and Valmont, she has increasing recourse to the *moi* on the one hand, and on the other to a series of classes and plurals, distinguishing her own situation from Valmont's but also from that of men in general: "Dites-moi donc, amant langoureux, ces femmes que vous avez eues, croyez-vous les avoir violées?" (X); "L'autre classe ... est celle des femmes qui, ayant eu un caractère et n'ayant pas négligé de nourrir leur raison, savent se créer une existence" (CXIII); "un homme de ma connaissance s'était empétré, comme vous, d'une femme qui lui faisait peu d'honneur" (CXLI); "je n'ai pas oublié que cette femme était ma rivale, que vous l'avez trouvée un moment préférable à moi, et qu'enfin vous m'aviez placée au-dessous d'elle" (CXLV). Obviously, these are to some extent staples of conventional usage, and we can also find them in the letters of certain other characters, but as was the case in the actualization of relatively dormant metaphors their importance here lies in the use the Marquise makes of them in a social world set to paper by characters who do not all master style and usage to the same degree. "Ecoutez, et ne me confondez pas avec les autres femmes" (LXXXV). In that sense one of the main ironies of the dénouement is to see how other characters using a similar turn of phrase can express a point of view so partial and so far from the whole truth of what has occurred socially, sexually and esthetically as to make one wonder just what edification they have extracted from it: "toutes les femmes l'y laissèrent seule. Ce mouvement marqué d'indignation générale fut applaudi de tous les hommes" (Madame de Volanges, CLXXIV); "on rougit d'être femme, quand on en voit une capable de semblables excès" (Madame de Rosemonde, CLXXI). Moreover, if one is to judge from letters exchanged by Laclos and Mme de Riccoboni on the publication of the novel, the chain of irony makes Merteuil as difficult for the female reader to accept as for the female character.[13] "Si, comme vous l'assurez, ce caractère affreux existe, je m'applaudis d'avoir passé mes jours dans un petit cercle" (p. 713); "Tant de dépravation irrite et n'instruit pas . . . On n'a pas besoin de prévenir contre les crimes, tout le monde en conçoit de l'horreur. Mais des règles de conduite seront toujours nécessaires, et ce sera toujours un mérite d'en donner" (p. 717).

While there is no doubt about the singular status Merteuil posits for herself, a formal and stylistic reading, attentive in particular to the use of antonomasia, tends nevertheless to highlight yet another hierarchy *en filigrane*, made up of levels and registers which represent a reworking which is more than travesty, parody or pastiche, of the social and ideological backdrop of the novel. (The most obvious anterior norm here, formally, thematically and philosophically is the *Nouvelle Héloïse*.)[14] In their very different ways Tourvel and Merteuil (whom Baudelaire saw characteristically as "Eve touchante" and "Eve satanique")[15] are both superior to Valmont, and as Merteuil's evocations of the "war" between the sexes and frequent recourse to antithesis imply (e.g., "née pour venger mon sexe et maîtriser le vôtre," LXXXI), women in general are superior to men, and in fact man, not

Tourvel, is Merteuil's ultimate enemy. (Danceny's selection for publication of the letter vindicating Prévan bears witness to the same antagonism.) Thus, even the status of Cécile is almost rehabilitated through the Marquise's perception of the character she might, as a woman, have become:

> si j'avais moins de mœurs, je crois qu'il [Belleroche] aurait dans ce moment un rival dangereux, c'est la petite Volanges. Je raffole de cet enfant: c'est une vraie passion. Ou je me trompe, ou elle deviendra une de nos femmes les plus à la mode ... nous lui donnerons une femme toute formée, au lieu de son innocente Pensionnaire ... (XX)

> elle est vraiment délicieuse! cela n'a ni caractère ni principes; jugez combien sa société sera douce et facile. (XXXVIII)

> Celle-ci a fait de son côté tout ce que j'attendais d'elle, scrupules évanouis, nouveaux serments d'aimer toujours, etc. ... mais le sot Danceny ... jamais personne ne fut plus susceptible d'une surprise des sens. Elle est vraiment aimable, cette chère petite! Elle méritait un autre Amant; elle aura une bonne amie, car je m'attache sincèrement à elle ... (LIV)

> renfermez-vous, en fille bien née, dans une parfaite soumission ... votre Danceny est gentil: mais c'est un de ces hommes qu'on a quand on veut et tant qu'on veut ... (CV)

There are admittedly other remarks and indeed other epithets to be taken into account (notably CVI), and no such remarks should be isolated from the novel's competitive context, with each author/character proposing his or her character/victim to the other reader/character. Yet stylistically the work seems to call for a rereading from a collective feminine viewpoint and in so doing leads one to wonder whether the lesbian overtones in Merteuil's assessment of Cécile are not, like the smallpox, to some extent a male author's way of marginalizing one of the major and most successful characters in the literature of the period.[16] The case is at any rate one to ponder as we move on to other patterns of person in which female characters (Silvia and the Princesse de Clèves) achieve or seek to achieve their fullest definition by a change in their formal and stylistic status within the works in which they appear.

Chapter VI

DISTINCTION, REPLICATION AND THE SELF IN *LE JEU DE L'AMOUR ET DU HASARD*

As the *Jeu* opens it is quickly apparent that as Frédéric Deloffre noted of Marivaux's theater in general, thematic considerations are a major source of information—marriage is "in the air" and indeed imminent—but our understanding of such a typical opening situation in comedy is not complete until we take note not only of what the characters are talking about but how they talk about it as well.[1] "Mais, encore une fois, de quoi vous mêlez-vous? Pourquoi répondre de mes sentiments?" Silvia's opening line is especially rich; we have arrived in the midst (*encore une fois*) of a rather heated debate (*se mêler*, and the questions which will be followed by another and by an exclamation), yet one in which the servant is in a sense deferent but equal. The *vouvoiement* by Silvia puts Lisette off—temporarily—at a certain angry distance from her usual station, but that distance is established as a possibility at the outset, and the fact that Lisette has meddled in Silvia's affairs sets up an opposition ("Pourquoi répondre de mes sentiments?") which will soon become a more generalized distinction between Silvia and the other characters ("Ce n'est pas à vous de juger de mon cœur par le vôtre").

When Lisette speaks it is readily apparent that her views on Silvia's impending marriage are radically opposed to those of her mistress and are a function of the domestic's down-to-earth willingness to settle for less ("Mon cœur est fait comme celui de tout le monde"), yet it is also rhetorically and dramaturgically significant that her speaking competence—how she couches her considerations, rather than what she says—is such that while we never lose sight of her position in life she is nonetheless an adequate interlocutor in the debate on marriage, and unlike Arlequin an appropriate substitute for her mistress in the game of disguise which will follow. In the meantime the game is a word game, the *marivaudage* in which as Deloffre also noted "l'originalité du dialogue . . . réside en grande partie dans la façon dont les répliques s'enchaînent . . . le fil qui passe de main en main est bien un mot que chacun des interlocuteurs reprend à l'autre" (p. 199). Thus Silvia plays on *oui/non, délicieuse, on dit,* and Lisette on *non/oui, cœur, tant pis, beau/fat, superflu, deux visages, glacée/ je gèle*. But this lexical competence is not so to speak democratically distributed or shared, and it is clear from Lisette's remarks that she is once again unwilling or unable to respect the nuances and motifs introduced by her mistress, that at the end of the scene she is still at a kind of platitudinous *degré zéro de la nuance*. Where marriage is concerned she will not only settle for less but a husband is what she wants and any man will do: "Un mari? c'est un mari, vous ne deviez pas finir par ce mot-là, il me raccommode avec tout le reste."

Silvia's position is diametrically opposed: she is not *raccommodée avec tout le reste* since it is not for Lisette, nor indeed for anyone else, to put words in her mouth or feelings in her heart: "c'est un *on-dit*, et je pourrais bien n'être pas de ce sentiment-là, moi" (one notes already the *on/je* distinction and the syntactic insistence on the first person which as we shall see contain the germ of the play's three-act structure). The portraits she draws of the husbands she has seen obviously partake of a literary tradition, but their dramatic function here is different from, say, Célimène's portraits in *Le Misanthrope* (II, 5): the latter's were improvised in the presence of suitors and therefore part of her coquetry, a means of maintaining her attractiveness but keeping suitors at a certain suspenseful distance at the same time. Silvia is speaking to her confidante (significantly, Célimène had—chose not to have?—no women to talk to), and if she squelches Lisette's versions of eligible males in a way reminiscent of Célimène's dispatching of a gallery of types, it is crucial to contrast her nubility with Célimène's independent status as a widow.

Marriage is a more likely and imminent event for Silvia, one her pride anticipates with trepidation, rather than the key to—or sign of—independence (as with Araminte's widowhood in *Les Fausses Confidences*). "Voilà ce que c'est que les hommes . . . Je la trouvai toute abattue, le teint plombé, avec des yeux qui venaient de pleurer, je la trouvai comme je serai peut-être; voilà mon portrait à venir, je vais du moins risquer d'en être une copie." The problem is a serious one and has led her to the limits of filial obedience: (*Lisette*) "Quoi! vous n'épouserez pas celui qu'il vous destine?" (*Silvia*) "Que sais-je? peut-être ne me conviendra-t-il point, et cela m'inquiète." In point of fact, in her father's presence (sc. 2) she will prove far less recalcitrant, and even tentative in suggesting the plan which will set the action of the play in motion, but the seriousness and stakes of the plan are well established in the opening scene. Contrary to Lisette and of course to Arlequin, she is in no hurry at all as the play opens: "je ne m'ennuie pas d'être fille," and as so often in classical comedy a fundamental dimension of characterization is expressed in one's attitude toward dramatic progression, to wit when—indeed whether—the marriage should take place.

Silvia is thus established at the outset as not so much a coquette as a *précieuse*: via the thematic opposition of love and marriage, and in her attention to nuances of language, she partakes of the *précieux* tradition, but in her case such theme and treatment, as in the preceding century, connote as well a set of underlying socio-sexual assumptions. The *précieuse* is at base "celle qui a ou se donne de la valeur, du prix," the woman who sets herself apart in an attempt to maintain a certain independence of status and initiative in a male-defined and male-regulated society. Writing on Marivaux as author of the *Journaux*, Paul Hoffmann sees coquetry for Marivaux as a kind of self-control that is part of women's nature and as the last example of an ideal shared with the *précieuse*, one that enables women to have the upper hand where love is concerned and to ensure a certain constancy in men.[2] He seems, however, to attribute too little importance to a sentence he quotes from Marivaux ("Notre malice n'est que le fruit de notre dépendence," p. 99) and his definition seems to me a faulty basis for a proper application of the term "feminism" (see my own definition below): as with Célimène such coquetry is more a holding action, contingent and contextual (whence Célimène's abhorrence of *le désert*). Valentini P. Brady on the other hand, seeing things as it were from behind the mask, takes a much more radical approach and speculates on the ramifications of the disguise ploy, since in a sense Silvia is known—and exceptional—only with respect to her apparent station as *soubrette*: where she comes to love a Dorante whose natural qualities have been tested and refined in the course of his *épreuve*, he has in fact fallen in love with Silvia-as-Lisette, not with Silvia.[3]

In Silvia's case and in terms of the play, the *précieuse* stance takes the form of an initial reluctance to play the game, followed by the decision that if play one must then let it at least be by rules of one's own devising. Deloffre points out (p. 212) that *marivaudage* occurs mainly in the early scenes of the plays. In the *Jeu* such language play is particularly intense in the first scene, but it remains a recurrent motif as well, and even a touchstone for the goings-on and particularly the merits of various characters. Lisette's comically inadequate and distorted résumé of Silvia's remarks (I, 2) is one example, but the main case is of course Arlequin. On his first appearance (I, 8) he is obviously peremptory and even disdainful in his remarks to a valet whose quality is already clear to a surprised Silvia and to the audience. His marital haste is such that he refers to "mon beau-père" and "ma femme," since after all "Je viens pour épouser" and the ceremony is a mere trifle. Silvia had already attempted to set the record straight, and no other exchange is more characteristic of the intertwining of basic attitudes: she is more attentive to the meaning of words, because she is "naturally" his superior but also because her vital interests are at stake in deferring the marriage:

> *Arlequin*
> ... il ne manque plus que la cérémonie, qui est une bagatelle.
> *Silvia*
> C'est une bagatelle qui vaut bien la peine qu'on y pense....
> *Arlequin*
> Et pourquoi ne pas dire mon beau-père, comme moi?
> *Silvia*
> C'est qu'il ne l'est pas encore.

Dorante
Elle a raison, monsieur, le mariage n'est pas fait.
Arlequin
Eh bien, me voilà pour le faire.
Dorante
Attendez donc qu'il soit fait.

Since the previous scene (I, 7), Silvia's theoretical reticence to marry her intended fiancé has acquired a personal and concrete set of reasons in Dorante, and the latter's siding with her to correct both Arlequin's language and his approach to (dramatic) action is evidence of nascent reciprocity in their feelings, already evident in their symmetrical disguise. Henceforth, Silvia not only waxes ironic but obviously need not be subtle about it.

Silvia
En effet, quelle si grande différence y a-t-il entre être mariée ou ne l'être pas? ... je cours informer votre beau-père de votre arrivée....
Arlequin
Croyez-vous que je plaise ici? Comment me trouvez-vous?
Silvia
Je vous trouve ... plaisant.

And henceforth Arlequin will only ensconce himself more firmly in the role of a pretentious domestic: confusing figurative usage with literal, quantitative with qualitative, the refined with the physical, and in his thirst and appetite offering an only too concrete expression of his nature and basic outlook (I, 10; II, 3, 5; III, 6).

Indeed, Arlequin's character is so broadly drawn à la Molière yet so integral a part of the main plot (different in that from the usual situation in Molière) that, as J.B. Ratermanis pointed out, Marivaux must limit the number and length of his conversations with Silvia lest what is clear to the audience become necessarily clear to Silvia.[4] By the same token, the second act suffices to reveal Dorante's true identity, lest similar problems of plausibility arise. In dramaturgic terms then, we have a double-disguise situation that is symmetrical and will at length become reciprocal, but one in which the elements are not equally interchangeable and which therefore necessitates shaping Arlequin's plot situation with all due care, although to that end his character need not be modified.

On the contrary, Arlequin will continue on basically unchanged, and one is constantly struck by a kind of echo construction in the *Jeu* where words are repeated in a *réplique*, with an extension of their meaning. Indeed projection onto the temporal axis of a basic mirror situation is a fundamental ingredient of the play's structure, and a particularly effective source of irony when one character level becomes a "comment" on another: not only when a master corrects a servant or a character rings a change on a repeated word, but also less literally in the many *déjà vu* (and *entendu*) aspects, such as Arlequin's various appearances; Lisette's summary (I, 2); Silvia quarreling a second time with Lisette (II, 7) or Dorante with Arlequin (III, 1); Arlequin's concern about her own project (II, 1) or the longevity of Arlequin's feelings (II, 5); Arlequin on his knees to Lisette (II, 5), followed by Dorante in the same position with Silvia (II, 9); Arlequin subdued by a word (the rhyming *faquin*, III, 6) recalling Lisette content with *mari* (I, 1); Orgon as dramatic advisor to Lisette (II, 1) and then to Silvia (II, 11). As we shall see in the specific case of Silvia, Orgon and Mario, such replication of words, situations and levels is a prime source of the play's effect, as the basic echo construction is itself replicated when Silvia extends the action into a third act of her own creation. At the same time, however, Orgon and Mario provide a certain image or replica of socio-familial structure, and the confrontation of the two points of view represents a major particularity of the play.

For the time being, symmetry is reserved for Silvia and Dorante, and it is particularly striking that, in contradistinction to the Silvia/Lisette and Silvia/Arlequin exchanges, we have in I, 7 equality of linguistic competence and at many points even a certain superiority on Dorante's part in the sense that it is more difficult to respond in kind than to initiate. Moreover, in its presentation their dialogue differs from the preceding scenes, since Dorante's wordplay—well-turned phrases, apt compliments, subtle extensions of meaning—also gives rise to asides in which Silvia expresses her astonishment: "mettons tout à profit, ce garçon-ci n'est pas sot ... Quel homme pour un valet! ... Il le mériterait ... Il ne tarit point; ... Mais en vérité, voilà un garçon qui me surprend, malgré que j'en aie." As the hallmark of one's

LE JEU DE L'AMOUR ET DU HASARD 109

qualities, language in Marivaux is a testing- and proving-ground, and Silvia's surprise at Dorante's merit, as evidenced by his ability to master language and of course to put language to use in his admiration of her, leads to other asides where we see that her astonishment has become a kind of paralysis, an inability to act as she should, and even to a certain *mauvaise foi.*

> *Silvia, à part*
> A la fin, je crois qu'il m'amuse... (*Haut*) Eh bien, Bourguignon, tu ne veux pas finir? Faudra-t-il que je te quitte? (*A part*) Je devrais déjà l'avoir fait.

This paralysis is shared:

> *Dorante*
> Attends, Lisette, je voulais moi-même te parler d'autre chose, mais je ne sais plus ce que c'est.
> *Silvia*
> J'avais de mon côté quelque chose à te dire, mais tu m'as fait perdre mes idées aussi à moi.

But via the asides the focus is on Silvia.

> *Silvia*
> ... je voudrais bien savoir comment il se fait que j'ai la bonté de t'écouter, car assurément, cela est singulier.
> *Dorante*
> Tu as raison, notre aventure est unique.
> *Silvia à part*
> Malgré tout ce qu'il m'a dit, je ne suis point partie, je ne pars point, me voilà encore, et je réponds! En vérité, cela passe la raillerie.

She will of course be at a similar loss in the second act, and the fact that she reappears only halfway through that act, and Dorante even later, gives the impression of a passage of time during which the feelings of the characters are evolving, an impression heightened by Lisette's panic (II, 1) at Arlequin's haste and by Silvia's lack of self-control in what appeared at first to be a simple echo scene with Lisette (II, 7). Significantly, in this latter scene the rhythm is reversed, and where in I, 1 she went from indignant apprehension to a certain mastery Silvia now marks the evolution of the general situation by moving from remonstration to crisis:

> *Lisette*
> Oh! Madame, dès que vous le défendez sur ce ton-là, et que cela va jusqu'à vous fâcher, je n'ai plus rien à dire.

Silvia
Dès que je le défends sur ce ton-là! Qu'est-ce que c'est que le ton dont vous dites cela vous-même? Qu'entendez-vous par ce discours? Que se passe-t-il dans votre esprit?
Lisette
Je dis, Madame, que je ne vous ai jamais vue comme vous êtes et que je ne conçois rien à votre aigreur...
Silvia
Voyez-vous le mauvais esprit! comme elle tourne les choses! Je me sens dans une indignation... qui... va jusqu'au larmes...
Silvia
... Que faut-il que je réponde à cela? Qu'est-ce que cela veut dire? A qui parlez-vous? Qui est-ce qui est à l'abri de ce qui m'arrive? Où en sommes-nous?
...
Silvia
... Retirez-vous, vous m'êtes insupportable, laissez-moi; je prendrai d'autres mesures.

The tables are turned, Silvia has lost her ability to deal with the language of the situation (as later she will lose her dramaturgic command, III, 8), and in almost Racinian terms "decides" to approach things in a different way.

Yet as soon as Dorante appears (II, 8) her tone softens: "mais ce n'est pas sa faute, le pauvre garçon, et je ne dois pas m'en prendre à lui." And if the softened tone continues in sc. 9 Silvia has not yet regained control, witness her inability to implement the most telltale of linguistic resolutions ("Bourguignon, ne nous tutoyons plus, je t'en prie") and her need to recall the necessities of her situation, as though to remind herself of her obligations, convince herself, and thereby come to a decision:

Tout cela doit m'être indifférent, et me l'est en effet... je devrais me dispenser de te le dire...; C'est par générosité que je te parle; mais il ne faut pas que cela dure... finissons, Bourguignon, finissons, je t'en prie. Qu'est-ce que cela signifie? c'est se moquer, allons, qu'il n'en soit plus parlé...; (*à part*) J'ai besoin à tout moment d'oublier que je l'écoute.

In fact, it is Dorante who moves along a situation which Silvia is unable to hold in stasis, first by getting down on his knees and forcing Silvia to make a muted declaration of her interest (sc. 10); then, after an interruption by Orgon and Mario (sc. 11) which only increases Silvia's anguish, in his announcement to her of his true identity (II, 12), at which Silvia acknowledges to herself both an understanding of her own feelings ("Ah! je vois

LE JEU DE L'AMOUR ET DU HASARD 111

clair dans mon cœur") but also a perhaps less conscious but equally accurate appraisal of her situation ("j'avais grand besoin que ce fût là Dorante"). And it is out of this need, this self-love, that Silvia will very quickly concoct her new plan ("Il me vient de nouvelles idées," sc. 13).

We have reached here a major linkage point between language and dramatic action, but find ourselves confronted as well with a variant of the *double registre* identified by Jean Rousset.[5] It takes in the novels the form of a narrator looking back with an experienced eye on an earlier self, but in the plays is lodged in secondary characters who as the playwright's representatives (*délégués indirects*, p. 54) erect a staging over and around the main action: "chaque pièce se développe sur un double palier, celui du cœur qui 'jouit de soi' et celui de la conscience spectatrice. Où est la vraie pièce? Elle est dans la surimpression et l'entrelacement des deux plans" (p. 56); "La pièce est finie quand les deux paliers se confondent, c'est-à-dire quand le groupe des héros regardés se voit comme les voyaient les personnages spectateurs" (p. 58). Rousset further points out the mirror effect achieved when the servant couple anticipates the sentimental evolution of their masters and, with respect to the *Jeu*, the fact that in the third act Silvia joins the spectators' camp (p. 56).

It is extremely unusual that one of the main characters act as *meneur de jeu*, and even more so that such a role should be taken on so late in the play. The third act was recognized at the play's first performances as a major particularity, one not necessarily to every critic's liking: "il ne s'agit que de satisfaire à la petite vanité de Silvia" (*Le Mercure*, January 1730).[6] Bernard Dort, on the other hand, considers the third act to be a hallmark of the Silvia character and prefers the character to the play as a whole.[7] Roger Navarri sees Silvia's motives in prolonging the action as "non pas tant pour mettre à l'épreuve les sentiments du jeune homme dont elle a déjà pu mesurer la force que pour satisfaire une certaine volonté de puissance."[8] Like Brady (pp. 261-64) and E.J.H. Greene,[9] I see Silvia's undertaking, whatever coquetry and self-satisfaction it may involve, as basically a more positive one, a search for an equality founded on separate autonomies; at the same time, however, I am less totally convinced than they that Silvia arrives at such a result.

It does seem plausible that had he so wished Marivaux could have developed the play in a two-act, ignorance/recognition structure, with the symmetrical situation leading to reciprocity in the two couples without need of a third act. In any case, the third act of the play as we have it is very clearly a willful prolonging by Silvia of an asymmetrical situation, as she goes even so far as to enroll her brother in her enterprise. As such it is homologous, at the level of plot and dramatic structure, to the extension of meaning which occurred earlier at the level of language and style. Having refused a certain leveling of nuance ("un mari, c'est un mari"), and equally disinclined to pull up short and settle for less ("ce mot-là ... me raccommode avec tout le reste") Silvia is now in command dramaturgically as well as linguistically, and intends to make full (if ultimately generous) use of the means at her disposal.

The third act is thus both an extension and encapsulation of the preceding action, more of the same yet different. Silvia's *précieux* penchant for establishing a trial situation, a marivaudian *mise à l'épreuve*, had appeared early on: "Dorante arrive ici aujourd'hui; si je pouvais le voir, l'examiner un peu sans qu'il me connût!" (I, 2), and once the uncertainty caused by Dorante's obvious merit in an inferior role has been dispelled she returns to formulations of the earlier dramaturgic type: "Cachons-lui qui je suis" (II, 2); "J'aurais besoin de vous aussi, mon frère ... il faudra feindre de m'aimer" (II, 13). Arlequin's inadequacies as detailed once again by an increasingly frustrated Dorante (III, 1) provide further echo-type continuity, as will the comic groping for adequate linguistic formulations between Lisette and Arlequin (III, 6).

At the same time, however, Silvia makes it abundantly clear that the play she is in a hurry to direct is the means to a very special end and thus something of a new departure: "Allons, mon frère, venez, ne perdons point de temps. Il n'est jamais rien arrivé d'égal à cela" (II, 13); cf. Dorante: "Tout ce qui se passe ici, tout ce qui m'y est arrivé à moi-même est incroyable" (III, 1).

LE JEU DE L'AMOUR ET DU HASARD 113

His consternation is the result of her undertaking and therefore the source of her pleasure (although like her initial mastery of language, her "directing" will also run into difficulties).

> *Dorante*
> Monsieur m'apprend qu'il vous aime, Lisette.
> *Silvia*
> Ce n'est pas ma faute.
> *Dorante*
> Et me défend de vous aimer.
> *Silvia*
> Il me défend donc de vous paraître aimable.
> *Mario*
> Je ne saurais empêcher qu'il ne t'aime, belle Lisette, mais je ne veux pas qu'il te le dise.
> *Silvia*
> Il ne me le dit plus, il ne fait que me le répéter.
> *Mario*
> Du moins ne te le répétera-t-il pas quand je serai présent. Retirez-vous, Bourguignon.
> *Dorante*
> J'attends qu'elle me l'ordonne. . . .
> *Mario*
> Eh bien, qu'il s'en aille!
> *Dorante, à part*
> Je souffre.
> *Silvia*
> Cédez, puisqu'il se fache.
> *Dorante, bas à Silvia*
> Vous ne demandez peut-être pas mieux? (III, 3)

To her father's surprise, she wants to take things as far as they can go: "Quoi! ma fille, tu espères qu'il ira jusqu'à t'offrir sa main dans le déguisement où te voilà?" Sure in her belief in their love's destiny, and in seeking to achieve *un mariage unique* (III, 4), she reveals an almost Cornelian side, anticipating pridefully a future of her own creation: "je serai charmée de triompher. Mais il faut que j'arrache ma victoire, et non pas qu'il me la donne, je veux un combat entre l'amour et la raison" (III, 4). Amid some humorous byplay she "gives away" Arlequin to Lisette, paving the way for other echoes when Lisette plays *meneuse de jeu* to Arlequin's character (sc. 6), and again in sc. 7, as Arlequin presumptuously and pretentiously deals likewise with his master: (*Lisette*) ". . . j'ai travaillé comme pour moi, et vous verrez de l'ouvrage bien fait . . . Que voulez-vous que j'en fasse à présent?" (III, 5); (*Arlequin*) ". . . Quand j'aurai épousé, nous vivrons but à but. Votre soubrette arrive. Bonjour, Lisette: je vous recommande Bourguignon, c'est un garçon qui a quelque mérite" (III, 7).

Thus it is that having finally arrived at her *scène à faire* (III, 8), Silvia nevertheless quickly finds herself in difficulty and in precisely those theatrical terms which shortly before expressed and prepared her victory. At the end of the dramaturgic chain, Dorante now turns inward in despair, taking as it were his direction from his own feelings: distant, prepared to abandon a lost cause, Dorante has been so humiliated that he prefers to leave rather than talk about it any longer (as he says a number of times). Language and presence on stage as the curtain goes up have thus become now not only the basic terms of the situation but the fundamental source of the new problem as well: (*A part*) "S'il part, je ne l'aime plus, je ne l'épouserai jamais." Despite what she knows about Dorante, Silvia is ready to throw it all over if he comes at too dear a price. Once again Silvia has moved, as in the first and second acts, from an equilibrium to a state of perplexity and exasperation before achieving a new resolution. The affair is out of her hands for a few brief moments at the crux of this penultimate scene, and her pride will therefore assert itself all the more strongly when Dorante decides not to leave. The rest of the scene will represent in a sense the application to a particular case, of the *précieux* point of view on men expressed in the opening debate with Lisette: "Quel dénoûement! Dorante reparaît pourtant; il me semble qu'il revient. Je me dédis donc; je l'aime encore . . . Feignons de sortir, afin qu'il m'arrête." Not only does Silvia push Dorante to the limit, making him "pay the price" of his love, but her lengthy speech in response to his "peux-tu douter que je ne t'adore?"—particularly in its shift from *vous* to *moi* at the midpoint—also recapitulates in its use of pronouns the move from men to women, and the obliteration of an apparent class difference which is at the heart of Silvia's whole undertaking and which Dorante comes finally to recognize. (*Silvia*) "Mais moi, monsieur. . . . Qui me dédommagera de votre perte . . . Savez-vous bien que si je vous aimais . . . Moi qui vous parle, je me ferais un scrupule de vous dire que je vous aime

..." Thus it is that Dorante comes to respect as well as love her, and that Silvia comes to the end of a trial of her own devising which tested and affected her almost as much as it did Dorante. Dorante's key promise of enduring love ("Ne disputons point, car je ne changerai jamais") is the direct result of Silvia's prolonging of the action, his *jamais* the word by which all the rest is in fact *raccommodé* to her grand design.

In pushing on, creating as it were a third act where she alone saw its necessity, Silvia's role appears finally not only *précieux* but "feminist," a term I should define as believing in the inherent equality (*through* difference or *despite* difference) of the female to the male, accompanied by a willingness to engage in intellectual, social and/or juridical activity in order to ensure the recognition of that equality. I once put such a question to students, i.e., why the third act? Is Silvia "liberated" and is this then a "feminist" play? We had just read *La Princesse de Clèves* along the lines I develop in my final chapter and conclusion, and as in that case the feminist problematic (once defined) not only generated a great deal of discussion but shed considerable light on the interplay of form and ideology. Basically, we found that if Silvia's role can be looked on as "feminist," the form of the play as a whole says otherwise. For reasons on which I shall now elaborate, the *Jeu* thus represents a midway point between the sensational but ultimately failed feminism of the Marquise de Merteuil and the unassuming rise to personal autonomy of the Princesse de Clèves.

Until now my discussion of the play has included little if any reference to either Orgon or Mario, a voluntary omission since it reproduces a typical first reading of the work, concentrating on the main characters. Brady reminds us (pp. 203-04) that where parents appear in Marivaux they are alone, i.e., there is only one parental attitude, and that in the case of fathers it is almost always a lenient and understanding attitude, reluctant to exercise authority.[10] And it is tempting to assess Orgon's role in terms of a somewhat overt and superficial content, as that of the indulgent and doting father, characteristic of an early eighteenth-century optimism: "Va! dans ce monde il faut être un peu trop bon pour l'être assez" (I, 2). True enough, Orgon's position in the *Jeu* is a far cry from a number of Moliéresque fathers in the New Comedy tradition, in the sense that they were not only blocking characters opposed to their son's or daughter's marriage (e.g., Orgon's namesake in *Le Tartuffe*), but compounded the felony on occasion by becoming rivals of their progeny as well (Harpagon in *L'Avare*).

Yet, if Orgon in the *Jeu* has a different and less central function, it is no less important to the meaning of the play as a whole. It is he who announces to an apprehensive Silvia the impending arrival of Dorante (I, 2) and who quickly accedes to her wish to examine her intended. Indeed, his only hesitation in granting that wish is to verbalize for us his reasons in doing so: (*A part*) "Son idée est plaisante . . . Si je le laisse faire, il doit arriver quelque chose de bien singulier, elle ne s'y attend pas elle-même." His permission, however generous, thus represents not only the necessary condition for the marriage and hence for the first two acts ("à condition que vous vous plairiez à tous deux") but also for the third. His superior knowledge, as expressed not only in "elle ne s'y attend pas elle-même" but in his "quelque chose de bien singulier" as well, thus overshadows the whole of the play's unfolding (cf. Silvia's consequently naïve if accurate references to her unique, singular, exceptional, etc., project).

More significant still for our perspective is the fact that in sc. 4, when after Silvia has rushed off to begin preparing for her project Orgon expands on the whole business to Mario, a number of references and echoes orient perception of the plot in a very particular way. Thus the son's answer "Ah! ah! cela sera plaisant" already echoes his father's "son idée est plaisante," even as the father is reiterating his superior point of view on things in order to share it with the son: "savez-vous rien de plus particulier que cela?" They will become spectators as Silvia sets out to "jouer ici la même comédie" (Orgon; Mario's like phrase is: "C'est une aventure qui ne saurait manquer de nous divertir"), a situation which will lead to Silvia's increasing irritation and exasperation at her brother's meddling in her affairs.[11]

LE JEU DE L'AMOUR ET DU HASARD 117

Mario
Dans quelle humeur es-tu, ma sœur? Comme tu t'emportes!
Silvia
C'est que je suis bien lasse de mon personnage, et je me serais déjà démasquée, si je n'avais pas craint de fâcher mon père.
Monsieur Orgon
Gardez-vous-en bien, ma fille, je viens ici pour le recommander....
Silvia
Mais que fais-je? de quoi m'accuse-t-on? Instruisez-moi, je vous en conjure; cela est-il sérieux? Me joue-t-on? se moque-t-on de moi? Je ne suis pas tranquille.
Silvia
Quel malheureux déguisement! Surtout que Lisette ne m'approche pas....
Silvia
... quand finira la comédie que vous vous donnez sur mon compte?
Monsieur Orgon
La seule chose que j'exige de toi, ma fille ... Attends encore, tu me remercieras du délai que je te demande, je t'en réponds.
Mario
Tu épouseras Dorante, et même avec inclination, je te le prédis ... (II, 11)

Knowing what we already do, *se donner la comédie* takes on considerable significance, illuminating the dramatic structure as do few other expressions and in a sense even coaching and prompting the audience toward a particular point of view. The play's action acquires an element of confirmation and predictability, a "Here we go again" dimension. And the fact that Orgon "guarantees" his daughter's happiness ("tu me remercieras du délai ... je t'en réponds") casts finally an ironic and condescending shadow on Silvia's initiative. However generous and comprehending, it is another reminder of paternal superiority and brings us back to the essential and symmetrical condition at the foundations of the dramatic action: two fathers, close friends of long standing, have arranged the marriage. The essential ambiguity of their paternal understanding appears clearly when in the letter from Dorante's father we find an echo of Orgon's "condition": his son intends to "saisir quelques traits du caractère de notre future ... suivant la liberté *que nous sommes convenus de leur laisser*" (I, 4). Freedom on sufferance is in fact not fully freedom, but a reiteration and reaffirmation of parental prerogative. Silvia further confirms the same at two critical junctures: "Vous avez fondé notre bonheur pour la vie, en me laissant faire" (III, 4), "Ah! mon père, vous avez voulu que je fussse à Dorante. Venez voir votre fille vous obéir avec plus de joie qu'on n'en eut jamais" (III, 9).[12]

The distribution of roles and sexes in the play offers further evidence that something other than the conflict of generations at the heart of many traditional comedies is at work here. On the one hand, the primary focus is on the daughter and the problematical "feminism" of her project, whereas in much of Molière for example the *dépit amoureux* is but one piece of evidence in the case against the father's foibles. On the other hand, the father here readily shares what he knows with his son (and with the absent father), creating a situation of complicity among the male secondary characters. (Moreover, Lisette is as much Orgon's servant as Silvia's, and Arlequin, who is somewhere between a main and a secondary character, is defined more by his social role and theatrical tradition than by his sex.) Indeed, it is striking to note that fairly late in the play, when Silvia is plotting to achieve recognition and respect for herself as an individual, the father and son still judge her wishes via a generalized sexual referent: (*Monsieur Orgon*) "... Quelle insatiable vanité d'amour-propre"! (*Mario*) "Cela, c'est l'amour-propre d'une femme, et il est tout au plus uni" (III, 4). One notes as well that the formulation in the *Mercure* article already quoted was an almost verbatim quotation, a remarkable instance of "echoed" response. No less than in the first scene, the play might be subtitled "Silvia et les hommes."

The *Jeu* is thus a very particular case of the *meneur-spectateur* function analyzed by Rousset and Koch, since Silvia's taking on the *meneur* function in the third act splits what in most of Marivaux's other love plays remains the perquisite of a single character-role. And in dealing with the highly gender-oriented theater of Marivaux, consideration of the sex of the characters in the role distribution points up how deeply into the play the paternal vision extends, how in this particular instance paternal and fraternal conjoin to share a male-defined, "paternalistic" attitude toward Silvia's endeavor, one that sets the tone for a certain spectator or reader reaction ("nous divertir," as Mario has it). True, the motives of the *meneur de jeu* are altruistic as well as egoistic (Koch, p. 24), but if the *meneurs* are both representatives of the playwright (Rousset, p. 54) and "in large measure a surrogate of the audience" (Koch, p. 27, n. 12), one wonders whether the split in the *meneur* function which coincides with a primarily sexual differentiation (Silvia/the males) allows of a single legitimate appreciation of the outcome.

The *Jeu* is finally a "frame play," in much the same way that we speak of a frame novel. That masters encompass the language and activities of servants is the normal state of affairs. But reversal of the linguistic and dramaturgic situation where Dorante-Bourguignon is concerned, the humorous echo effect of Lisette's dramaturgic apprehensions, indeed the cyclical vicissitudes of Silvia's situation in general, are all followed by an audience attuned to—and by—the paternalistic frame, and the result is a comedy that generates above all a condescending smile, the corroboration of the paternal wisdom on which the play's action is founded. Greene insists quite properly and at times even eloquently on the authenticity of Silvia's enterprise, on Marivaux's "giving dramatic expression to a critical moment in the life of every person who aspires to be a *personne*, an individual in his own right" (p. 134), and on "marriage as a union freely entered into by equals for mutual pleasure and enrichment" (p. 132). But while one may subscribe to this as the legitimacy of Silvia's outlook, Greene's reference to "an individual in *his* own right" is already a significant choice of terms (see my concluding note on the problems raised by such pronominal orientation); and his admonition to see her not as a coquette but through Dorante's eyes (p. 132) in fact shifts the frame rather than removes it. Even if Silvia's undertaking is "feminist" insofar as her one-act extension supersedes the paternal conditions for two-act structure, the play as a whole, in its granting of initiative and perspective through a paternalistic frame, is not.

Chapter VII

SPEECH AND AUTONOMY IN *LA PRINCESSE DE CLEVES*

Despite varying emphases and approaches, there has come to be general critical agreement on most aspects of *La Princesse de Clèves*: its overriding theme of *amour-passion* portrays an emotion which as its etymology indicates has a life of its own, is suffered and undergone at the expense and to the detriment of one's wishes, one's obligations, one's autonomy. Moreoever, not only is the court as agitated by *galanteries* as by political intrigue, but love and marriage are in total opposition. It is the Princess' lot to learn all this slowly and painfully in an emotional apprenticeship developed rhythmically and structurally in a remarkable union of psychological analysis and formal economy.[1]

Even as the court oscillates between the political and the amatory, the main character is continually subjected to a back-and-forth movement: between Clèves and Nemours, and between the public scrutiny of the court and precious moments of solitary respite in her room or at a country home. The novel thus quickly accustoms the reader to an "interiority" and indirection which are in a sense its hallmarks. As we move continually from social spectacle to its impact on the individual, and from representation to commentary, we sense not only the character's plight but the narrator's superior ability to articulate her feelings and situation, as a variety of types of discourses lead to a "shaping of the reader's perspective" which appears in the light of recent criticism to be far more elaborate and accomplished than was once assumed to be the case.[2]

Rather than static, however, or merely oscillatory and complementary, the various patterns and strategies are set in a progression, an evolving situation whose most obvious outward sign is the falling away of the two characters who in their different ways serve as confidants and mentors to the Princess, and of course as screens between her and Nemours: her mother dies having alerted her to what she has begun to sense herself only vaguely, and her husband's demise is ultimately a function of her admission to him that she loves another. The novel empties the personal space surrounding the Princess at the same time that it moves her inexorably toward a confrontation with Nemours.

Yet the dénouement—the Princess' decision not to marry and her attendant retirement—has evoked great divergences in critical reaction and some of criticism's harshest judgments, as though earlier debates about the propriety and verisimilitude of the Princess' *aveu* to her husband were now supplanted by similar puzzlement and/or socio-esthetic disapproval concerning the outcome of the novel. I shall attempt here to develop a formal approach to the final confrontation with Nemours as a key to the dénouement, and shall speculate in a concluding chapter on the role of the person of the reader in the various interpretations of that dénouement. Briefly, my thesis is that a detailed examination of the use of direct speech and dialogue will show that the Princess' decision is a victory for autonomy rather than a mutilation, and will in the same process re-establish the textual and stylistic underpinnings which even some critics who cite a triumph have tended to neglect, but without which the notion of such a triumph remains necessarily somewhat abstract and imposed.

A prime early example is the scene between the Princess and her mother on the latter's deathbed. It is a scene in the sense that we have a relatively lengthy quotation from a character rather than interpretation by the narrator, Madame de Chartres representing of course a major relay of the analytical instance in the novel as she delineates theme and situation for her daughter.

   Vous avez de l'inclination pour M. de Nemours; je ne vous demande point de me l'avouer: je ne suis plus en état de me servir de votre sincérité pour vous conduire ... vous êtes sur le bord du précipice ... Songez ce que vous devez à votre marie; songez ce que vous vous devez à vous-même, et pensez que vous allez perdre cette réputation que vous vous êtes conquise ... retirez-vous de la cour ... vous voir tomber comme les autres femmes ...[3]

It is also typical of this early stage of the novel that conversation should be in fact one-sided, that the Princess, overwhelmed by the relevance of what she is hearing, should burst into tears but say nothing. Thus, while the crucial terms of the situation are laid out by only one character, it bears stressing that direct discourse is the mark of a "heard" scene, a *récit de paroles* creating so to speak an aural focus in which non-narrated speech provides the bulk of the information (albeit one-sidedly for the moment), rather than a "sight" scene where the character's point of view —literal or figurative—is for the most part related to us by a mediator.[4]

The narrator's return contains an important re-establishing of overt contact with the reader: "Mme de Clèves sortit de la chambre de sa mère en l'état que l'*on* peut *s*'imaginer"(p. 278), thus further reminding us that the two levels of apprehension—characterial and narratorial—are distinct and distinguishable in the text.[5] But as the novel progresses, the fact that other characters as well as the narrator will be analyzing the Princess' situation (her husband will also, and Nemours will attempt to in the final scene) will be further accompanied by a shift whereby the Princess herself will take over that role. It is this evolution and shift from interpretive commentary to direct aural representation, rather than any axiomatic superiority of one mode over the other, that leads to a particular foregrounding of her situation. With commentary and visual presentation at a minimum in her final confrontation with Nemours, she will not only tell Nemours (and us) what she has learned but by speaking for herself will offer demonstrable proof that she has indeed learned.

Of those critics who have analyzed speech in the novel, Gougenheim deals with what in the language of the time was called "discourse," i.e., both conversation and monologue, and his article is a description of the verbs which introduce such "speech."[6] Fabre deals mainly with analysis and indirection and finds the direct speech of the novel definitely lifeless and inferior: "Au lieu de libérer la parole pour lui donner les apparences de la vie, il s'agit de la soumettre à un cérémonial qui l'en éloigne ... a-t-on jamais entendu une amante parler de la sorte à un tel moment?"[7] Rousset underscores in a second study the text's insistence that the final scene is in fact the first time the Princess and Nemours can and do speak freely and openly, but concerns himself otherwise with the veiled, oblique and indirect exchanges of which Nemours is the initiator and the Princess the recipient or victim.[8] Alain Niderst asserts that dialogue is where the profoundest truths are encountered, that dialogue is more frequent than action, and that the longer the dialogue the less the novelist attempts to reveal the thoughts of her characters, but his remarks are mainly concerned with what he considers the high degree of stylization of dialogue in the novel.[9] For Roger Francillon, the final scene is exceptional, since for the most part the Princess is dominated and silence is therefore the rule, but his remarks are essentially thematic.[10] Kuizenga sees direct discourse as enjoining the reader to share the heroine's point of view, or to step back to gain ironic distance; she also sees increased use of dialogue as a sign of increased consciousness on the part of the characters.[11] From my point of view here, speaking is also and primarily an element of characterization: where narrator and reader step back, the character steps forward to fill the gap and for the Princess to speak will be finally to act. But in order to assess properly and fully the meaning of a final verbal confrontation, we must not only look closely at the fact that the main character speaks but at the basic modes of her speech and how they evolve as well, and in so doing trace the move from a syntax of the character to a sense of the character in the syntax of the text as a whole.

In a typology of the "spoken" we have first the silent scenes, including some of the most important in the work: Clèves's first catching sight of Mlle de Chartres at the jeweler's, the forging of the substitute letter, the Princess observed by Nemours in the garden, etc. On a second level come those moments when she either listens but does not speak, or is spoken to directly but does not reply, unwilling or unable to respond verbally to the situation. The element common to both is that the Princess is usually strongly affected: surprised by what she hears, embarrassed, distraught: "n'était plus maîtresse de cacher ses sentiments . . . la laissa si étonnée et dans un si grand saisissement . . ." (pp. 307-08); "Le trouble et l'embarras de Mme de Clèves étaient au-dela de tout ce que l'on peut s'imaginer" (pp. 345-46); "Le nom de M. de Nemours surprit Mme de Clèves et la fit rougir" (p. 378); "... lui fit une idée de M. de Nemours ... qui lui donna un trouble confus, dont elle ne savait même pas la cause" (p. 379).

The scenes in which the Princess does speak can of course be measured first in quantitative terms: relative length (here, the *aveu* stands out noticeably as the longest save the final scene, which is twice as long again), or number of exchanges (few number more than three or more by each speaker).[12] The range of interlocutors is quite limited: four exchanges with her mother (pp. 264, 274, 275, 277), five with the reine Dauphine (pp. 262, 289, 298, 326, 344), eight with her husband (pp. 258, 279, 334, 339, 341, 348, 361, 374), four with Nemours prior to the final scene (pp. 293, 323, 341, 371). Extremely few exchanges occur outside her presence, spoken or otherwise. In terms of order and distribution, the mother is limited to the first section of the novel, the reine Dauphine mainly to the second and third, while Nemours and the Prince span all four sections. Finally, direct discourse represents 31, 64, 42 and 33 percent of the respective sections (Kuizenga, p. 131).

The subject matter is virtually always the same: the ways and means of love. (If this is not surprising, it is nonetheless worth noting that the political theme is presented almost solely in narration, resulting in greater actualization of the love theme than if both were distributed more or less equally between the two modes of presentation.) Love is also the manifest or latent subject of the subnarratives in their connection to the Princess, and significantly on four of five occasions the reine Dauphine is talking about Nemours. In both cases the reader is naturally more aware than a given character of how closely the subject concerns the Princess, but the theme is also evoked by characters in direct reference to their relationship to her: her mother sounds the alert, and thereafter Clèves and Nemours do battle verbally with her "duty" and her emotions.

Consideration of a number of common denominators in the function and texture of the exchange leads to a more qualitative assessment of the Princess' presence and role. Thus in all but a

LA PRINCESSE DE CLEVES 125

few exchanges (even most of these come in the second half of the novel), the Princess is not the first to speak but is responding, as she does in so many of the scenes where she does not speak at all. This is especially significant since in slightly more than half of the exchanges her interlocutor speaks once more than she, i.e., both opens and closes the conversation.

Passivity is further evidenced in the style of her response, in what amounts to verbal equivalents of her involuntary reactions. On some occasions the subject is quite simply beyond her:

Je vous assure, Madame, reprit Mme de Clèves, qui paraissait un peu embarrassée, que *je ne devine pas* si bien que vous pensez. (p. 262)

Je n'eusse jamais soupçonné cette haine. (p. 264)

Vous m'étonnez, reprit Mme de Clèves ... *apprenez-moi* je vous en supplie, ce qui vous a détrompé de Mme de Tournon ... L'on ne peut être plus surprise que je le suis. (pp. 279-80)

Elle m'en a dit quelque chose, répondit Mme de Clèves; mais *je ne vois* pas ce que cette lettre a de commun. ... *J'ai peine à comprendre* ... à moins que vous n'ayez quelque raison que *je ne sais point*. ... Mme de Clèves témoigna par son silence qu'elle était prête à l'écouter. (pp. 324-25)

Je ne sais, Madame, comment vous ferez, répondit-elle. (p. 327)

Je ne sais que vous répondre, lui dit-elle; je meurs de honte en vous parlant. (p. 339)

More often still a number of remarks are heavily "modalized," underscoring her diffidence, her uncertainty, her insecurity.[13]

Je ne sais ce que vous pouvez souhaiter au-delà de ce que je fais, et *il me semble* que la bienséance ... (p. 258)

Il est vrai, repartit Mme de Clèves, qu'elle l'a remarqué, et je crois lui en avoir ouï dire quelque chose. (p. 293)

il me semble aussi, reprit Mme de Clèves, que l'on dit qu'elle était née en France. (p. 299)

je crois que la prudence ne veut pas que je vous le nomme. ... *Il me semble*, répondit-elle, que vous devez être content de ma sincérité. (p. 335)

il me semble que vous devriez essayer de faire choisir quelque autre. (p. 341)

Je crois, Madame, lui répondit-elle, que je ne dois pas vous remercier de cette impatience et qu'elle est *sans doute* causée par quelque autre chose ... (p. 344)

Je ne croyais pas, reprit Mme de Clèves ... que vous puissiez me faire des reproches de ne l'avoir pas vu. (p. 362)

Je ne crois pourtant pas, reprit Mme de Clèves, que M. de Nemours y ait jamais entré. ... *Je ne me souviens point*, lui dit-elle, de vous y avoir vu ... c'est *sans que je l'aie su*. (p. 371)

Structurally, thematically, stylistically, we have then a character who is the focal point of the novel, yet who is forever reacting rather than acting: listening rather than speaking, submitting to another's subject matter rather than initiating, answering rather than addressing, modalizing rather than asserting, who is unable much of the time even to close off by her own means a painful discussion. What becomes of such a character at the dénouement?

The final confrontation very clearly occupies a special place in the novel: not simply because it comes after the death of the Princess' husband, but because it occurs in fact several months later, a major hiatus in the narrated time, albeit not long enough for the Princess' feelings for Nemours to have died out: "La pensée que c'était M. de Nemours changea entièrement la situation de son esprit, elle ne se trouva plus dans un certain triste repos qu'elle commençait à goûter, elle se sentit inquiète et agitée ... Quelle passion endormie se ralluma dans son cœur et avec quelle violence!" (pp. 379-80). The narrator is at further pains to underscore the exceptional nature of the coming encounter: "Plus de devoir, plus de vertu, qui s'oppossassent à ses sentiments, *tous les obstacles étaient levés* ... Toutes ces idées furent *nouvelles* à cette princesse..." (p. 380). The barriers have fallen; the narrator gives us the mental state of both characters (pp. 380-81), a rare occurrence in the case of Nemours; and they thus arrive equally moved at the final scene: "L'on ne peut exprimer ce que sentirent M. de Nemours et Mme de Clèves de se trouver seuls et en état de se parler *pour la première fois*" (p. 382).

Thematically, the scene represents a culmination, as the *devoir, repos* and *retraite* motifs come together once again after having been formulated explicitly for her in her mother's deathbed scene.[14] A second group of thematic references also plays a major role in the discussion, as mention of the passage of time appears throughout the scene. Here again the scene is a culmination in the sense that from the beginning of the novel "agitation" and inconstancy have been presented as hallmarks of life at court, where time and love are mutually exclusive. But what occurs here is more than a thematic tying-together at the resolution of the plot, and it is crucial to note that for the duration of the scene the disposition of these issues is left up to the main character. The "falling away" process results finally in a tight circumscription of the reader's attention around the Princess' personal situation: the collective, political themes have given way to the story of individual passion, the secondary narrative episodes have disappeared, the Princess' mother and husband are gone.

Stated another way, a semantic approach via delineation of key themes and concepts is a necessary but not sufficient approach, since the meaning of the scene is equally a function of its syntax, in the exercise by the main character of analytical faculties which until now have been the prerogative of the narrator. The distance traveled by the character since the story's inception is best measured by the fact that thanks to her experience, terms and motifs which she took on faith at the outset now become the tools and the means to analyze that experience. The exercise of her newfound ability to articulate provides dramatic proof of her competence as she applies it.[15]

In terms of earlier assessments of the "spoken," several characteristics set this scene apart: its considerable length compared to other exchanges and particularly to the other scenes with Nemours; its preponderance within Part IV; the number and relative symmetry of the individual exchanges; the absence of visual references and the extremely limited intervention by the narrator.[16] After the preliminary remarks and once the conversation is joined, it is she who assumes the initiative: "Puisque vous voulez que je vous parle et que je m'y résous, répondit Mme de Clèves, je le ferai avec une sincérité... Je ne vous dirai point ..." (p. 383); "Il commença à lui conter... mais elle l'interrompit avant qu'il eût achevé" (p. 384); "Ne vous excusez point, reprit-elle, il y a longtemps que je vous ai pardonné" (p. 384); "Je veux vous parler encore, avec la même sincérité... mais je vous conjure de m'écouter sans m'interrompre" (p. 386); "Elle sortit en disant ces paroles, sans que M. de Nemours pût la retenir" (pp. 389-90). Such firmness of tone does not of course preclude concessions to Nemours, and her frankness and openness will be obvious throughout. Her use of the verb *avouer* is one more link to the *aveu* to her husband, an earlier and crucial *prise de parole*, yet here her concessions are assumed in a much more active way and are couched in a context of lucidity which was lacking previously: "J'avoue, répondit-elle, que les passions peuvent me conduire; mais elles ne sauraient m'aveugler" (p. 387). The Princess now speaks from a new certitude, emphasizing throughout what she has learned, what she now knows, and this change is all the more striking for representing a shift from Nemours's knowing ways: "Je ne vous dirai point que je n'ai pas vu l'attachement que vous avez eu pour moi . . . Je vous avoue donc, non seulement que je l'ai vu . . . mais je voudrais bien savoir . . ." (p. 383).[17] Thus, she may still blush, but at the same time her imperatives now orient the discussion rather than flee from it. Her questions too represent active probing, not a screen thrown up in order to gain time, and she will integrate the answers into a new and active comprehension, one of her own elaboration and based on her experience:

Ne m'en dites pas davantage, lui dit-elle; *je vois* présentement . . . (p. 384)

. . . des raisons qui *vous sont inconnues*. (p. 385)

Je sais bien que ce n'est pas la même chose à l'égard du monde, mais au mien il n'y a aucune différence puisque *je sais* que c'est par vous qu'il est mort. (p. 385)

Rien ne me peut empêcher de *connaître* que vous êtes né avec toutes les dispositions pour la galanterie. (p. 387)

mon *expérience* me ferait croire qu'il n'y en a point à qui vous ne puissez plaire. (p. 388)

Moreover, this new certainty is the stronger and the more lucid for its recognition of the situation ("Je sais bien qu'il n'y a rien de plus difficule que ce que j'entreprends," p. 388) and is present not only through affirmation and allusion but also in examples of discrimination and analysis found heretofore only in the narratorial point of view.

Her newfound autonomy is thus based on a lucid recognition of her emotions rather than an absence of feeling, a perspective evidenced by her ability both to name those emotions and to discriminate among them in a way familiar to us from earlier narratorial analysis, and from contemporary *moraliste* literature as well.

Je ne sais même si je ne vous le dis point plus pour *l'amour de moi* que pour *l'amour de vous*. (p. 385) les *raisons de mon devoir* ne me paraîtraient pas si fortes sans cette distinction. (p. 386)

mes actions involontaires, *ou* les choses que le hasard vous a apprises, vous ont donné assez d'espérance. (p. 387)

Par vanité *ou* par goût, toutes les femmes souhaitent de vous attacher. (p. 388)

Je vous croirais toujours *amoureux* et *aimé* et je ne me tromperais pas souvent. (p. 388)

Ce que je crois *devoir* à la mémoire de M. de Clèves serait faible s'il n'était soutenu par l'intérêt de mon *repos*, et les raisons de mon *repos* ont besoin d'être soutenues de celles de mon *devoir*. (pp. 388-89)

It is further striking to note that the same Nemours who was once master of the *double-entendre* and general wisdom applied to a particular situation, now finds no answer to the *repos* argument but throws himself at her feet, shedding tears and uttering words which are referred to only indirectly in the text.

Her experience and these insights further engender a firm confidence in her ability to predict and therefore to generalize:

Vous vous repentirez, peut-être, de l'avoir obtenue, et *je me repentirai* infailliblement de vous l'avoir accordée. Vous méritez une destinée plus heureuse que celle que vous avez eue jusques ici et que celle que vous pouvez *trouver à l'avenir* . . . (p. 383)

c'est elle [her singling out of Nemours] qui me fait *envisager des malheurs* à m'attacher à vous. (p. 386)

la seule fois de ma vie où je me donnerai la liberté de vous les faire paraître . . . puis-je me mettre en état de voir *certainement finir* cette passion . . . Vous avez déjà eu plusieurs passions, vous en auriez *encore*; je *ne* ferais *plus* votre bonheur. (p. 387)

Painful experience has been transformed into a keen, *moraliste*'s sense of time's effect on the emotions, and we find now an incipient ability to emit general truths and observations; incipient rather than the finished products of the *moralistes*, but nonetheless the single most striking evidence of how far the character has come from her initial silence.

je suivrai les règles que mon devoir m'impose. (p. 385)

je vais passer par-dessus toute la retenue et toutes les délicatesses que je devrais avoir dans une première conversation. (p. 386)

Mais les hommes conservent-ils de la passion dans ces engagements éternels? (p. 387)

toutes les qualités qui sont propres à y donner des succès heureux . . . je ne serais pas même assurée de n'avoir point le malheur de la jalousie. (pp. 387-88)

Perhaps no formulation better traces the heroine's trajectory than her own words spoken at the outset of the scene: "je vous avoue que vous m'avez inspiré des sentiments qui m'étaient inconnus devant que vous avoir vu, et dont j'avais même si peu d'idée qu'ils me donnèrent d'abord une surprise qui augmentaient encore le trouble qui les suit toujours" (p. 384). Many elements prepare here what is to follow: the initial innocence, the surprise and the passion, emotions working in tandem, frank admission of them. One notes in particular how several past tenses lead to a generalizing present and absolute adverb ("qui les suit toujours") in striking contrast to other more relative possibilities (*a suivi, suivrait* or even *suivra*) and to the interpretive role fulfilled earlier by the narrator (cf. for example "elle [the Princess] se trompait elle-même; et ce mal, qu'elle trouvait si insupportable, était la jalousie avec toutes les horreurs dont elle peut être accompagnée," p. 310).[18]

The falling-away process leads then to a special moment when the narrator too recedes into the background, supplanted by the main character, and when Nemours, the only other important character, is not only kept at bay but transcended. This *prise de parole*, the lucid expression of her analytical competence, therefore represents the thematic and stylistical authority which embodies formally and on the level of character what critics have often seen as failure, mutilation and symbolic suicide when assessing the dénouement. But it is precisely important to recall that if her remarks in the final scene contain concessions and admissions of her feelings they are fitted by the character herself into a new scheme of things, a personal perspective achieved by her over and against great emotion, where only a few paragraphs earlier her feelings were suddenly reawakened and still required a narrator's ordering ("Toutes ces idées furent nouvelles à cette princesse . . . cette persuasion, qui était un effet de sa raison et de sa vertu, n'entraînaient pas son cœur," pp. 380-81). Now she is feeling but also thinking on her (own) feet, voicing both what she feels and her appraisal of it.

The alternating event-analysis rhythm of the plot thus changes radically in the final encounter, as analysis now *becomes* the event. This is at the same time, however, a culmination of the outward-to-inward movement of the text and it is perhaps this paradox which has made assessment of the dénouement so problematic: what on the level of meaning culminates in the primacy of the internal (self) over the external (the Other, and socially determined behavior) occurs stylistically and structurally in an *exteriorization*, an explicitation, as the Princess completes the passage from inchoate and amorphous feeling to overt expression and delineation in dialogue. Analytical competence shifts briefly from the narrator to the eponymous character and will shortly be restored to the narrator, as the character repairs to a new silence; but the meaning of the work has been established, since the character's journey to lucidity is now irreversible. There is nothing unheroic about the strength of her feelings in the final pages of narration, nor in the way in which sickness lessens desire, nor indeed in her retreat itself. When she breaks off she still loves Nemours, and as her "vues plus grandes et plus éloinées" attest (p. 393), the separation is a rising above more than an amputation or a mutilation, her "occupations plus saintes" (p. 395) confirmation of the same rather than compensation. The Princess has chosen integrity over integration. Her retirement is not anti-climactic but post-climactic, and the confrontation scene is one of ascendancy and victory, ascendancy over one's surroundings and one's feelings, and victory over the silence which once enveloped both.

CONCLUDING NOTE ON THE PERSON OF THE READER

The final confrontation between Madame de Clèves and Nemours is only part of the dénouement of *La Princesse de Clèves*, rather like the main scene of an Act IV, the ultimate crisis which necessitates a sorting out and detailing of fates. Moreover, I hope to have shown in the previous chapter that in its illustration of the Princess' new lucidity the confrontation is also the *sine qua non* of the resolution and that without detailed stylistic consideration of her exchange with Nemours we cannot properly assess the motivation and the meaning of her withdrawal at the novel's end. Thanks to her growth throughout the plot, she goes off rather like Cléopâtre to a certain "grandeur," a culmination and a confirmation of the changes that have occurred and indeed that she has wrought. Her *retraite* is the ultimate stage of the "approach/avoidance dialectic" which Susan Tiefenbrun sees as the most basic structural pattern in the novel and, as Robert N. Nicolich has remarked, her new perspective—"des vues plus grandes et plus éloignées" (p. 393)—represents a transposition of the earlier "seeing" motif onto a loftier, quasi-religious plane where an earlier alternation becomes a sublime unity.[1] "Elle passait une partie de l'année dans cette maison religieuse et l'autre chez elle, mais dans une retraite et dans des occupations plus saintes que celles des couvents les plus austères" (p. 395).

At the same time, it is clear from the remarks of readers concerning the dénouement that something rather special is at work in *La Princesse de Clèves* and criticism of it, that by repairing to her "maison religieuse" the Princess leaves many of those readers puzzled and even frustrated. By reviewing briefly critical comments over the last twenty-odd years, I should like now to conclude with some reflections on the "person" of the reader and its relationship to the textual person.

A good starting place is a remark in Francis L. Lawrence's review of earlier criticism.

Unless the activities of court—ambition, galanterie, intrigue, license—are held as the definition of life, I fail to see how the resolution can be interpreted as a rejection of life, or a retreat into nothingness.... The individual, exercising a salutary, non-destructive selfishness, may freely choose and work out his happiness.[2]

On a first level, Lawrence was clearly taking the point of view I have referred to earlier as my own, namely that the dénouement must be seen as an example of a justifiedly self-oriented initiative and therefore a positive moment in the "career" of this particular textual person. At the same time, however, Lawrence's choice of terms, specifically the reference to "The individual . . . *his* happiness," must give one pause. His remarks were of course written well before *his/her* became common usage, yet surely the situation at the end of the novel calls for a "his or her," not to mention an even more probable "her." We are after all witnesses to a singular he/she confrontation which no other character sees or hears, and to which even the narrator adds only a bare minimum of information and no commentary. The "his" thus seems overly abstract here, if not an unwarranted displacement of primary interest onto the male participant (who moreover fails notably to "work out his happiness," as we have seen). Still, other critics have been even less circumspect, taking a more blatantly sexual stance in their approach to the characters.

Claude Vigée, for example, gives what is doubtless an extreme example of a chauvinistic interpretation, one that is pro-male as such: the main character's decision is not considered or assessed but judged, as a flight from the real, fatal to personal development, a privation, morbid, impotence, protectionist, guilty, egocentric and egomaniacal, a defeat, a negation, inflexible, etc.[3] A polemicist could hardly hope for a better formulation to expose than the following: "elle accepte la mutilation la plus cruelle, celle de ses affections humaines, de son bonheur de femme" (p. 740). Yet in its way so excessive a remark represents more a difference in degree than in kind.

In his influential article, traces of which appear in several others, Serge Doubrovsky subsumes—not improperly but at some sacrifice to formal considerations—the Princess' destiny into a psychological and existential schema which tends to focus on liberty and sincerity, with an attendant lessening of the role of the character's initial subjectedness, and of lucidity as an ethico-esthetic vector of the text.[4] Only the "style" is referred to, very quickly and with more reference to author than to narrator or character, as a skillful achievement ("en soi-même une prouesse et un triomphe," p. 51). While the Princess is rightly seen as wanting to answer only to herself ("ne dépendre que d'elle," p. 47) such a preference is without "chaleur ni élan, pas un seul instant elle ne pense à Nemours et à son bonheur à lui . . . Il ne lui reste plus de solution, ou plutôt il n'en reste qu'une: *le suicide*" (p. 48; emphasis in the text). Even a critic at pains to delineate explicitly the differences of reaction in seventeenth-century readers and those in our time[5] speaks of the Princess naively babbling, of a fear of spontaneity, of the Princess immuring herself behind walls in "a form of living death," a "death in life."[6]

There is a lack of élan here, of sheer response to life, as well as the incapacity of the gift of self . . . ; the fair Princess' final withdrawal is more than retreat, for which we might superficially blame her; it is retrenchment, a truncation and semi-suicidal mutilation of the self that results in the traumatism that goes by the name of *repos*.[7]

Elsewhere, for Georges Poulet the dénouement is the result of the search for self-preservation in a negative state, outside passion, an asceticism.[8] Martin Turnell sees the Princess as "condemned to unhappiness . . . and whether or not she really believes that M. de Nemours would abandon her, it is this that she simply cannot face . . . an attitude of complete negation, a refusal to take any further part in life. It is a sign of the miraculous clairvoyance of the seventeenth century that the Princess admits it."[9] For Erich Kahler her decision is an ultimate surrender,[10] for Bernard Beugnot it represents the "sanction douloureuse d'un échec" as her "repos, qui, proche du vide de l'être, nie l'intensité passionnelle hors de laquelle pourtant, aux yeux de Madame de Clèves, la vie perd tout sens . . . une impasse affective où se rencontrent l'ennui et la mort."[11] Bernard Pingaud speaks of "cette mort involontaire . . . le pouvoir suprême qu'elle permet d'obtenir étant celui de s'écarter de soi, non pas pour se mêler à un autre et trouver son bonheur en lui, mais pour remonter . . . à ce lieu du vrai *repos* qui est à la fois notre origine et notre perte."[12] For Niderst, "la retraite finira par vaincre la cour, mais ce sera presque un suicide," although a few years later he seems to find reasons which are more justifiable, even if they receive only a rather half-hearted endorsement on his part: "L'extrême abdication peut paradoxalement restaurer une forme de liberté, et donner le repos à la place du bonheur. Elle permet, en tout cas, d'éviter cet écartèlement qu'inflige le monde en imposant un idéal, qu'il rend en même temps impossible."[13] Roger Francillon sees the Princess' final state as an emptiness to be filled by a religious conversion, but no less death-like: "comme la passion est cause d'aliénation, il semblerait, à première vue, que le repos implique la reconquête de l'identité perdue. Mais ce ne sont que des hypothèses. Lorsqu'enfin, l'héroïne trouve le repos dans la retraite, la narratrice cesse de l'intérioriser, si bien que le lecteur à l'impression d'un certain vide, qu'illustre d'ailleurs la nouvelle de sa mort qui met un point final au roman."[14]

As late as 1975, Jean Cordelier showed an irritation intolerant of silence or opacity on the part of a female character, and resorted to reckless interpolation and extrapolation.[15] Thus we learn that the Princess' ultimate refusal goes back in part to the trauma of her husband's "grossièreté" on their wedding night, that since she cites more than one reason for her retirement none of the reasons is valid, that on her deathbed "Malade boudeuse, malade obstinée, elle se retourne dans son lit contre le mur." We even get to hear the arguments Nemours should have used: ". . . en refusant de m'épouser, c'est vous-même qui me démontrez la faiblesse de votre inclination pour moi puisque vous me refusez la seule preuve décisive de votre amour . . . Nemours, au lieu de se jeter à ses pieds, aurait mieux fait de la prendre dans ses bras, quitte à la chiffonner un peu" (p. 51). In other words, "If you loved me, you'd do it . . . Lean back and enjoy it."

Cordelier's assimilation of us into his frustration via a collective *nous* ("nous, lecteurs naïfs," p. 46; "Silence qui nous laisse dans le mystère," p. 47) is a reminiscence if not an analogue of Nemours's attempt to annex and therefore subdue the Princess' resistance via the same generalizing pronoun: "Il est plus difficile que vous ne le pensez, Madame, de résister à ce qui *nous* plaît et à ce qui *nous* aime" (p. 388). Those who find the Princess cold or cruel in the final scene, or feel she is rejecting her only route to happiness, might also compare her sincere frankness ("Je ne sais même si je ne vous le dis point plus pour l'amour de *moi* que pour l'amour de *vous*," p. 385) to Nemours's revealing pronominal usage: "quel fantôme de devoir opposez-*vous* à *mon* bonheur" (p. 385); "*Vous* seule *vous* opposez à *mon* bonheur" (p. 389). The characters share a passion but with Nemours it leads to *amour-propre*, with the Princess to *amour de soi*.[16]

In an early and more or less direct rejoinder to Vigée's comments, Simone Fraisse set them in a more appropriate perspective while at the same time pointing out that Jean Delannoy had left the whole notion of *repos* out of his film version of the novel (Delannoy: "J'ai voulu raconter une très belle histoire où les femmes ne sont pas bafouées").[17] Fraisse shows as well that an historical reading of the text allows us to see *repos* (and the seventeenth-century convent) in its own context and then in our own, and that inclination to understand historically is to be less inclined to judge: "Prenons l'œuvre telle qu'elle nous est offerte" (p. 563); "Ce qu'elle appelle devoir est la fidélité au souvenir de son mari, le repos est une fidélité à soi-même, une conquête sur le désordre intérieur" (p. 565); ". . . l'outrance même [Vigée's] montre combien aujourd'hui l'éthique de Madame de la Fayette est dépassée . . . Mais le film a laissé échapper—volontairement sans doute—l'éthique qui donnait au roman son sens et sa singularité" (p. 567). A year later Marie-Jeanne Durry traced clearly the character's path from feeling to knowledge, her "clairvoyance conquise": ". . . d'abord naïve. Eveillée ensuite, avant l'incident de la lettre perdue, mais déjà par la jalousie, l'intelligence de soi va s'approfondir, et à travers les contradictions intérieures, les erreurs complaisantes ou involontaires, les illusions répétées de délivrance, devenir enfin souveraines."[18] And of the large number of female critics who have written on the *Princesse de Clèves* more recently, the first set down two very pointed reminders (note here "the reader . . . he"):

The complete success of Mme de La Fayette's novel requires that the reader participate in the heroine's triumph in living up to the ideals which she has accepted, but to do this, he must also be aware of those ideals. . . . To impose the standard of another epoch, another society, could only constitute a falsification. The real triumph in the novel is not the heroine's rejection of her love for Nemours, but rather her attainment of the perspective which allows this rejection, the perspective of eternity.[19]

Possible explanations for the divergence in interpretation of the dénouement surely include the familiar dangers of anachronism and excessive abstraction evident in much of the critical comment I have been quoting. A more specific element in the case of *La Princesse de Clèves* is the perhaps unavoidably negative connotations, for some readers, of *retraite*. (Gabriel Bounoure, for example, prefers *"retirance . . .* retraite ayant des harmoniques militaires et religieux.")[20] One could also cite a certain male propensity to speak of the Princess' *refus*, where female critics emphasize *repos* (see the titles of the Vigée, Fraisse and Cordelier articles), although this is as much an effect as a cause.

The greatest pitfall seems to be that some readers ally naturally with Nemours, even though the novel's perspective is largely in sympathy with the Princess or simply neutral. Its most outlandish expression is the revealing use of pronouns in the passage by Jean Cordelier already cited, but Jean Rousset also speaks of "le dénouement qu'attendent Nemours et le lecteur," and Niderst appears to understate the sharing of the Princess' perspective and to portray objectivity as superiority: "Nous épousons et dominons les raisonnements de la princesse. Nous sommes, si l'on ose dire, à la fois 'dedans' and 'dehors.'"[21] The narrative perspective thus seems to generate a potential confusion of point of view on the Princess' situation, a temptation to mix the superior "objective" knowledge of the narrator with the exterior and therefore less demonstrable superiority of Nemours's viewpoint.

One would do well to bear in mind here the full import of Jules Brody's demonstration that the reader's understanding of Nemours's true feelings remains problematic.[22] Thanks to the primary narrative mode of the work we "know" the Princess better in fact than we know Nemours, but her direct speech represents a complicating factor. Specifically, that her lucid defense of the internal (her self) should occur as an externalization is a formal situation which necessitates close attention to both modes of presentation, but we have seen that critical tradition has heretofore been far more concerned with the novel's indirection. This aspect is perhaps more spectacular in its rich development, but attention to it at the expense of the Princess' speech has led to a situation where reliance on determination by the narrator may make one unaware of, or unreceptive to, self-determination by the character. That is, the critic accustomed to elucidating the being-seeing dichotomy, or evaluating the narrator's technique in doing so, becomes so used to sharing the knowing faculty which such delineation implies that there may result a reluctance to recognize the Princess' emancipation, or a tendency simply to overlook the exteriorization and to judge her *retraite* from the same "superior" viewpoint as earlier. Whereas in fact the Princess comes to know herself in a moment when, through the "falling away" process and her direct speech, we can only take her word(s) for it. Her emergent lucidity swings around as it were to face Nemours and by extension the reader. If we are in a sense "closer" to Nemours in the pages following the final scene it is because the Princess is quite literally looking the other way, and because she goes off where the male character (and reader) find it difficult to follow, to a place and a self of her own.[23]

Her new silence seems to represent both a temptation to speak for her and a frustration, a special case of the "indeterminacy" Wolfgang Iser sees as part of "the reader's transformation of signals sent out by the text" and "steered by two main structural components within the text: first a repertoire of familiar literary patterns and recurrent literary themes, together with allusions to familiar social and historical contexts; second, techniques or strategies used to set the familiar against the unfamiliar."[24] A case in point is Jean Fabre, whose judgment on the lifeless "cérémonial" of the spoken word was cited earlier, and who referred to the Princess in a colloquium discussion as ultimately a "morte vivante."[25] Later in *L'Art de l'analyse* his attitude becomes one of even more explicit frustration.

> Et, libre aux yeux du monde, pourquoi ne pas épouser Nemours? ... [among other possible reasons] parce qu'elle a manqué sa vie, parce qu'elle a trop souci de son repos pour vivre et qu'elle en meurt. Cette âme translucide emporte avec elle son secret; une âme pleine de ténèbres et de tempêtes nous eût peut-être livré le sien.* [*Telle Madame de Merteuil des *Liaisons*. Ce cœur monstrueux est moins énigmatique que celui de Madame de Clèves.][26]

It is almost as though, like Cordelier, Fabre saw the number of reasons as invalidating any and all, rather than seeing the ability to cite and articulate those reasons as the prerequisite for her decision. Similarly, "translucide" implies, not seeing by the character but a character seen through.

Yet when we turn to Fabre's essay on the *Liaisons dangereuses* his treatment of Merteuil compels one to ponder the personal basis for his preference and indeed the whole question of male readers and female characters.

Une telle promotion [admiration by the reader of her force of character] équivaut en effet à mettre la Merteuil hors du jeu, du grand jeu ironique qui donne aux *Liaisons* leur unité, leur totalité et, sans doute, leur signification. Moralement hors du commun, elle ne saurait échapper, littérairement, à la commune loi qui soumet à la sanction de l'ironie tous les personnages du roman ... Ce n'est après tout, qu'une femme et l'on serait tenté d'ajouter: une pauvre femme, si le choix d'un si insolite adjectif n'impliquerait pour son prestige une dégradation plus mortifiante que la flétrissure mondaine et que la pseudo-colère du ciel. ... [Mertueil] ne sent que trop ce par quoi Mme de Tourvel l'emporte sur elle, invinciblement: la féminité, cette faiblesse et grâce de la nature, contre laquelle ne cesseront de s'insurger, après elle, les plus ardentes et pathétiques militantes du mouvement qui se présente comme une libération de leur sexe.[27]

Now in this essay Fabre was also railing against the "ingénieurs de la 'littérairété'" for whom "*Les Liaisons* sont semblables à un jouet de luxe, 'meccano' ou central téléphonique, dont on démonte savamment les connexions pour en faire admirer l'agencement aux badauds, sans se soucier autrement du message que l'appareil a pour fonction de transmettre" (pp. 652-53). There are thus generational and institutional components to his reaction as well as sexual, but one notes once again the reader's desire to wield the ironic structure and ultimately to confer meaning on the text. Moreover, as in the case of his allusion to the "morte vivante" in a discussion, it is precisely in such a *papier d'humeur* that one gets more of the person of the reader. Here, as with the *Princesse de Clèves*, a (male) reader seems to confuse a sexually oriented story with a sexually determined one, and to see as a battle of the sexes what is even more fundamentally a battle for the self, a movement from self-consciousness to *self*-consciousness. The cardinal sin for the character thus becomes disinclination to remain framed and in (her) place, and by resisting the typical socio-formal closure of marriage to escape possession not only by the male character but by the reader as well. The reader's classic (but superficial) frustration-by-suspense is unrelieved since the trajectories of Nemours and the Princess ultimately prove tangential rather than convergent, and the *Princesse de Clèves* ends not so much "dénouée" as "hors nœud." Free to marry is equally free not to.

Now it is hardly my intent to assert that one must be a woman in order to achieve a full and proper reading of *La Princesse de Clèves*, and along the way I have mentioned a number of acute studies by male critics. There do remain, however, some extraordinary elements in the novel's critical dossier. Perhaps the two most obvious are that a work by a woman should have joined so early the canon of French masterpieces, and even more that female critics of the novel should be about equal in number to the males. Furthermore, male and female readings of the dénouement have not only diverged along almost consistently sexual lines, but have done so continuously throughout the last twenty years. Thus, even if the exceptional number of females in the pool of critics of the novel is to some extent a function of the recent American university situation (the necessity to publish, and a more legitimized female approach to literary texts than seems yet to be the general case in France), such a reading does not seem to be necessarily or uniquely a function of evolving critical trends. It also bears noting, however, that female critics of late have often tended to take an explicitly formal approach as the most appropriate route to meaning, and two in particular have recently elucidated the textual components of a certain readerly frustration:

> C'est la présence de Nemours ainsi que le travail du lecteur qui menacent la solitude et augmentent l'érotisme par le tabou attaché au voyeurisme. A la fin de la scène [Madame de Clèves is contemplating the cane and the portrait] les pensées et les sentiments de Nemours nous sont révélés par le biais du narrateur-voyeur et omniscient ... ; Le fantasme ... s'accomplit à l'aide d'une œuvre d'art. La princesse regarde un portrait tandis que nous, lecteurs-voyeurs, lisons de même un roman.[28]
>
> ... l'attente du lecteur, son désir de savoir si oui ou non ils s'avoueront jamais leur amour ... est entretenue par un narrateur qui peut, à son gré, reculer le moment de l'aveu. Structure donc de désir et d'attente, qui captive l'intelligence du lecteur et, éveillant aussi en lui un certain intérêt érotique, renforce constamment son besoin de posséder la fin du texte.... Le texte se dérobe, refuse, lui aussi, d'être totalement possédé.[29]

The competent reader of *La Princesse de Clèves* must naturally take into account both theme and technique, but more pertinently the fact as well that the erotic "content" of the novel includes necessarily a very special focal system among characters, that the reader is willy-nilly drawn into that *abyme* of desire, and that having done so the reader may consequently gravitate toward the character of his or her own sex. Two generations later, *La Princesse de Clèves* might well have been related in memoir form, presumably from the convent to which the Princess has repaired and perhaps addressed to a singular and explicit narratee.[30] For the time being, the narrator appears as a *je* only once (p. 242) and remains consistently asexual, thus reinforcing a certain sexual indeterminacy and a concomitant ambiguity in the implicit relationship between the textual persons and the person of the reader.

I grouped together my studies of the *Liaisons dangereuses*, *Jeu de l'amour et du hasard*, and *Princesse de Clèves* because all deal with the story of a nubile young woman, but also because they display in various degrees a framing element at work which now appears crucial in any consideration of the textual person. *La Princesse de Clèves* makes especially clear as well that the reader may be as inclined to establish a personal contextual frame as to be conditioned by an existent intratextual one. Like the more banal reader preferences with which we have long been familiar—individual and generational tastes in matters of theme, of form, of style—there may also be, even with more sophisticated readers, a problematic relationship on an earlier and deeper level of sexual predisposition to a particular textualization of person.

This fits rather well perhaps with the current search for a "feminist hermeneutic ... an interpretive strategy along a feminist/non-feminist axis by analyzing the critic's stance toward his/her findings: does he/she identify with the narrator/narratee? 'buy' the message? project into the text? The key lies not so much in the critic's gender (although that is often the case), but attitude towards gender."[31] One could also see in the Princess a prime example of the "special" woman who suffers on her way to "self-expression rather than self-abnegation,"[32] and her story appears to include what have been proposed as two feminine modes: "reflexive perceptions" (discovery of self in situations one cannot fully comprehend), and "inversion" (isolation as a means to self-knowledge and contentment).[33] At the same time, however, "sexual" reading unaccompanied by, or overshadowing, formal considerations may simply reverse the problem.

Harriet Allentuch, starting from a clear and critical sense of the male reader's point of view and of the temptation to contemplate the female character as "fictional counterparts of the loving, self-sacrificial wife," sees the Princess as "less interested in acting upon others than in dwelling upon her inner turbulence."[34] From there it is a short step to the dénouement as "sacrificial suicide . . . an end in isolation and despair. . . . Both [characters] crave sainthood. To cure herself of Nemours, she rations her human relationships, buries herself in solitude and meets a premature death, alone, in some far distant convent beyond the reach of the world she had known" (p. 182). One misses in her analysis the historical distinction between *amour-propre* and *amour de soi*, and the formal one between the narrator's point of view and the character's.

Paul Genuist, on the other hand, perhaps because he is so convinced from the start of the novel's feminism, makes statements about it which are not so much inaccurate as abstracted and aprioristic.[35] In order to set up a contrast he posits a bit quickly and rhetorically a modern feminist interpretation ("se retirer dans une maison religieuse, quelle féministe ne verrait là, d'abord, un réflexe de peur . . . il s'agit aujourd'hui de satisfaire ses désirs immédiats, existentiels," p. 136) but more importantly his preconceptions lead to an overly voluntaristic interpretation of the Princess' actions: "nous suggérons de voir l'amour dans ce livre plutôt comme l'instrument par lequel l'homme ou la femme pourront s'affirmer ou triompher l'un de l'autre. Notons que c'est Madame de Clèves qui, en repoussant les avances de l'homme, fait de la femme la grande maîtresse du jeu" (p. 137). Closer consideration of the work's structure would show to what extent passion is the primary agent, and that the Princess moves painfully from passive silence to overt analysis in the conquest of herself, indeed in a repossession of herself from passion. Yet Genuist constantly describes her situation in terms of decision-making, as a kind of quasi-military ethical campaign, and because he chooses male characters as the measure of the Princess' actions, the *aveu*, for example, becomes a conscious and almost manipulatory triumph (p. 246): "Cette joie provient sans doute de la réussite à avoir dominé sa passion . . . n'oublions pas que c'est aux dépens de M. de Nemours" (p. 147). The work as a whole is reduced to a demonstration ("Madame de Lafayette nous prouvera que la voie du bonheur ne passe ni par le mariage ni par l'amour," p. 141), rather than the image of an experience, the conquest of a personhood depicted through the givens of a particular historical (including sexual) situation.[36]

And finally, in a polemical essay on male-dominated reading, Michael Danahy chooses to sum up his arguments with the case of *La Princesse de Clèves*, "ouvrage écrit par une femme à propos d'une femme":

> Il a fallu trois siècles pour qu'une femme [Helen Kaps] suggère que les intérêts personnels de la princesse sont certainement aussi valables que ceux de son amant . . . ; comme fait l'héroïne, nous devrions accepter ses sentiments pour ce qu'ils se donnent. Dans les romans écrits par les hommes, les héroïnes vivent leurs passions jusqu'au bout, en sont alors punies et se perdent. *La Princesse de Clèves* est le seul classique de la littérature française que je connaisse où l'héroïne soit envisagée avec une sympathie compatissante et où la passion puisse être tempérée sans se trahir elle-même.[37]

By my count Danahy is off by a few years (see Fraisse, Durry, Lawrence), but he is only too accurate in his remarks on the significance of the novel's outcome and its treatment by the vast majority of (male) critics. And yet a stylistic quirk in the translation of his text points up, rather like Lawrence's *his*, a particularity of the problem which should not be lost sight of.

> Personne n'a déclaré à haute voix . . . que le roman se comporte comme une femme soit-disant [sic] "typique." (p. 87)

> Helen Kaps a montré avec force et clarté que ce parangon de la masculinité [Nemours] que repousse la princesse, soit-disant [sic] a cause de ses craintes sublimées ou subconscientes, est en realité froid et égoiste, égocentrique et calculateur, décidé à se ménager des chances maximales de succès. (pp. 103-04)

The "soit-disant" is of course not only a misspelling but loose usage pointing to a debatable interpretation. Would-be, "qui se dit, se prétend, tell ou telle," *soi-disant* not only makes a poor adverb but at the very least should refer to an explicit and proper antecedent rather than appear in dangling, ambiguous fashion, and should further clarify whether the writer wishes to actualize the term's latent implication of dubiety (i.e., "so-called").[38] The text should thus read "prétendument" (allegedly, supposedly) or otherwise indicate that the woman is not the source of the affirmations, especially since in the case of the Princess (and Silvia, and *a contrario* Cécile) we have in fact a young woman *qui se dit*, and who acquires her definition and ultimate textual significance through that process. "Self-styled" implies here a style of the self.[39]

What I hope to have suggested then is the importance of a stylistic and formal approach to the question of the person in the text, and more particularly to what I have called the syntax of the person and the person in the Syntax. It is obviously not enough to elucidate the semic aspect of character (young + female + unmarried, etc.), nor even sufficient to trace what becomes of those traits in the course of the plot. Based on a reading of these three works, and as I have been attempting to emphasize throughout, a problematic of the (female) character and of any textual person necessitates attention to the primacy of language: how language articulates the relationship between writer, person and reader, and how and to what degree—indeed *whether*—the person assumes language and linguistic competence. As two recent titles would have it in the case of female writer-characters, a *parole de femme* entails *les mots pour le dire*.[40]

NOTES

Introduction

1. See Leo Spitzer, *Linguistics and Literary History* (Princeton: Princeton Univ. Press, 1948).

2. Some bibliographical remarks here may help further situate my approach. While character, the main avatar of the textual person, perhaps remains "the major aspect of the novel to which structuralism has paid least attention and has been least successful in treating" (Jonathan Culler, *Structuralist Poetics* [Ithaca: Cornell Univ. Press, 1975], p. 230), a major renewal of interest did occur in the mid-1960s with publication of works by Benveniste, Greimas and Harvey, and the now classic *Communications* 8 (see my bibliography on the textual person for complete references). What followed, however, has been for the most part, and despite differences which would surely seem crucial to the critics and theorists I lump together here, either an analysis of the impact of action and especially narrative (Alexandrescu, Bremond, Greimas, Lotman, much of Todorov) or a delineation of levels of production of the character (Ferrara, Greimas again, Ubersfeld). In another tradition, W.J. Harvey's elaboration of the ethico-logical "constitutive categories" of character (pp. 21-23) was a very explicit rejoinder to the then recent creative and critical "retreat from character" and the "attack on the concept of character as the basis of a critical approach" (Harvey, pp. 191-217). For Rawdon Wilson, whose survey is most useful alongside Philippe Hamon's, the English (notably Bayley and Harvey, whose approach Wilson prefers as more complete) have tended to analyze "the imaginative re-creation of character in one's mind," while Americans (Gass, Price, Barroll) tend rather more toward character as artificial, "a fictional construct" (Wilson, p. 735). Attention to character and person at the surface of the text—Todorov's "niveau verbal" (*Décaméron*, p. 18), Gass's "character as instrument of verbal organization" (p. 44), Greimas' "grammaire narrative superficielle" (*Du sens*, pp. 166 ff.)—has usually meant analysis of physical description (Kempf, Mitterand, Resch, Vannier); identification of the semic or thematic components of the figure, as in Barthes's *S/Z* and his earlier work on "indices" in *Communications* 8, and in Chatman (*Story*, pp. 115-34); or pursuance of the perspectives opened up by Benveniste on the deictic and especially pronominal dimension of "l'homme dans la langue" and on the *énoncé/énonciation* distinction (e.g., Bruss, Butor, Lecointre-Le Galliot, Sumi, Todorov). Todorov and Chatman (*Story*, pp. 10-11) distinguish explicitly between style and "verbal level," on the one hand, and the deeper, "syntactic" analysis with which their works are concerned, on the other. A good discussion of the importance and relevance of attention to surface patterning is Josephine Miles, "Forest and Trees: Or, the Sense at the Surface," *NLH*, 4 (1972), 35-45. In the same issue of *NLH* George Steiner reminds us of a problem in terms—"the notion of 'deep structure' conveys a powerful valuation and that of 'surface' is inherently pejorative" (p. 33)—and I cannot resist introducing here a popular version of the same question which I encountered while preparing

these studies: Blondie: "Ed Truffles ran away with the schoolteacher." Dagwood: "It wasn't Ed ... It was his brother Ted. And he didn't run away with a schoolteacher ... she was a seamstress." Blondie: "Who cares about the details as long as I had the facts!"

3. Nor am I using "person" in Michel Zéraffa's sense: "l'homme et sa présence dans le monde tels que le romancier les perçoit d'abord, les conçoit ensuite ..."; "personnage est du côté du fonctionnel, la personne de celui du notionnel" (*Personne et personnage*, pp. 10, 12).

4. Michael Riffaterre, *Essais de stylistique structurale* (Paris: Flammarion, 1971), p. 81.

5. The "figure/ground" distinction is borrowed from Rudolf Arnheim, *Art and Visual Perception* (Berkeley: Univ. of California Press, 1954), pp. 177-85. The "figure in the carpet" is my appropriation of Henry James's metaphor for the writer's hidden design, in the novella of that title.

6. David Lodge, *The Language of Fiction* (London: Routledge and Kegan Paul, 1966), p. 79.

7. *Isotopie*: "Un ensemble redondant de catégories sémantiques qui rend possible la lecture uniforme du récit" (Greimas, *Du sens*, p. 188). On the concept and its various definitions, see especially Culler, pp. 79-83, 87-95, and Michel Arrivé, "Pour une théorie des textes poly-isotopiques," *Langages*, 31 (1973), 53-63. In a later version, Greimas distinguishes many types of *isotopie*, including "grammaticale" and "sémantique"; see Greimas and J. Courtés, *Sémiotique: Dictionnaire raisonné de la théorie du langage* (Paris: Hachette, 1979), p. 197.

8. The proper name or noun (*nom propre*) is a recurrent motif in the theory of the person and the character. See, for example, Barthes, *S/Z*, pp. 98-102; Bremond, p. 126; Chatman, *Story*, pp. 131-32; *Communications* 8, p. 18; Culler, pp. 236-37; and Todorov, *Décaméron*, pp. 24-27, "Grammaire du récit," p. 96, and "Personnage," p. 288. See also Barthes on Proust, Bonnet, Compagnon, Démoris, Le Huenen-Perrot, Richard, Vannier.

9. "... un certain type de textes renverse les perspectives habituelles et substitue à la 'communication verbale' une 'communication musicale' ..."; "dans la langue-discours, il peut arriver que des actants prosodiques prennent le relais d'actants narratifs défaillants. I. Fonagy dit de son côté dans son article sur la transparence verlainienne: 'Dans la poésie lyrique ce plan musical se substitue aux événements, il constitue une sorte d'action lyrique'" (J.-C. Coquet, "Sémiotiques," *Langages*, 31 [1973], 9). The remark by Fonagy is in the same volume, p. 98.

10. Roland Barthes, "Style and Its Image," in *Literary Style: A Symposium*, ed. Seymour Chatman (New York: Oxford Univ. Press, 1971), p. 10. (Barthes was referring to style as one of the layers or codes of the text's discourse.) Cf., as an example of the semic construction theory of person: "Rappelons-nous le film *L'homme invisible*: quand on avait fini de dérouler les bandages entourant sa tête, on ne découvrait rien. C'est un peu le contraire qui se passe pour l'œuvre romanesque vue sous l'angle de la personne: à mesure que nous lisons un roman des espèces de bandages humains se forment, s'épaississent, façonnent une personne qui devient concrète" (Zéraffa, in Meyerson, p. 274).

Chapter 1

1. Claude Abraham, *Pierre Corneille* (New York: Twayne, 1972), p. 86.

2. Corneille, *Discours de l'utilité et des parties du poème dramatique*, in *Trois Discours sur le poème dramatique*, ed. Louis Forestier (Paris: SEDES, 1963), p. 55.

3. Robert Nelson, *Corneille: His Heroes and Their Worlds* (Philadelphia: Univ. of Pennsylvania Press, 1963), p. 159.

4. Lucien Goldmann, "Le Problème du mal," in *Structures mentales et création culturelle* (Paris: Editions Anthropos 10/18, 1970), p. 137. On amorality, see also Jacques Schérer, ed., *Rodogune* (Paris: Droz, 1945), p. xx; Serge Doubrovsky, *Corneille et la dialectique du héros* (Paris: Gallimard, 1963), pp. 295 ff.; Octave Nadel, "L'Exercice du crime chez Corneille," in *A mesure haute* (Paris: Mercure de France, 1964), pp. 47-58; and André Stegmann, *L'Héroïsme cornélien* (Paris: Colin, 1968), pp. 371-72, 423-29, 598-601.

5. *Discours*, ed. Forestier, pp. 89-90.

6. Jacques Schérer has pointed out that "invocations à des sentiments personnifiés" were a staple of classical drama and were more frequent than the addressing of material objects (*La Dramaturgie classique en France* [Paris: Nizet, 1950], pp. 251-52). See also Peter France, *Racine's Rhetoric* (Oxford: Oxford Univ. Press, 1965), pp. 75-87, and Roland Barthes on "la fonction meurtrière de l'objet," in "Tacite et la baroque funèbre," in *Essais critiques* (Paris: Seuil, 1964), p. 110.

7. Schérer's section on the history of the monologue (pp. 256-60) traces a marked evolution away from the monologue in the course of the century. From *Polyeucte* on, Corneille's monologues became much shorter and far fewer in number (see also the "Examen de *Clitandre*"), and as recently as *Cinna* they were distributed evenly among the characters. Thus, while his theater as a whole is typical of the historical trend, *Rodogune* represents an exception on all counts.

8. As examples of confidants divulging privileged information, Schérer cites (pp. 49-50) Euphorbe in *Cinna*—and Laonice. Transfer of such information from confidant to confidant was the more common situation. The case of Narcisse in *Britannicus* is different in that it involves outright spying, and he is in fact a (crucial) secondary character rather than simply a confidant.

9. In his *Pratique de théâtre* (1657), D'Aubignac urged that apostrophes be short and warned against apostrophes which were too numerous or possibly disrespectful of the authority figures in whose presence they might occur (ed. Pierre Martino, [Algiers: Carbonnel, 1927], pp. 349-51). They are in fact long and relatively frequent in *Rodogune*, but are restricted to Cléopâtre, occur in monologues, and include both people and personifications (cf. Schérer, n. 7). They are thus no threat to the proprieties, verisimilitude or interest, and in fact represent a salient quality in the characterization of Cléopâtre. In his remarks on the function of monologue in tragedy, Pierre Larthomas underscores the frequency of apostrophe, which is certainly the case here, and cites Emilie's monologue in *Cinna* I, 1, the closest analogous example to that of Cléopâtre. He sees such recourse to apostrophe as a reduction of the *écart* of figurative language, a kind of naturalizing (my term) of the rhetorical situation, maintaining the solitude inherent in the tragic situation, but allowing in certain cases the character to seek reassuring support at critical moments. This seems much less true of *Rodogune*, where all of the functions mentioned serve as the backdrop which is ultimately transcended by Cléopâtre's *moi*. See Larthomas, *Le Langage dramatique* (Paris: Colin, 1972), pp. 346-48, 369-79.

10. Cf. Octave Nadal: "Ame absolument dénaturée, mais par volonté, par irrévocable décision: 'Sors de mon cœur, nature' est un cri plus total que celui de Lady Macbeth, 'Ote-moi mon sexe.' Il dépouille plus radicalement Cléopâtre; la vertu qu'il exige la place soudain dans une lumière qui ne semble plus être de ce monde . . . Ce

n'est pas une tare, une fatalité, un instinct de cruauté . . . C'est une cause toute différente qu'il faut reconnaître: une volonté, une lucidité, une liberté, telle est l'action de Cléopâtre dans sa source" (pp. 53-54).

11. In his *Commentaire sur Rodogune*, Voltaire registered a strong demurral concerning the verisimilitude of this episode (as well as a complaint about a Queen talking to poison): ". . . il n'est pas naturel que Séleucus en mourant ait prononcé quatre vers entiers sans nommer sa mère" (quoted in Schérer, p. 372). Despite attempts at certain logistical and rhetorical explanations, Schérer is obliged to concede the conventional nature of the device; he might also have referred, however, to Corneille's own *parti pris* not to name her, since in the full context of the play it is neither idle idiosyncrasy nor even in fact a flaw.

Chapter 2

1. On appositive in Racine, see Henri Bremond, *Racine et Valéry* (Paris: Grasset, 1930), pp. 201-07; Marcel Raymond, "Le Discours poétique de Racine," in *Génies de France* (Neuchâtel: La Baconnière, 1942), p. 120; Leo Spitzer, "L'Effet de sourdine dans le style classique: Racine," in *Etudes de style*, ed. Jean Starobinski (Paris: Gallimard, 1970), pp. 274-75; Peter France, *Racine's Rhetoric* (Oxford: Oxford Univ. Press, 1965), pp. 146-48, 153-63. Spitzer grouped appositive constructions, including participials, among the devices which create the "distancing" effect in Racine and stressed as well the retardant, tension-creating effect of such insertions, seeing their use in *récits* as creating a Latinate, "medallion" effect. France stresses particularly the elimination of conjunctions and subordinate clauses which apposition permits and the resultant movement, which is less rational or intellectual, better suited to the portrayal of changing emotions, and often lyrical or reflective. In her *Sentence Structure and Characterization in Racine* (Rutherford, N.J.: Fairleign Dickinson Univ. Press, 1979), Mary Lynne Flowers documents an exceptionally high number of first-person-singular subjects, particularly in Phèdre's references to herself, and frequent internal punctuation, a category which includes questions and exclamations as well as commas, colons and semi-colons. Her categories do not otherwise allow for a statistical indication or verification of the importance of apposition.

2. On the preference for participial constructions, see also Seymour Chatman, "Milton's Participial Style," *PMLA*, 83 (1968), 1386-99. Chatman found that in Milton such constructions referred implicitly to God as agent.

3. Kuentz, "Lecture d'un fragment de *Britannicus*," *Langue Française*, 7 (September 1970), 20-27. "Nous n'avons ni affaire à un 'récit' ni à une 'description,' mais bien à une 'mise en scène' . . . Son 'amour,' c'est ce discours qu'il tient en ce moment même sur la scène . . ." (pp. 26-27). Serge Doubrovsky sees this same passage as the *théâtralisation* of Néron's Oedipal dilemma and Junie as identified phantasmatically with Agrippine: "L'Arrivée de Junie dans *Britannicus*: La tragédie d'une scène à l'autre," *Papers on French Seventeenth Century Literature*, No. 10, Part 2 (1978-1979), 223-66. On the expression/narration distinction as it applies to Racine, see also Bremond and Raymond; France, p. 163; Roland Barthes, *Sur Racine* (Paris: Seuil, 1963), pp. 115-22, 135-44. Another example is Robert Langbaum, "Character vs. Action in Shakespeare," in *The Poetry of Experience* (New York: Norton, 1957), pp. 160-81. The expressive/narrative distinction is an appropriation from Roman Jakobson's discussion of language functions in his "Linguistics and Poetics," in *Style and Language*, ed. Thomas Sebeok (Cambridge, Mass.: M.I.T. Press, 1960), pp. 350-77.

4. On saying vs. silence in *Phèdre*, see especially Barthes. pp. 115-22.

5. Sayce, "Racine's Style: Periphrasis and Direct Statement," in *The French Mind: Studies in Honor of Gustave Rudler*, ed. Will Moore (Oxford: Clarendon Press, 1952), pp. 70-89.

6. In his *Commentaires de textes français modernes* (Paris: Didier, 1965), pp. 130-37, Marcel Galliot sees this moment as analogous to cinematic "surimpression" and psychological transference. He does not, however, delineate appositional function or in fact even mention it as such, with a lessened appreciation, therefore, of both stylistic detail and its importance to the whole. For France, the speech becomes more and more dreamlike and "after 'J'aime' floats away in six lines of apposition in which Phèdre gradually identifies Thésée with Hippolyte" (p. 157).

7. In his "La Vivante Arabesque de la voix," *Littérature*, 35 (October 1979), 57-74, Stéphane Vogel seeks to effect a reading of lines from IV, 6, "qui, en intégrant et en dépassant le niveau de l'expressivité immédiate, sache reconnaître un fonctionnement proprement structural des figures—et cela non seulement dans le cadre souvent trop étroit ou bien trop général de la nomenclature traditionnelle, mais surtout dans la convergence des mouvements phoniques, sémantiques et syntaxiques..." (p. 70). While apposition is not distinguished as such, the results presented here are consonant with his and vice versa. A more strictly metaphorical and rhetorical, structuralist approach to the constitution and transformation of "figures" in *Phèdre* can be found in Danielle Kaisergruber, *et al.*, *"Phèdre" de Racine: Pour une sémiotique de la représentation classique* (Paris: Larousse, 1972). With reference to the present considerations, see especially pp. 22-28, 113-39.

8. For other approaches to identity in Racine, see J.D. Hubert, "L'Identité tragique dans *Iphigénie*," in *Essai d'exégèse racinienne* (Paris: Nizet, 1956), pp. 181-99; Paul Bonnet, "Les Diverses Manières d'appeler Néron dans *Britannicus*," *Bulletin de Liaison Racinienne*, 6 (1958), 16-18; and Barthes on *Athalie*, pp. 126-32.

9. On the latter, see particularly Barthes, and Charles Mauron, *Phèdre* (Paris: Corti, 1968). Mauron elaborates the intrapsychic unity of Racine's theater by superimposition of dominant dramatic situations. For his remarks on personal analogies and identifications, see especially pp. 66-91.

Chapter 3

1. On the portrait, see Jean D. Lafond, "Les Techniques du portrait dans le 'Recueil des portraits et éloges' de 1659," *CAIEF*, 18 (1966), 139-48, and discussion, pp. 270-75; Peter Brooks, *The Novel of Worldliness* (Princeton: Princeton Univ. Press, 1969), pp. 48-82; Jacqueline Plantié, "La Mode du portrait littéraire en France dans la société mondaine (1641-1681)" (diss. Université de Paris-IV, 1975); E. Heier, "'The Literary Portrait' as a Device of Characterization," *Neophilologus*, 60 (1976), 321-33; Wendy Steiner, "The Semiotics of a Genre," *Semiotica*, 21 (1977), 111-19. The present chapter is a partial reworking, for the purpose of the "person" problematic I am seeking to develop here, of material from my *Jean de La Bruyère* (New York: Twayne, 1973), reprinted with the permission of Twayne Publishers, a division of G.K. Hall & Co., Boston. Where relevant, I have incorporated mention of criticism published in the interim, but I refer the reader to that edition for a more complete set of references, particularly since the examples I cite here are representative rather than exhaustive. Hereafter I use the standard abbreviations of chapter titles: *BF* ("Des biens de fortune"), *C* ("De la cour"), *CH* ("De la chaire"), *Cœur* ("Du cœur"), *EF* ("Des esprits

forts"), *F* ("Des femmes"), *G* ("Des grands"), *H* ("De l'homme"), *J* ("Des jugements"), *M* ("De la mode"), *MP* ("Du mérite personnel"), *OE* ("Des ouvrages de l'esprit"), *QU* ("De quelques usages"), *SC* ("De la société et de la conversation"), *SR* ("Du souverain ou de la république"), *V* ("De la ville").

    2. *Rhetorica ad Herennium*, trans. Harry Caplan, Loeb Classical Library (Cambridge, Mass.: Harvard Univ. Press, 1954), IV, 49-50.

    3. The word *caractère* appears in *OE*, 24, 52; *MP*, 36; *SC*, 1, 13, 20, 28, 37; *BF*, 69; *V*, 7; *C*, 96; *G*, 26; *SR*, 12, 13; *H*, 7, 52, 140, 141, 147; *J*, 26; *CH*, 24; *EF*, 36. See also Louis Van Delft, "Du caractère, de Théophraste à La Bruyère," *Papers on French Seventeenth Century Literature*, No. 14 (1981), pp. 165-88.

    4. "Air de famille" is used by Jules Brody, "La Bruyère: Le style d'un moraliste," *CAIEF*, 30 (1978), 151. This and two earlier ground-breaking articles by Brody which appeared in *L'Esprit Créateur* have been incorporated as "Phrases," "Images" and "Contextes" in *Du style à la pensée: Trois études sur les* Caractères *de La Bruyère*, French Forum Monographs, 20 (Lexington, Ky.: French Forum, Publishers, 1980). See also useful works such as those by Doris Kirsch, *La Bruyère ou le style cruel* (Montreal: Presses de l'Université de Montréal, 1977); André Stegmann, *Les Caractères de La Bruyère: Bible de l'honnête homme* (Paris: Larousse, 1972); and Robert Garapon, *Les Caractères de La Bruyère: La Bruyère au travail* (Paris: CDU-SEDES, 1978)—although the latter two tend somewhat toward catalogues of device-and-effect, whereas I continue to feel that the overall meaning of the work can only emerge through elucidation of its patterning as a structured continuum. On the evolution of *caractère* technique throughout the various editions, see Michael Koppisch, *The Dissolution of Character: Changing Perspectives in La Bruyère's* Caractères, French Forum Monographs, 24 (Lexington, Ky.: French Forum, Publishers, 1981).

    5. The most rigorous treatments of accumulation and juxtaposition are in Brody ("Phrases"), and Serge Doubrovsky, "Jean de La Bruyère," in *Explication de texte*, ed. Jean Sareil (Englewood Cliffs, N.J.: Prentice-Hall, 1970), I, 131-37 (also in *Poétique*, 1 [1970], 195-201). See also part two of Jacqueline Hellegouarc'h, *La Phrase dans les "Caractères" de La Bruyère* (Paris: Champion, 1975); and, on the varieties of rhythm segmentation in La Bruyère's *style coupé*, John Porter Houston, *The Traditions of French Prose Style* (Baton Rouge: Louisiana State Univ. Press, 1981), pp. 100-06.

    6. Of all the devices and techniques commented on here, this strikes me as the most essentially "caracterial" and relatively the most neglected in La Bruyère criticism. The iterative nature of the *caractère*'s behavior is what primarily distinguishes it from the static and permanent characterization of the portrait, on the one hand, and from the individual "destiny" of the traditional narrative protagonist, on the other. See Gérard Genette, *Figures III* (Paris: Seuil, 1972), pp. 145-56; and Knox, pp. 100-16. Brody comments on the automatic and inevitable impression created by inversions in "Phrases," pp. 15-18.

    7. Todorov, *Grammaire du Décaméron* (The Hague: Mouton, 1969), p. 28.

    8. On the importance of metaphor in general and the relevance of the Cartesian background concerning animals and machines, see Brody ("Images"), Doubrovsky, and Kirsch (pp. 69-88). For references on the various types of metaphor, see Knox, pp. 128-29.

    9. Using the convergence of a number of stylistic features outlined here (accumulation, juxtaposition, extension, hyperbole, metaphor, and conclusion) as a definition of *caractère*, the most successful and significant are: Arrias (*SC*, 9), Théodecte

(*SC*, 12), Hermagoras (*SC*, 74), Giton/Phédon (*BF*, 83), Sannion (*V*, 10), the man of the court (*C*, 20), Théodote (*C*, 61), Théognis (*G*, 48), Pamphile (*G*, 50), Ménalque (*H*, 7), Gnathon (*H*, 121), Télèphe (*H*, 141), the collectors (*M*, 2), and Hermippe (*QU*, 64).

10. Kirsch, p. 110. See also Brody's explication of the coded proliferation of the Sannions (in "Contextes," pp. 59-64).

11. On this *monde paradoxal*, see Kirsch, pp. 29-65, and a number of commentaries in *Papers on Seventeenth Century French Literature*, No. 15 (1981), pp. 193-216.

12. Mouton, "La Bruyère: Le recours à l'objet," in *Les Intermittences du regard chez l'écrivain* (Paris: Desclée de Brouwer, 1973), pp. 35-54. In contrast, see Kirsch, pp. 101-29.

13. Barthes, *Essais critiques* (Paris: Seuil, 1964), p. 232. On the emptiness at the center of the *caractère*, see Brody ("Phrases" and "Images"); Doubrovsky, p. 137; and Kirsch, pp. 115-23.

14. La Bruyère sees "disproportion" as basically an earlier, stable society's disruption by money (*BF*, esp. 5 and 58). On the relevance of the socio-historical background, see Erica Harth, "Classical Disproportion: La Bruyère's *Caractères*," and Michael Koppisch, "The Ambiguity of Social Status in La Bruyère's *Caractères*," both in *From Humanism to Classicism*, *L'Esprit Créateur*, 15 (1975), 189-210 and 211-20 respectively.

Chapter 4

1. Starobinski, *Jean-Jacques Rousseau: La transparence et l'obstacle* (Paris: Gallimard, 1971), pp. 285-86.

2. Jean-Jacques Rousseau, *Les Rêveries du promeneur solitaire*, ed. Marcel Raymond, in *Oeuvres complètes*, I, eds. B. Gagnebin and Marcel Raymond (Paris: Gallimard, 1959), p. 996. All subsequent quotations from the *Rêveries* will refer to this edition.

3. Spitzer, *Linguistics and Literary History* (Princeton: Princeton Univ. Press, 1948), p. 175. The whole notion of prose rhythm, including its definition, has been a subject of considerable debate and controversy. See Yvette Louria, *La Convergence stylistique chez Proust* (Geneva: Droz, 1967), pp. 1-9; Jean Mourot, *Le Génie d'un style: Chateaubriand. Rythme et sonorité dans "Les Mémoires d'outre-tombe"* (Paris: Colin, 1960), pp. 5-22, 89-120; Marcel Cressot, *Le Style et ses techniques*, 5th ed. (Paris: Presses Universitaires de France, 1965), pp. 200-27; Pierre Larthomas, *Le Langage dramatique* (Paris: Colin, 1972), pp. 50-80, 308-29; Michael Riffaterre, "Comment décrire le style de Chateaubriand?" *Romanic Review*, 53 (1972), 128-38; Mourot, "Stylistique des intentions et stylistique des effets," *CAIEF*, 16 (1964), 71-79; Daniel Delas and Jacques Filliolet, *Linguistique et poétique* (Paris: Larousse, 1973), pp. 139-50; Michael Riffaterre, "Modèles de la phrase littéraire," in *Essais sur la stylistique* (Paris: Flammarion, 1971), pp. 133-51; Jean Milly, *La Phrase de Proust* (Paris: Larousse, 1975), pp. 14-22.

4. Jean Guéhenno, "La Dernière Confession de Jean-Jacques," *NNRF* (November 1955), pp. 837-49; Basil Munteano, *Solitude et contradictions de Jean-Jacques Rousseau* (Paris: Nizet, 1975), p. 56, first published in *Annales de la Société Jean-Jacques Rousseau*, 31 (1946-1949), 132; Robert J. Ellrich, *Rousseau and His Reader:*

The Rhetorical Situation of the Major Works (Chapel Hill: Univ. of North Carolina Press, 1969), p. 95. See also *Oeuvres complètes,* I, 1763-64.

5. Batlay, "Rousseau's 'Les Rêveries du promeneur solitaire': A Reading" (diss. Columbia University 1977), p. 67. See also her other comments on the structure of sentences in the *Rêveries,* pp. 67-69, 79-83, 108-11, 118-33.

6. For other remarks on style and rhythm in the *Rêveries* and/or elsewhere in Rousseau, see Robert Osmont, "Contribution à l'étude psychologique des *Rêveries*: La vie du souvenir. Le rythme lyrique," *Annales de la Société Jean-Jacques Rousseau,* 23 (1934), 7-135; Marcel Galliot, *Commentaires de textes français modernes* (Paris: Didier, 1965), pp. 185-91; Monique Parent, "Diversité et unité dans la 'Deuxième Promenade,' " *Neuphilologische Mitteilungen,* 66 (1965), 519-35; Roland Derche, *Etudes de textes français,* IV (Paris: SEDES, 1966), pp. 241-83; Jean-Louis Lecercle, *Rousseau et l'art du roman* (Paris: Colin, 1969), pp. 247-63; Marie-Hélène Cotoni, "Les Valeurs rythmiques dans la 'Lettre à Christophe de Beaumont,' " *Annales de la Société Jean-Jacques Rousseau,* 38 (1969-1971), 61-103; Claude Bellessort, "Les *Lettres de la Campagne* de Tronchin et les *Lettres de la Montagne* de Rousseau: Critères stylistiques de jugement," in *Jean-Jacques et son temps,* ed. Michel Launay (Paris: Nizet, 1969), pp. 159-72, esp. 166-69; Launay, "L'Art de l'écrivain dans le *Contrat social,*" in *Jean-Jacques et son temps,* pp. 125-50, esp. 144; J.-P. Seguin, "Pour une étude comparative de textes semblables: Un point de méthode stylistique," *Le Français Moderne,* 39 (1971), 33-43; Yves Lehir, *Styles* (Paris: Klincksieck, 1972), pp. 62-71. Launay pointed out several years ago that "seule l'analyse stylistique des rythmes qu'on peut déceler dans la totalité de l'œuvre de Rousseau permettra peut-être d'apporter des conclusions" (in *Jean-Jacques Rousseau: Problèmes et recherches* [Paris: Klincksieck, 1964], pp. 346-47). But if we are further along now than we were then, the major autobiographical works have not yet been fully examined from that point of view, nor have any rhythmic constants emerged, save perhaps the importance of rhythm in general in Rousseau's writing and the sense that greater emotional "expressivity" is to be found in ternary than in binary structures. Nor are the definitions of rhythm and its structures completely homogeneous. For examples of contrasting values in another writer, see R.A. Sayce, "The Style of Montaigne: Word-Pairs and Word Groups," in *Literary Style: A Symposium,* ed. Seymour Chatman (New York: Oxford Univ. Press, 1971), pp. 383-405.

7. Spitzer refers at several points to the "innervation of language by emotion" in Diderot. See also E.L. Epstein's remarks on "subjective and self-reflexive mimesis" in *Style and Structure in Literature,* ed. Roger Fowler (Ithaca: Cornell Univ. Press, 1975), pp. 49-78, and his *Language and Style* (London: Methuen, 1978), pp. 64-78. For accounts of Rousseau's relationship to the reader, see Jean Terrasse, "Public fictif et public réel: *Les Rêveries du promeneur solitaire,*" *Revue Belge de Philologie et d'Histoire,* 3 (1966), 925-35; and Juliet Fowler MacCannell, "The Post-Fictional Self: Authorial Consciousness in Three Texts by Rousseau," *MLN,* 89 (1974), 560-99.

8. On this paradoxical and crucial presence in memory of what has theoretically been cast out, see Starobinski, pp. 72-77, 291-97; and Ellrich, pp. 100-01.

9. *Dédommagement* appears on pp. 996, 1019, 1020, 1047, 1088; *dédommager,* pp. 1002, 1021, 1089, 1096. See also Starobinski, "Sur Rousseau et Baudelaire: Le dédommagement et l'irréparable," in *Le Lieu et la formule* (Neuchâtel: La Baconnière, 1978), pp. 47-59.

10. On concentricity, oscillation and circumscription of the self: Georges Poulet, *Métamorphoses du cercle* (Paris: Plon, 1971), pp. 102-32; Marcel Raymond,

Jean-Jacques Rousseau: La quête de soi et la rêverie (Paris: Corti, 1972), pp. 137-40, 192-92; Muntéano and Henri Gouhier, " 'Expansion' et 'resserrement' selon J.-J. Rousseau," in *De Ronsard à Breton: Hommages à Marcel Raymond* (Paris: Corti, 1967), pp. 116-25. On the island and insularity: Michel Butor, "L'Ile au bout du monde," in *Répertoire III* (Paris: Editions de Minuit, 1968), pp. 59-101; Marc Eigeldinger, *Jean-Jacques Roseau et la réalité de l'imaginaire* (Neuchâtel: La Baconnière, 1972), pp. 137-62; Marie-José Southworth, "La Notion de l'île chez Rousseau," *SVEC*, 70 (1970), 177-92; and Eigeldinger, *Jean-Jacques Rousseau: Univers mythique et cohérence* (Neuchâtel: La Baconnière, 1978), pp. 277-86, 303-04.

11. Starobinski, *Transparence*, pp. 419-29. The "convertir la douleur en volupté" phrase is from the Huitième Promenade, p. 1074.

12. On botany in Rousseau, see Starobinski, pp. 197, 278-82; Claude Lévi-Strauss, "Jean-Jacques Rousseau, fondateur des sciences de l'homme," in anon., *Jean-Jacques Rousseau* (Neuchâtel: La Baconnière, 1972), pp. 239-48; Yves Le Hir, *Styles*, pp. 62-71; Bento Prado, "Philosophie, musique, et botanique de Rousseau à Lévi-Strauss," in *Echanges et communications: Mélanges offerts à Claude Lévi-Strauss*, ed. Jean Pouillon (The Hague: Mouton, 1970), I, 572-80, and "Entretien avec Michel Butor," in *Index-Concordance des "Rêveries du promeneur solitaire,"* eds. Gilbert Fauconnier and Michel Launay (Geneva: Slatkine, 1978), pp. 1-7. See also, of course, the Cinquième Promenade and Rousseau's other writings on botany, collected in *Oeuvres complètes*, vol. IV.

13. "Les arbres, les arbrisseaux, les plantes sont la parure et le vétement de la terre . . ." (p. 1062), "Attiré par les rians objets qui m'entourent, je les considére, je les contemple, j'apprends enfin à les classer, et me voila tout aussi botaniste qu'a besoin de l'être . . ." (p. 1068), "Il se promene, il erre librement d'un objet à l'autre, il fait la reveue de chaque fleur avec intérest et curiosité, et sitot qu'il commence à saisir les loix de leur structure il goute à les observer un plaisir sans peine aussi vif que s'il lui en coûtoit beaucoup" (p. 1069), "Là je trouvai la Dentaire heptaphyllos, le ciclamen, le nidus avis, le grand laserpitium et quelques autres plantes qui me charmérent et m'amusérent longtems" (p. 1071).

14. These remarks were written before encountering Jean Starobinski's "Rousseau's Happy Days," *NLH*, 11 (1979), 148-66. His elucidation of "symbolic correspondences," "isomorphic approximations" and "analogical relationships" among the exterior and internal worlds, memory and writing in the *Rêveries* confirms at other levels of the text the results of this stylistic approach.

15. See also "un engouement . . . qui me fait rire moi-même quand j'y reflechis" (p. 1060), "Me Voila donc à mon foin pour toute nourriture, et à la botanique pour toute occupation" (ibid.), ". . . vieux, radoteur, déjà caduque et pesant . . . aux exercices de la jeunesse et aux lecons d'un écolier" (p. 1061), "je me regardois presque comme un autre Colomb" (p. 1071), ". . . je finis par rire en moi-même et de ma vanité puerile et de la maniere comique dont j'en avois été puni" (ibid.), and the highly oratorical developments, pp. 1066-68, ending in a matching but sarcastic and even domineering "Quel appareil affreux . . . des cadavres puans, de baveuses et livides chairs, du sang. . . . Ce n'est pas là, sur ma parole, que J.J. ira chercher ses amusements" (p. 1068). We are at quite the other end of the scale from the pained "Me voici donc" of the first line.

16. See, for example, ". . . une grande sagesse et meme grande vertu: c'est le moyen de *ne laisser germer* dans mon cœur aucun levain de vengeance ou de haine" (p. 1061), "Plus la solitude où je vis alors est profonde, plus il faut que quelque objet

en *remplisse* le vuide .... Le plaisir d'aller dans le desert chercher de nouvelles plantes *couvre* celui d'échaper a mes persécuteurs ..." (p. 1070).

Chapter 5

1. See Jean-Luc Seylaz, *Les "Liaisons dangereuses" et la création romanesque chez Laclos* (Paris: Droz, 1958), esp. chap. 4; Yves Le Hir, ed., *Les Liaisons dangereuses* (Paris: Garnier, 1959), pp. xxv-xxvii (ed. of reference for this chapter); Jean Rouset, "Le Roman par lettres," in *Forme et signification* (Paris: Corti, 1964), pp. 93-99; Laurent Versini, *Laclos et la tradition: Essais sur les sources et la technique des "Liaisons dangereuses"* (Paris: Klincksieck, 1968), pp. 311-43.
2. See Georges May, "The Witticisms of Valmont," *L'Esprit Créateur*, 3 (1963), 181-87.
3. See Martin Turnell, *The Novel in France* (New York: Vintage, 1958), pp. 49-79; Versini, pp. 92-95, 356-66, 377-80; Roger Mercier, "Les Personnages des *Liaisons dangereuses* et le regard d'autrui," in *Missions et démarches de la critique: Mélanges offerts au Professeur J. Vier* (Paris: Klincksieck, 1973), pp. 673-81; Christine Belcikowski, *Poétique des "Liaisons dangereuses"* (Paris: Corti, 1972); Maurice Roelens, "Le Texte et ses 'conditions d'existence': L'exemple des *Liaisons dangereuses*," *Littérature*, 1 (1971), 73-81. Maurice Roelens has taken Versini to task for intertextual laxity, for not having seen technique as the result of a dialectic between the functional necessities of the text itself and borrowings from tradition.
4. Versini answers in "Laclos épistolier ou la préméditation," *CAIEF*, 29 (1977), 187-203.
5. See also Sylvère Lontringer's remarks on social and moral *langue* and the "idiolecte passionnel," in "Vice de forme," *Critique*, 17 (1971), pp. 202-07 (he is reviewing Versini and T. Todorov, *Littérature et signification* [Paris: Larousse, 1967]).
6. Michel Butor, "Sur *Les Liaisons dangereuses*," in *Répertoire II* (Paris: Editions de Minuit, 1964), p. 150. See also Seylaz, pp. 106-07; and Peter Brooks, *The Novel of Worldliness* (Princeton: Princeton Univ. Press, 1969), pp. 176 ff.
7. Nancy K. Miller, "Female Sexuality and Narrative Technique in *La Nouvelle Héloïse* and *Les Liaisons dangereuses*," *Signs*, 1 (1976), 609.
8. On "time-lag" and epistolary form, see especially Janet Altman, *Epistolarity: Approaches to a Form* (Columbus: Ohio State Univ. Press, 1982), pp. 117-42.
9. For different character levels and ranking, see Tzvetan Todorov, *Littérature et signification* (Paris: Larousse, 1967), pp. 58-67, and Jean Fabre, " 'Les Liaisons dangereuses,' roman de l'ironie," in *Missions et démarches de la critique: Mélanges offerts au Professeur J. Vier* (Paris: Klincksieck, 1973), pp. 656 ff.
10. Considering Tourvel to be the book's heroine, Lotringer reminds us aptly that her conversion of Valmont is in fact a reciprocal sacrifice of earlier personal visions: "A mesure que Mme de Tourvel apprend à se dissocier des principes de la morale, lui aussi s'écarte de son projet libertin" ("Vice de forme," p. 208). See also Georges Poulet's often-quoted remark that the story of Tourvel's seduction becomes in fact "un autre roman, inattendu, imprévisible, qui est celui de la conquête non préméditée du séducteur par la victime," in *La Distance intérieure* (Paris: Plon, 1952), p. 77.
11. We arrive here at the point, mentioned in my introduction, where analysis of stylistic detail leads us—as will the next two chapters—into consideration of a

"Syntax" of the whole and an appreciation of how person functions as a major element of coherence between sub- and trans-phrastic levels, and even as a locus of the shift between the two. On the "internal" publication I referred to earlier and the publication of the correspondence, see especially Todorov, pp. 48-49. See also the reservations of Fredric Jameson, *The Prison House of Language* (Princeton: Princeton Univ. Press, 1972), pp. 198-201.

12. See Alfred Owen Aldridge, "Essai sur les personnages des *Liaisons dangereuses* en tant que types littéraires," *Archives des Lettres Modernes*, 31 (1960), 3-56; Aram Vartanian, "The Marquise de Merteuil: A Case of Mistaken Identity," *L'Esprit Créateur*, 3 (1963), 175; and Versini, pp. 135-46.

13. Laclos, *Oeuvres complètes*, ed. Maurice Allem (Paris: Gallimard, 1951), pp. 710-22. To me it is not altogether clear from Laclos's letters just what he felt he had done in the work, i.e., whether his assertion of its moral value was sincere, ironic or ambivalent, and whether he realized to what extent his character would take on a "heroic" status beyond the confines of the work. See also Ronald C. Rosbottom, *Choderlos de Laclos* (Boston: Twayne, 1978), pp. 47-49.

14. See, in addition to the studies in literary history already mentioned, Peggy Kamuf, "Detour Signs: *Les Liaisons dangereuses*," in *Fictions of Feminine Desire: Disclosures of Heloise* (Lincoln: Univ. of Nebraska Press, 1982), pp. 123-47. In a less strictly historical perspective, another remarkable predecessor (in a comic mode) is *L'Ecole des femmes*: in the initial supra-human attitude, one character reducing another to sub-human status; the expression of the pseudo-heroic project in a network of dramaturgical and religious allusions and figures; the simultaneous need for secrecy and for someone to share it; the ironic turning back of the system onto its perpetrator, in the very terms in which that system was conceived and expressed.

15. Charles Baudelaire, "Notes sur *Les Liaisons dangereuses*," in *Oeuvres complètes*, ed. Marcel Ruff (Paris: Seuil, 1968), p. 645.

16. Vartanian sees her as hermaphrodite (p. 176); René Démoris, as *mère phallique* (*femme phallique + mère adoptive*), in "La Symbolique du nom dans 'Les Liaisons dangereuses,'" *Littérature*, 36 (December 1979), 104-19. See also Todorov on "le procès d'énonciation [qui] désigne le triomphe de l'auteur, sa victoire sur les personnages" (p. 49), and Nancy Miller: "In the imaginary universe of the novel there is no room for the exceptional woman who calls into question the ground rules of the oldest game in the world" ("The Exquisite Cadavers: Women in Eighteenth-Century Fiction," *Diacritics*, 5, No. 4 [1975], 43).

Chapter 6

1. Deloffre, *Une Préciosité nouvelle: Marivaux et le marivaudage* (Paris: Les Belles Lettres, 1955), p. 207.

2. Hoffmann, "Marivaux féministe," *Travaux de Linguistique et de Littérature*, 15 (1977), 91-100.

3. Brady, *Love in the Theatre of Marivaux* (Geneva: Droz, 1970), pp. 47-53.

4. Ratermanis, *Etude sur le comique dans le théâtre de Marivaux* (Geneva: Droz, 1961), p. 228.

5. Rousset, "Marivaux ou la structure du double registre," in *Forme et signification* (Paris: Corti, 1964), pp. 45-64.

6. Quoted in F. Deloffre, ed., *Théâtre complet de Marivaux* (Paris: Garnier, 1978), p. 793.

7. In Jacques Scherer, ed., *Théâtre complet de Marivaux* (Paris: Seuil, 1964), p. 275.
8. Navarri, "Marivaux réactionnaire?" *Europe* (November-December 1963), pp. 70-71.
9. Greene, *Marivaux* (Toronto: Univ. of Toronto Press, 1965), pp. 131-35.
10. See also Bernard Dort, "A la recherche de l'amour et de la vérité: Esquisse d'un système marivaudien," in *Théâtre public* (Paris: Seuil, 1967), esp. pp. 48-49.
11. On the importance of such second-degree play-acting, see Robert J. Nelson, *The Play within a Play* (New Haven: Yale Univ. Press, 1958), pp. 76-87, and especially Philip Koch, "On Marivaux's Expression 'se donner la comédie,'" *Romanic Review*, 56 (1965), 22-29. Koch underscores what I have called echo construction by recalling the other use of the expression in Silvia's "quand finira la comédie que vous vous donnez sur mon compte?" (III, 11).
12. See also the photograph of a Comédie Française dénouement (Petits Classiques Bordas, p. 132): the father is standing upright between the two couples, who are bowing and curtsying—a most . . . paternal figure.

Chapter 7

1. For an overview of the criticism on the novel, including quotation and excerpts, see Maurice Laugaa, *Lecture de Mme de Lafayette* (Paris: A. Colin, 1971), and Marie-Odile Sweetser, "*La Princesse de Clèves* devant la critique contemporaine," *Studi Francesi*, 18 (1974), 13-29. The authoritative bibliography is J.W. Scott, *Madame de La Fayette: A Selective Critical Bibliography* (London: Grant and Cutler, 1974).
2. The "shaping of the reader's perspective" is one of the components of narrative strategy referred to by Donna Kuizenga, *Narrative Strategies in* La Princesse de Clèves, French Forum Monographs, 2 (Lexington, Ky.: French Forum, Publishers, 1976), p. 5. Hers is the fullest treatment of the subject. On interiority, see especially Jean Rousset, *Forme et signification* (Paris: Corti, 1964), pp. 20-25. The modes of indirection have been dealt with on several occasions, unfortunately with a certain amount of terminological hesitation concerning *monologue* and *soliloque*. See Jean Fabre, *L'Art de l'analyse dans la "Princesse de Clèves"* (Paris: Ophyris, 1970); Marie-Jeanne Durry, "Le Monologue intérieur dans *la Princesse de Clèves*," in *La Littérature narrative d'imagination, des genres aux techniques d'expression* (Paris: Presses Universitaires de France, 1959); Claudette Delhez-Sarlet, "Style indirect libre et 'point de vue' dans *La Princesse de Clèves*," *Cahiers d'Analyse Textuelle*, 6 (1964), 70-80; Georges Kassaï, "L'Indirect dans la 'Princesse de Clèves,'" *Lettres Nouvelles* (May-June 1970), pp. 123-32; Michèle Respaut, "Un Texte qui se dérobe: Narrateur, lecteur et personnages dans *La Princesse de Clèves*," *L'Esprit Créateur*, 19 (1979), 64-73.
3. Mme de Lafayette, *Romans et nouvelles*, ed. Emile Magne; Chronologie, introduction et bibliographie par Alain Niderst (Paris: Garnier, 1970), pp. 277-78. All references are to this edition.
4. "Récit de paroles" is from Gérard Genette, *Figures III* (Paris: Seuil, 1972), pp. 189 ff. On scene and commentary, see Genette, pp. 183-94; Wayne Booth, *The Rhetoric of Fiction* (Chicago: Univ. of Chicago Press, 1971), pp. 154-65; and Seymour Chatman, *Story and Discourse* (Ithaca: Cornell Univ. Press, 1978), chs. 4 and 5. On seeing in *La Princesse de Clèves*, consult especially Robert N. Nicolich, "The

Language of Vision in *La Princesse de Clèves*: The Baroque Principle of Control and Release," *Language and Style*, 4 (1971), 279-96.

5. Greater attention to the *je* of the narrator ("Ceux que je vais nommer étaient ..." [p. 242]) and the narrative framing which results from it might also have obviated the tendency to confuse author and narrator which mars much criticism of the novel. Kuizenga, pp. 13-14, and Respaut are consistent and welcome exceptions.

6. Georges Gougenheim, "La Présentation du discours direct dans *La Princesse de Clèves* et dans *Dominique*," *Le Français Moderne*, 6 (1938), 205-20.

7. Fabre, pp. 49-50 (he is not discussing the final scene).

8. Rousset, "Echanges obliques et 'paroles obscures' dans *La Princesse de Clèves*," in *Littérature, histoire, linguistique: Recueil d'études offert à Bernard Gagnebin* (Lausanne: L'Age d'Homme, 1973), pp. 97-106.

9. Alain Niderst, *La Princesse de Clèves: Le roman paradoxal* (Paris: Larousse, 1973).

10. Roger Francillon, *L'Oeuvre romanesque de Madame de La Fayette* (Paris: Corti, 1973).

11. Kuizenga, esp. pp. 21-28, 49-54.

12. The aural equivalent of the pavilion scene is, of course, the *aveu*, when Nemours eavesdrops on the Princess' words as well as her gestures and mood.

13. I use "modalize" here to refer to the process (*la modalisation*) by which the character expresses the modalities of uncertainty. On modalization in general, see John Lyons, *Introduction to Theoretical Linguistics* (Cambridge: Cambridge Univ. Press, 1968), pp. 307-09; E. Benveniste, "L'Appareil formel de l'énonciation," *Langages*, 17 (March 1970), 12-18; and A. Meunier, "Modalités et communications," *Langue Française*, 21 (February 1974), 8-25.

14. See Domna N. Stanton, "The Ideal of Repos in Seventeenth-Century Literature," *L'Esprit Créateur*, 15 (Spring-Summer 1975), 79-104; and Bernard Beugnot, "Y a-t-il une problématique féminine de la Retraite?" in *Onze Etudes sur l'image de la femme dans la littérature française du dix-septième siècle*, ed. Wolfgang Leiner (Paris: Jean-Michel Place, 1978), pp. 28-49.

15. We reach here the point at which surface modalization is replaced by modal "competence" in Greimas' narrative theory: "Sur le plan narratif, nous proposons de définir la *compétence comme le vouloir et/ou pouvoir et/ou savoir-faire du sujet* que présuppose son faire performanciel" ("Les Actants, les acteurs et les figures," in Claude Chabrol, et al., *Sémiotique narrative et textuelle* [Paris: Larousse, 1973], p. 164, italics in the original). See also his articulation of the two notions: "A partir de la définition traditionnelle de la modalité entendue comme 'ce qui modifie le prédicat' d'un énoncé, on peut concevoir la modalisation comme la production d'un énoncé dit modal, surdéterminant un énoncé descriptif," in Greimas et J. Courtés, *Sémiotique: Dictionnaire raisonné de la théorie du langage* (Paris: Hachette, 1979), p. 230.

16. On the latter, see Nicolich, pp. 288-89, and Kuizenga, pp. 64-65, respectively. Jules Brody points out the narrator's calling attention to the fact that the Princess is seated during this scene, and makes a number of pertinent remarks on style and language, in "*La Princesse de Clèves* and the Myth of Courtly Love," *University of Toronto Quarterly*, 38 (1969), 126-30.

17. On certitude and lucidity, see Kuizenga, pp. 82-83, and Brody, pp. 126-30. Kuizenga points out that concession of the *il est vrai* type is relatively banal usage for the period and, in any case, represents implicit rectification of the perceptions of

one's interlocutor (p. 79). See also a number of apt remarks on the difference between "observing self" and "affected self," and the ultimate disappearance of the latter, in Manfred Kusch, "Narrative Technique and Cognitive Modes in *La Princesse de Clèves*," *Symposium*, 30 (1976), 308-24.

18. In her examination of general truths in the novel, Jeanne Goldin omits the one on p. 384 and a number of others uttered by the Princess (pp. 333, 349, 352, 375, 393): "Maximes et fonctionnement narratif dans *La Princesse de Clèves*," *Papers on French Seventeenth-Century Literature*, 10, No. 2 (1978-1979), 155-76. As the next chapter should make clear, this is an ironic omission for a female critic, since at the same time Goldin takes Gérard Genette properly to task for having seriously missed the importance of "maxims" in the work (in his "Vraisemblance et motivation," in *Figures II* [Paris: Seuil, 1969], pp. 71-99).

Conclusion

1. Tiefenbrun, *A Structural-Stylistic Analysis of* La Princesse de Clèves (The Hague: Mouton, 1976), pp. 117-20; Nicolich, "The Language of Vision in *La Princesse de Clèves*: The Baroque Principle of Control and Release," *Language and Style*, 4 (1971), 288-90. Quotations from the novel again refer to the Emile Magne edition, *Romans et nouvelles* (Paris: Garnier, 1970).

2. Lawrence, "*La Princesse de Clèves* Reconsidered," *French Review*, 39 (1965), 21.

3. Vigée, "*La Princesse de Clèves* et la tradition du refus," *Critique*, 159-60 (1960), 723-54.

4. Doubrovsky, "*La Princesse de Clèves*: Une interprétation existentielle," *La Table Ronde*, 138 (1959), 36-51. This is all the more curious since the Sartrean distinction Doubrovsky cites (p. 42) between *prendre conscience* and *prendre connaissance* applies well, if a bit abstractly.

5. Stirling Haig, *Madame de Lafayette* (New York: Twayne, 1970), pp. 119, 133.

6. Ibid., pp. 115, 123, 131.

7. Ibid., pp. 132, 133.

8. Poulet, "Mme de La Fayette," in *Etudes sur le temps humain* (Paris: Plon, 1950), pp. 122-32.

9. Turnell, *The Novel in France* (New York: Vintage, 1958), p. 46.

10. Kahler, *The Inward Turn of Narrative*, trans. Richard and Clara Winston (Princeton: Princeton Univ. Press, 1973), p. 33.

11. Beugnot, "L'Héroïsation des vertus solitaires," in *Héroïsme et création littéraire*, Colloque de la Société d'Etude du XVIIe Siècle (Paris: Klincksieck, 1974), p. 181, and "Y a-t-il une problématique féminine de la retraite?" in *Onze Etudes sur l'image de la femme dans la littérature française du dix-septième siècle*, ed. Wolfgang Leiner (Paris: Jean-Michel Place, 1978), p. 41.

12. Pingaud, *Mme de La Fayette par elle-même* (Paris: Seuil, 1959), pp. 104-05.

13. Alain Niderst, in Mme de Lafayette, *Romans et nouvelles*, ed. Emile Magne (Paris: Garnier, 1970), Introduction, p. xxxvi, and *La Princesse de Clèves: Le roman paradoxal* (Paris: Larousse, 1973), p. 190.

14. Francillon, *L'Oeuvre romanesque de Madame de La Fayette* (Paris: Corti, 1973), p. 177. For more "positive" male readings of the dénouement in addition to

those of Lawrence and Nicolich, see my references below to Brody and Danahy. See also Christian Garaud, "Le Geste et la parole: Remarques sur la communication amoureuse," *XVIIe Siècle*, 121 (October-December 1978), 257-68; and, in a more abstract, theoretical mode, René Girard, *Mensonge romantique et vérité romanesque* (Paris: Grasset, 1961), pp. 179-80, 293-96, 308-12; Gérard Genette, *Figures II* (Paris: Seuil, 1969), pp. 71-99; and Sylvère Lotringer, "La Structuration romanesque," *Critique*, 26 (1970), esp. 516-21.

15. Cordelier, "Le Refus de la Princesse," *XVIIe Siècle*, 108 (1975), 43-57. The remarks alluded to are on pp. 48-51, 55.

16. On the importance of the *amour-propre/amour de soi* distinction, see Marie-Odile Sweetser, "*La Princesse de Clèves* devant la critique contemporaine," *Studi Francesi*, 18 (1974), 28.

17. Fraisse, "Le 'Repos' de Mme de Clèves," *Esprit*, 11 (1961), 56-67. Delannoy is quoted in Maurice Laugaa, *Lectures de Madame de Lafayette* (Paris: Colin, 1971), p. 346.

18. Durry, *Madame de La Fayette* (Paris: Mercure de France, 1962), pp. 42-43.

19. Helen Kaps, *Moral Perspective in* La Princesse de Clèves (Eugene: Univ. of Oregon Press, 1968), pp. 53, 86. See also Sweetser, "*La Princesse de Clèves* et son unité," *PMLA*, 87 (1972), 488-89, and "*La Princesse de Clèves* devant la critique contemporaine," pp. 25-26.

20. Bounoure, "La Perle blanche," *Mercure de France*, 352 (1964), 431.

21. Rousset, *Forme et signification* (Paris: Corti, 1964), pp. 24-25. See also Niderst, *La Princesse de Clèves*, p. 78, and the case of another *roman de femme*: "We took up *Jane Eyre* one winter's evening, somewhat piqued at the extravagant commendations we had heard, and sternly resolved to be as critical as Croker. But as we read on we forgot both commendations and criticism, identified outselves with Jane in all her troubles, and finally married Mr. Rochester about four in the morning" (William G. Clark, *Fraser's* [December 1849], cited in Wolfgang Iser, *The Implied Reader: Patterns in Communication in Prose Fiction from Bunyan to Beckett* [Baltimore: Johns Hopkins Univ. Press, 1974], pp. 291-92). One notes the difference in reader reaction created by the first-person, retrospective viewpoint in Brontë's novel.

22. Brody, "*La Princesse de Clèves* and the Myth of Courtly Love," *University of Toronto Quarterly*, 38 (1969), 105-35.

23. On "proximity" in the final pages, see Kaps, pp. 63-64, and Donna Kuizenga, *Narrative Strategies in* La Princesse de Clèves (Lexington, Ky: French Forum, Publishers, 1976), pp. 65-67. After an "epicurean" reading Nicole Boursier concludes that the ending is "open" and allows the reader to believe in a positive, satisfactory dénouement for the Princess, in "Une Lecture de *la Princesse de Clèves*," *Lettres Romanes*, 33 (1979), 61-72. In an analysis published after this study was completed, Michael Danahy elucidates a network of "genderized spaces" which lead to a similar interpretation of the Princess' *retraite* as a liberation, in "Social, Sexual and Human Spaces in *La Princesse de Clèves*," *French Forum*, 6 (1981), 212-24.

24. Iser, p. 289. The reference to the reader's "transformation of signals" is from his "Indeterminacy and the Reader's Response," in *Aspects of Narrative*, English Institute Essays, ed. J. Hillis Miller (New York: Columbia Univ. Press, 1971), p. 3.

25. Fabre, in *Roman et lumières au XVIIIe siècle* (Paris: Editions Sociales, 1970), p. 111.

26. Fabre, *L'Art*, p. 71. The asterisk represents a footnote in the original.

27. Fabre, " 'Les Liaisons dangereuses': Roman de l'ironie," in *Mission et*

démarches de la critique: Mélanges offerts au Professeur J. Vier (Paris: Klincksieck, 1973), p. 664.

28. Tiefenbrun, "Les Transformations littéraires d'un érotisme classique," *Papers on French Seventeenth-Century Literature*, 10, No. 1 (1978-1979), 125-26, 139.

29. Michèle Respaut, "Un Texte qui se dérobe: Narrateur, lecteur et personnages dans *La Princesse de Clèves*," *L'Esprit Créateur*, 19 (1979), 67, 73. See also Marie-Rose Carré, "La Rencontre inachevée: Etude sur la structure de *La Princesse de Clèves*," *PMLA*, 87 (1972), 475-82. Another possible explanation, suggested first by Genette, namely that women's writing may follow a different "thematic structuration," is developed at length in Nancy K. Miller, "Emphasis Added: Plots and Plausibilities in Women's Fiction," *PMLA*, 96 (1981), 36-48. On the "inaccessibility of female meaning to male interpretation," see also Annette Kolodny, "A Map for Rereading: Or, Gender and the Interpretation of Literary Texts," *NLH*, 11 (1980), 451-65, 587-91. Other recent approaches have emphasized the link between mother and daughter. See, for example, Marianne Hirsch, "A Mother's Discourse: Incorporation and Repetition in *La Princesse de Clèves*," *Yale French Studies*, 62 (1981), 67-87; and Peggy Kamuf, "A Mother's Will: *The Princesse de Clèves*," in *Fictions of Feminine Desire: Disclosures of Heloise* (Lincoln: Univ. of Nebraska Press, 1982), pp. 67-96. My own reading finds the Princess as exceptional and extraordinary as her mother had hoped—"une personne où l'on ne pouvait atteindre" (p. 260)—but in ways and for reasons that are not, strictly speaking, her mother's.

30. In the rest of the passage already quoted from his *Princesse de Clèves*, Niderst entertains the notion with respect to the novel as it is: ". . . à la fois 'dedans' et 'dehors.' Faut-il justifier cela en disant que le roman est comme une autobiographie, et que nous considérons l'héroïne, comme elle se voit elle-même aux yeux du souvenir? Cette explication, nous l'avons vu, convient à certains passages; elle ne saurait rendre compte de la structure générale de l'œuvre . . ." (p. 78). See also Rousset, *Forme et signification*, p. 39, on the first-person mode vs. authorial interventions, and the remark by Manfred Kusch that the Princess "dreams, one might say, of being her own historian" ("Narrative Technique and Cognitive Modes in *La Princesse de Clèves*," *Symposium*, 30 [1976], 320).

31. Nancy K. Miller, "Exquisite Cadavers: Women in Eighteenth-Century Fiction," *Diacritics*, 5, No. 4 (1975), 41.

32. Patricia Meyer Spacks, "Afterword," in *The Female Imagination* (New York: Knopf, 1972), p. 408.

33. Kolodny, "Feminist Literary Criticism," *Critical Inquiry*, 2 (Autumn 1975), 78-81.

34. Allentuch, "Pauline and the Princesse de Clèves," *MLQ*, 30 (1969), 180.

35. Genuist, "Pour une interprétation féministe de la *Princesse de Clèves*," *Papers on French Seventeenth-Century Literature*, 9 (1977), 135-49.

36. In her commentary on the novel, Béatrice Didier situates the work's feminism in its portrait of a female character resolved to maintain her independence and in the "author's" presentation through the character's eyes—"le *elle* de la princesse, qui a presque l'intériorité d'un *je*"—creating thereby an original and specifically feminine literary work ("Le Silence de la Princesse de Clèves," in *Ecriture-femme* [Paris: Presses Universitaires de France, 1981], p. 77; rpt. from the introduction to the Livre de Poche edition [1972], p. 282). On the *mise en question* of marriage as a feminist theme in the classical novel, "le seul corpus . . . dans lequel la femme, et le point de

vue de la femme, prédominent," see A. Kibedi Varga, "Romans d'amour, romans de femmes, à l'époque classique," *Revue des Sciences Humaines*, 44 (1977), 517-24.

37. Danahy, "Le Roman est-il chose femelle?" *Poétique*, 25 (1976), 103-04.

38. For examples of the possible, unintentionally humorous effects of such referential ambiguity, see Adolphe V. Thomas, *Dictionnaire des difficultés de la langue française* (Paris: Larousse, 1971), p. 386. (For the record, Danahy's text was translated—by a woman—and the term in the original was "supposedly.")

39. In her *Voleuses de langue* (Paris: Grasset, 1975), Claudine Herrmann refers frequently to *La Princesse de Clèves* in the context of language and the female experience, but, with the exception of her remarks on the male characters (pp. 46, 121-22), her comments on the novel strike me as forced and somewhat distorted. See, once again, *L'Ecole des femmes* as predecessor: "le véritable combat . . . [est] celui qu'Agnès mène contre Arnolphe pour conquérir une parole enfin libérée de la toute puissante censure du tuteur-prétendant," "l'échec d'Arnolphe: son discours est mal fondé, parce qu'il est fondé sur le silence d'autrui et ne peut renvoyer qu'à lui-même" (Bernard Magné, "L'Ecole des Femmes ou la conquête de la parole," *Revue des Sciences Humaines*, 37 [1972], pp. 126, 139).

40. Annie Leclerc, *Parole de femme* (Paris: Grasset, 1974); Marie Cardinal, *Les Mots pour le dire* (Paris: Grasset, 1975).

BIBLIOGRAPHY

1. Works Cited

Abraham, Claude. *Pierre Corneille*. New York: Twayne, 1972.

Aldridge, Alfred Owen. "Essai sur les personnages des *Liaisons dangereuses* en tant que types littéraires." *Archives des Lettres Modernes*, 31 (1960), 3-56.

Allentuch, Harriet. "Pauline and the Princesse de Clèves." *MLQ*, 30 (1969), 171-82.

Altman, Janet. *Epistolarity: Approaches to a Form*. Columbus: Ohio State Univ. Press, 1982.

d'Aubignac, Abbé. *Pratique du théâtre*. Ed. Pierre Martino. Algiers: Carbonnel, 1927.

Barthes, Roland. *Essais critiques*. Paris: Seuil, 1964.

———. "Style and Its Image." In *Literary Style: A Symposium*. Ed. Seymour Chatman. New York: Oxford Univ. Press, 1971, pp. 3-10.

———. *Sur Racine*. Paris: Seuil, 1963.

Batlay, Jenny. "Rousseau's 'Les Rêveries du promeneur solitaire': A Reading." Diss. Columbia University, 1977.

Baudelaire, Charles. "Notes sur Les Liaisons dangereuses." In *Oeuvres complètes*. Ed. Marcel Ruff. Paris: Seuil, 1968, pp. 638-46.

Belcikowski, Christine. *Poétique des "Liaisons dangereuses."* Paris: Corti, 1972.

Bellessort, Claude. "Les *Lettres de la Campagne* de Tronchin et les *Lettres de la Montagne* de Rousseau: Critères stylistiques de jugement." In *Jean-Jacques et son temps*. Ed. Michel Launay. Paris: Nizet, 1969, pp. 159-72.

Benveniste, Emile. "L'Appareil formel de l'énonciation." *Langages*, 17 (March 1970), 12-18.

Beugnot, Bernard. "L'Héroïsation des vertus solitaires." In *Héroïsme et création littéraire*. Colloque de la Société d'Etude du XVIIe Siècle. Paris: Klincksieck, 1974, pp. 173-82.

———. "Y a-t-il une problématique féminine de la retraite?" In *Onze Etudes sur l'image de la femme dans la littérature française du dix-septième siècle*. Ed. Wolfgang Leiner. Paris: Jean-Michel Place, 1978, pp. 28-49.

Bonnet, Paul. "Les Diverses Manières d'appeler Néron dans *Britannucus.*" *Bulletin de Liaison Racinienne*, 6 (1958), 16-18.
Booth, Wayne. *The Rhetoric of Fiction*. Chicago: Univ. of Chicago Press, 1971.
Bounoure, Gabriel. "La Perle blanche." *Mercure de France*, 352 (1964), 426-35.
Boursier, Nicole. "Une Lecture de *la Princesse de Clèves.*" *Lettres Romanes*, 33 (1979), 61-75.
Brady, Valentini P. *Love in the Theatre of Marivaux*. Geneva: Droz, 1970.
Bremond, Henri. *Racine et Valéry*. Paris: Grasset, 1930.
Brody, Jules. *Du style à la pensée: Trois études sur les* Caractères *de La Bruyère*. French Forum Monographs, 20. Lexington, Ky.: French Forum, Publishers, 1980.
———. "*La Princesse de Clèves* and the Myth of Courtly Love." *University of Toronto Quarterly*, 38 (1969), 105-35.
Brooks, Peter. *The Novel of Worldliness*. Princeton: Princeton Univ. Press, 1969.
Butor, Michel. "L'Ile au bout du monde." In *Répertoire III*. Paris: Editions de Minuit, 1968, pp. 59-101.
———. "Sur *Les Liaisons dangereuses.*" In *Répertoire II*. Paris: Editions de Minuit, 1964, pp. 146-51.
Caplan, Harry, trans. *Rhetorica ad Herennium*. Loeb Classical Library. Cambridge, Mass.: Harvard Univ. Press, 1954.
Cardinal, Marie. *Les Mots pour le dire*. Paris: Grasset, 1975.
Carré, Marie-Rose. "La Rencontre inachevée: Etude sur la structure de *La Princesse de Clèves.*" *PMLA*, 87 (1972), 475-82.
Chabrol, Claude, *et al. Sémiotique narrative et textuelle*. Paris: Larousse, 1973.
Chatman, Seymour. "Milton's Participial Style." *PMLA*, 83 (1968), 1386-99.
———. *Story and Discourse*. Ithaca: Cornell Univ. Press, 1978.
Clark, William G. In *Fraser's* (December 1849), cited in Wolfgang Iser, *The Implied Reader: Patterns in Communication in Prose Fiction from Bunyan to Beckett*. Baltimore: Johns Hopkins Univ. Press, 1974.
Cordelier, Jean. "Le Refus de la Princesse." *XVIIe Siècle*, 108 (1975), 43-57.
Corneille, Pierre. *Discours de l'utilité et des parties du poème dramatique*. In *Trois Discours sur le poème dramatique*. Ed. Louis Forestier. Paris: SEDES, 1963.
Cotoni, Marie-Hélène. "Les Valeurs rythmiques dans la 'Lettre à Christophe de Beaumont.'" *Annales de la Société Jean-Jacques Rousseau*, 38 (1969-1971), 61-103.

Cressot, Marcel. *Le Style et ses techniques*. 5th ed. Paris: Presses Universitaires de France, 1965 (1947).
Culler, Jonathan. *Structuralist Poetics*. Ithaca: Cornell Univ. Press, 1975.
Danahy, Michael. "Le Roman est-il chose femelle?" *Poétique*, 25 (1976), 85-106.
———. "Social, Sexual and Human Spaces in *La Princesse de Clèves*." *French Forum*, 6 (1981), 212-24.
Delas, Daniel, and Jacques Filliolet. *Linguistique et poétique*. Paris: Larousse, 1973.
Delhez-Sarlet, Claudette. "Style indirect libre et 'point de vue' dans *La Princesse de Clèves*." *Cahiers d'Analyse Textuelle*, 6 (1964), 70-80.
Deloffre, Frédéric, ed. *Théâtre complet de Marivaux*. Paris: Garnier, 1978.
———. *Une Préciosité nouvelle: Marivaux et le marivaudage*. Paris: Les Belles Lettres, 1955.
Démoris, René. "La Symbolique du nom dans 'Les Liaisons dangereuses.'" *Littérature*, 36 (December 1979), 104-19.
Derche, Roland. *Etudes de textes français*. Vol. IV. Paris: SEDES, 1966.
Derrida, Jacques. *De la grammatologie*. Paris: Editions de Minuit, 1967.
Didier, Béatrice. *L'Ecriture-femme*. Paris: Presses Universitaires de France, 1981.
Dort, Bernard. "A la recherche de l'amour et de la vérité: Esquisse d'un système marivaudien." In *Théâtre public*. Paris: Seuil, 1967, pp. 41-70.
Doubrovsky, Serge. *Corneille et la dialectique du héros*. Paris: Gallimard, 1963.
———. "Jean de La Bruyère." In *Explication de texte*. Ed. Jean Sareil. Englewood Cliffs, N.J.: Prentice-Hall, 1970, I, 195-201.
———. "*La Princesse de Clèves*: Une interprétation existentielle." *La Table Ronde*, 138 (1959), 36-51.
———. "L'Arrivée de Junie dans *Britannicus*: La tragédie d'une scène à l'autre." *Papers on French Seventeenth Century Literature*, 10, No. 2 (1978-1979), 223-66.
Durry, Marie-Jeanne. *Madame de la Fayette*. Paris: Mercure de France, 1962.
———. "Le Monologue intérieur dans la *Princesse de Clèves*." In *La Littérature narrative d'imagination, des genres littéraires aux techniques d'expression*. Paris: Presses Universitaires de France, 1959, pp. 87-93.
Eigeldinger, Marc. *Jean-Jacques Rousseau et la réalité de l'imaginaire*. Neuchâtel: La Baconnière, 1972.
———. *Jean-Jacques Rousseau: Univers mythique et cohérence*. Neuchâtel: La Baconnière, 1978.
Ellrich, Robert J. *Rousseau and His Reader: The Rhetorical Situation of the Major Works*. Chapel Hill: Univ. of North Carolina Press, 1969.

Epstein, E.L. *Language and Style*. London: Methuen, 1978.
Fabre, Jean. *L'Art de l'analyse dans la "Princesse de Clèves."* Paris: Ophrys, 1970.
———. " 'Les Liaisons dangereuses': Roman de l'ironie." In *Mission et démarches de la critique: Mélanges offerts au Professeur J. Vier*. Paris: Klincksieck, 1973, pp. 651-72.
———. *Roman et lumières au XVIIIe siècle*. Paris: Editions Sociales, 1970.
Fauconnier, Gilbert, and Michel Launay, eds. *Index-Concordance des "Rêveries du promeneur solitaire."* Geneva: Slatkine, 1978.
Flowers, Mary Lynne. *Sentence Structure and Characterization in Racine*. Rutherford, N.J.: Fairleigh Dickinson Univ. Press, 1979.
Fowler, Roger, ed. *Style and Structure in Literature*. Ithaca: Cornell Univ. Press, 1975.
Fraisse, Simone. "Le 'Repos' de Mme de Clèves." *Esprit*, 11 (1961), 56-67.
France, Peter. *Racine's Rhetoric*. Oxford: Oxford Univ. Press, 1965.
———. *Rhetoric and Truth in France*. Oxford: Oxford Univ. Press, 1972.
Francillon, Roger. *L'Oeuvre romanesque de Madame de La Fayette*. Paris: Corti, 1973.
Galliot, Marcel. *Commentaires de textes français modernes*. Paris: Didier, 1965.
Garapon, Robert. *Les Caractères de La Bruyère: La Bruyère au travail*. Paris: CDU-SEDES, 1978.
Garaud, Christian. "Le Geste et la parole: Remarques sur la communication amoureuse." *XVIIe Siècle*, 121 (October-December 1978), 257-68.
Genette, Gérard. *Figures II*. Paris: Seuil, 1969.
———. *Figures III*. Paris: Seuil, 1972.
Genuist, Paul. "Pour une interprétation féministe de la *Princesse de Clèves*." *Papers on French Seventeenth Century Literature*, 9 (1977), 135-49.
Girard, René. *Mensonge romantique et vérité romanesque*. Paris: Grasset, 1961.
Goldin, Jeanne. "Maximes et fonctionnement narratif dans *La Princesse de Clèves*." *Papers on French Seventeenth Century Literature*, 10, No. 2 (1978-1979), 155-76.
Goldmann, Lucien. "Le Problème du mal." In *Structures mentales et création culturelle*. Paris: Editions Anthropos 10/18, 1970, pp. 131-41.
Gougenheim, Georges. "La Présentation du discours direct dans *La Princesse de Clèves* et dans *Dominique*." *Le Français Moderne*, 6 (1938), 305-20.
Greene, E.J.H. *Marivaux*. Toronto: Univ. of Toronto Press, 1965.
Greimas, A.-J., and J. Courtés. *Sémiotique: Dictionnaire raisonné de la théorie du langage*. Paris: Hachette, 1979.

Guéhenno, Jean. "La Dernière Confession de Jean-Jacques." *NNRF* (November 1955), pp. 855-66.
Haig, Stirling. *Madame de Lafayette*. New York: Twayne, 1970.
Harth, Erica. "Classical Disproportion: La Bruyère's *Caractères*." In *From Humanism to Classicism. L'Esprit Créateur*, 15 (1975), 189-210.
Heier, E. "The Literary Portrait as a Device of Characterization." *Neophilologus*, 60 (1976), 321-31.
Hellegouarc'h, Jacqueline. *La Phrase dans les "Caractères" de La Bruyère*. Paris: Champion, 1975.
Herrmann, Claudine. *Voleuses de langue*. Paris: Grasset, 1975.
Hirsch, Marianne. "A Mother's Discourse: Incorporation and Repetition in *La Pricesse de Clèves*." *Yale French Studies*, 62 (1982), 67-87.
Hoffmann, Paul. "Marivaux féministe." *Travaux de Linguistique et de Littérature*, 15 (1977), 91-100.
Houston, John Porter. *The Traditions of French Prose Style*. Baton Rouge: Louisiana State Univ. Press, 1981, pp. 100-06.
Hubert, J.D. "L'Identité tragique dans *Iphigénie*." In *Essai d'exégèse racinienne*. Paris: Nizet, 1956, pp. 181-99.
Iser, Wolfgang. "Indeterminacy and the Reader's Response." In *Aspects of Narrative*. English Institute Essays. Ed. J. Hillis Miller. New York: Columbia Univ. Press, 1971, pp. 1-45.
Jakobson, Roman. "Linguistics and Poetics." In *Style and Language*. Ed. Thomas Sebeok. Cambridge, Mass.: MIT Press, 1960, pp. 350-77.
Jameson, Fredric. *The Prison House of Language*. Princeton: Princeton Univ. Press, 1972.
Kahler, Erich. *The Inward Turn of Narrative*. Trans. Richard and Clara Winston. Princeton: Princeton Univ. Press, 1973.
Kaisergruber, Danielle, et al. *"Phèdre" de Racine: Pour une sémiotique de la représentation classique*. Paris: Larousse, 1972.
Kamuf, Peggy. *Fictions of Feminine Desire: Disclosures of Heloise*. Lincoln: Univ. of Nebraska Press, 1982.
Kaps, Helen. *Moral Perspective in* La Princesse de Clèves. Eugene: Univ. of Oregon Press, 1968.
Kassaï, Georges. "L'Indirect dans la 'Princesse de Clèves.'" *Lettres Nouvelles* (May-June 1970), pp. 123-32.
Kirsch, Doris. *La Bruyère ou le style cruel*. Montreal: Presses de l'Univ. de Montréal, 1977.
Knox, Edward C. *Jean de La Bruyère*. New York: Twayne, 1973.
Koch, Phillip. "On Marivaux's Expression 'se donner la comédie.'" *Romanic Review*, 56 (1965), 22-29.
Kolodny, Annette. "Feminist Literary Criticism." *Critical Inquiry*, 2

(Autumn 1975), 75-92.

———. "A Map for Rereading: Or, Gender and the Interpretation of Literary Texts." *NHL*, 11 (1980), 451-65, 587-91.

Koppisch, Michael. "The Ambiguity of Social Status in La Bruyère's *Caractères*." In *From Humanism to Classicism*. *L'Esprit Créateur*, 15 (1975), 211-20.

———. *The Dissolution of Character: Changing Perspectives in La Bruyère's Caractères*. French Forum Monographs, 24. Lexington, Ky.: French Forum, Publishers, 1981.

Kuentz, Pierre. "Lecture d'un fragment de *Britannicus*." *Langue Française*, 7 (September 1970), 20-27.

Kuizenga, Donna. *Narrative Strategies in* La Princesse de Clèves. French Forum Monographs, 2. Lexington, Ky.: French Forum, Publishers, 1976.

Kusch, Manfred. "Narrative Technique and Cognitive Modes in *La Princesse de Clèves*." *Symposium*, 30 (1976), 308-24.

Laclos, Choderlos de. *Oeuvres complètes*. Ed. Maurice Allem. Paris: Gallimard, 1951.

Lafayette, Mme de. *Romans et nouvelles*. Ed. Emile Magne. Chronologie, introduction et bibliographie par Alain Niderst. Paris: Garnier, 1970.

Lafond, Jean D. "Les Techniques du portrait dans le 'Recueil des portraits et éloges' de 1659." *CAIEF*, 18 (1966), 139-48, 270-75.

Langbaum, Robert. "Character vs. Action in Shakespeare." In *The Poetry of Experience*. New York: Norton, 1957, pp. 160-81.

Larthomas, Pierre. *Le Langage dramatique*. Paris: Colin, 1972.

Laugaa, Maurice. *Lectures de Mme de Lafayette*. Paris: Colin, 1971.

Launay, Michel. "L'Art de l'écrivain dans le *Contrat social*." In *Jean-Jacques et son temps*. Paris: Nizet, 1969, pp. 125-50.

———. *Jean-Jacques Rousseau: Problèmes et recherches*. Paris: Klincksieck, 1964.

Lawrence, Francis L. "*La Princesse de Clèves* Reconsidered." *French Review*, 39 (1965), 15-21.

Lecercle, Jean-Louis. *Rousseau et l'art du roman*. Paris: Colin, 1969.

Le Hir, Yves, ed. *Les Liaisons dangereuses*. Paris: Garnier, 1959.

———. *Styles*. Paris: Klincksieck, 1972.

Lévi-Strauss, Claude. "Jean-Jacques Rousseau, fondateur des sciences de l'homme." In anon., *Jean-Jacques Rousseau*. Neuchâtel: La Baconnière, 1972, pp. 239-48.

Lotringer, Sylvère. "La Structuration romanesque." *Critique*, 26 (1970), 498-529.

———. "Vice de forme." *Critique*, 27 (1971), 195-209.

Louria, Yvette. *La Convergence stylistique chez Proust*. Geneva: Droz, 1967.
Lyons, John. *Introduction to Theoretical Linguistics*. Cambridge: Cambridge Univ. Press, 1968.
MacCannell, Juliet Flower. "The Post-Fictional Self: Authorial Consciousness in Three Texts by Rousseau." *MLN*, 89 (1974), 560-99.
Magné, Bernard. "L'Ecole des Femmes ou la conquête de la parole." *Revue des Sciences Humaines*, 37 (1972), 125-40.
Mauron, Charles. *Phèdre*. Paris: Corti, 1968.
May, Georges. "The Witticisms of Valmont." *L'Esprit Créateur*, 3 (1963), 181-87.
Mercier, Roger. "Les Personnages des *Liaisons dangereuses* et le regard d'autrui." In *Missions et démarches de la critique: Mélanges offerts au Professeur J. Vier*. Paris: Klincksieck, 1973, pp. 673-81.
Meunier, A. "Modalités et communication." *Langue Française*, 12 (February 1974), 8-25.
Miller, Nancy K. "Emphasis Added: Plots and Plausibilities in Women's Fiction." *PMLA*, 96 (1981), 36-48.
———. "The Exquisite Cadavers: Women in Eighteenth Century Fiction." *Diacritics*, 5, No. 4 (1975), 37-43.
———. "Female Sexuality and Narrative Technique in *La Nouvelle Héloïse* and *Les Liaisons dangereuses*." *Signs*, 1 (1976), 609-38.
Milly, Jean. *La Phrase de Proust*. Paris: Larousse, 1975.
Muntéano, Basil. *Solitude et contradictions de Jean-Jacques Rousseau*. Paris: Nizet, 1975. (First published in *Annales de la Société Jean-Jacques Rousseau*, 31 [1946-1949]).
Mourot, Jean. *Le Génie d'un style: Chateaubriand. Rythme et sonorité dans "Les Mémoires d'outre-tombe."* Paris: Colin, 1960.
———. "Stylistique des intentions et stylistique des effets." *CAIEF*, 16 (1964), 71-79.
Mouton, Jean. "La Bruyère: Le recours à l'objet." In *Les Intermittences du regard chez l'écrivain*. Paris: Desclée de Brouwer, 1973, pp. 35-54.
Nadal, Octave. "L'Exercice du crime chez Corneille." In *A mesure haute*. Paris: Mercure de France, 1964, pp. 47-58.
Navarri, Roger. "Marivaux réactionnaire?" *Europe* (November-December 1963), pp. 65-71.
Nelson, Robert J. *Corneille: His Heroes and Their Worlds*. Philadelphia: Univ. of Pennsylvania Press, 1963.
———. *The Play within a Play*. New Haven: Yale Univ. Press, 1958.
Nicholich, Robert N. "The Language of Vision in *La Princesse de Clèves*: The Baroque Principle of Control and Release." *Language and Style*,

4 (1971), 279-96.
Niderst, Alain, introd. *Romans et nouvelles.* By Mme de Lafayette. Ed. Emile Magne. Paris: Garnier, 1970.
———. *La Princesse de Clèves: Le roman paradoxal.* Paris: Larousse, 1973.
Osmont, Robert. "Contribution à l'étude psychologique des *Rêveries*: La vie du souvenir. Le rythme lyrique." *Annales de la Société Jean-Jacques Rousseau,* 23 (1934), 7-135.
———. "Les Théories de Rousseau sur l'harmonie musicale et leurs relations avec son art d'écrivain." In *Jean-Jacques Rousseau: Problèmes et recherches.* Paris: Klincksieck, 1964, pp. 329-44.
Parent, Monique. "Diversité et unité dans la 'Deuxième Promenade.'" *Neuphilologische Mitteilungen,* 66 (1965), 519-35.
Pingaud, Bernard. *Mme de la Fayette par elle-même.* Paris: Seuil, 1959.
Plantié, Jacqueline. "La Mode du portrait littéraire en France dans la société mondaine (1641-1681)." 3 vols. Diss. Université de Paris-IV, 1975.
Poulet, Georges. *La Distance intérieure.* Paris: Plon, 1952.
———. "Mme de La Fayette." In *Etudes sur le temps humain.* Paris: Plon, 1950, pp. 122-32.
———. *Métamorphoses du cercle.* Paris: Plon, 1971.
Prado, Bento. "Philosophie, musique, et botanique de Rousseau à Lévi-Strauss." In *Echanges et communications: Mélanges offerts à Claude Lévi-Strauss.* Ed. Jean Pouillon. The Hague: Mouton, 1970, I, 572-80.
Ratermanis, J.R. *Etude sur le comique dans le théâtre de Marivaux.* Geneva: Droz, 1971.
Raymond, Marcel. "Le Discours poétique de Racine." In *Génies de France.* Neuchâtel: La Baconnière, 1942, pp. 116-23.
———. *Jean-Jacques Rousseau: La quête de soi et la rêverie.* Paris: Corti, 1972.
Respaut, Michèle. "Un Texte qui se dérobe: Narrateur, lecteur et personnages dans *La Princesse de Clèves.*" *L'Esprit Créateur,* 19 (1979), 64-73.
Riffaterre, Michael. "Comment décrire le style de Chateaubriand?" *Romanic Review,* 53 (1972), 128-38.
———. *Essais de stylistique structurale.* Paris: Flammarion, 1971.
———. "Modèles de la phrase littéraire." In *Essais sur la stylistique.* Paris: Flammarion, 1971, pp. 133-51.
Roelens, Maurice. "Le Texte et ses 'conditions d'existence': L'exemple des *Liaisons dangereuses.*" *Littérature,* 1 (1971), 73-81.
Rosbottom, Ronald C. *Choderlos de Laclos.* Boston: Twayne, 1978.
Rousseau, Jean-Jacques. *Les Rêveries du promeneur solitaire.* Ed. Marcel Raymond. In *Oeuvres complètes,* I. Eds. B. Gagnebin and Marcel Raymond. Paris: Gallimard, 1959.

Rousset, Jean. "Echanges obliques et 'paroles obscures' dans *La Princesse de Clèves*." In *Littérature, histoire, linguistique: Recueil d'études offert à Bernard Gagnebin*. Lausanne: L'Age d'Homme, 1973, pp. 97-106.
———. *Forme et signification*. Paris: Corti, 1964.
Sayce, R.A. "Racine's Style: Periphrasis and Direct Statement." In *The French Mind: Studies in Honor of Gustave Rudler*. Ed. Will Moore. Oxford: Clarendon Press, 1952, pp. 70-89.
———. "The Style of Montaigne: Word-Pairs and Word Groups." In *Literary Style: A Symposium*. Ed. Seymour Chatman. New York: Oxford Univ. Press, 1971, pp. 383-405.
Schérer, Jacques. *La Dramaturgie classique en France*. Paris: Nizet, 1950.
———, ed. *Rodogune*. Paris: Droz, 1945.
———, ed. *Théâtre complet de Marivaux*. Paris: Seuil, 1964.
Scott, J.W. *Madame de La Fayette: A Selective Critical Bibliography*. London: Grant and Cutler, 1974.
Seguin, J.-P. "Pour une étude comparative de textes semblables: Un point de méthode stylistique." *Le Français Moderne*, 39 (1971), 33-43.
Seylaz, Jean-Luc. *Les "Liaisons dangereuses" et la création romanesque chez Laclos*. Paris: Droz, 1958.
Southworth, Marie-José. "La Notion de l'île chez Rousseau." *SVEC*, 70 (1970), 177-91.
Spacks, Patricia Meyer. "Afterword." In *The Female Imagination*. New York: Knopf, 1972, pp. 404-14.
Spitzer, Leo. "L'Effet de sourdine dans le style classique: Racine." In *Etudes de style*. Ed. Jean Starobinski. Paris: Gallimard, 1970, pp. 274-85.
———. *Linguistics and Literary History*. Princeton: Princeton Univ. Press, 1948.
Stanton, Domna N. "The Ideal of *Repos* in Seventeenth-Century Literature." *L'Esprit Créateur*, 15 (1975), 79-104.
Starobinski, Jean. *Jean-Jacques Rousseau: La transparence et l'obstacle*. Paris: Gallimard, 1971.
———. "Rousseau's Happy Days." *NLH*, 11 (1979), 147-66.
———. "Sur Rousseau et Baudelaire: Le dédommagement et l'irréparable." In *Le Lieu et la formule*. Neuchâtel: La Baconnière, 1969, pp. 47-59.
Stegmann, André. *Les Caractères de La Bruyère: Bible de l'honnête homme*. Paris: Larousse, 1972.
———. *L'Héroïsme cornélien*. Paris: Colin, 1968.
Steiner, Wendy. "The Semiotics of a Genre." *Semiotica*, 21 (1977), 111-19.
Sweetser, Marie-Odile. "*La Princesse de Clèves* devant la critique contemporaine." *Studi Francesi*, 18 (1974), 13-29.
———. "*La Princesse de Clèves* et son unité." *PMLA*, 87 (1972), 483-91.
Terrasse, Jean. "Public fictif et public réel: *Les Rêveries du promeneur*

solitaire." *Revue Belge de Philologie et d'Histoire*, 3 (1966), 925-35.
Thomas, Adolphe V. *Dictionnaire des difficultés de la langue française.* Paris: Larousse, 1971.
Tiefenbrun, Susan. *A Structural-Stylistic Analysis of* La Princesse de Clèves. The Hague: Mouton, 1976.
———. "Les Transformations littéraires d'un érotisme classique." *Papers on French Seventeenth Century Literature*, 10, No. 1 (1978-1979), 121-41.
Todorov, Tzvetan. *Grammaire du Décaméron*. The Hague: Mouton, 1969.
———. *Littérature et signification*. Paris: Larousse, 1967.
Turnell, Martin. *The Novel in France*. New York: Vintage, 1958.
Van Delft, Louis. "Du caractére, de Théophraste à La Bruyère." *Papers on French Seventeenth Century Literature*, 14, No. 2 (1981), 165-88.
Varga, A. Kibedi. "Romans d'amour, romans de femmes à l'époque classique." *Revue des Sciences Humaines*, 54 (1977), 517-24.
Vartanian, Aram. "The Marquise de Merteuil: A Case of Mistaken Identity." *L'Esprit Créateur*, 3 (1963), 172-80.
Versini, Laurent. "Laclos épistolier ou la préméditation." *CAIEF*, 29 (1977), 187-203.
———. *Laclos et la tradition: Essais sur les sources et la technique des "Liaisons dangereuses."* Paris: Klincksieck, 1968.
Vigée, Claude. *"La Princesse de Clèves* et la tradition du refus." *Critique*, 159-60 (1960), 723-54.
Vogel, Stéphane. "La Vivante Arabesque de la voix." *Littérature*, 35 (October 1979), 57-74.

2. Works of Criticism and Theory Touching Directly or Indirectly on the Notion of "Person"

Adam, Jean-Michel, and Jean-Pierre Goldenstein. *Linguistique et discours littéraire*. Paris: Larousse, 1976, esp. ch. 6.
Alexandrescu, Sorin. *La Logique du personnage: Réflexions sur l'univers faulknérien*. Tours: Mame, 1974.
Auerbach, Erich. "L'Humaine Condition." In *Mimesis*. Trans. Willard Trask. New York: Doubleday/Princeton Univ. Press, 1953, pp. 249-73.
Bakhtine, Mikhail. *La Poétique de Dostoievski*. Paris: Seuil, 1970. English version: *Problems of Dostoevsky's Poetics*. Ann Arbor, Mich.: Ardis, 1973.
Barroll, J. Leeds. *Artificial Persons: The Formation of Character in the Tragedies of Shakespeare*. Columbia: Univ. of South Carolina Press, 1974.

Barthes, Roland. "Introduction à l'analyse structurale des récits." *Communications*, 8 (1966), esp. pp. 8-18.
———. "Proust et les noms." In *To Honor Roman Jakobson*. The Hague: Mouton, 1967, I, 150-58.
———. *S/Z*. Paris: Seuil, 1970.
Bayley, John. *The Character of Love: A Study in the Literature of Personality*. New York: Collier, 1963 (1960).
———. "Character and Consciousness." *NLH*, 5 (1974), 225-35.
Beaujour, Michel. *Miroirs d'encre*. Paris: Seuil, 1980.
Benveniste, Emile. "L'Homme dans la langue." In *Problèmes de linguistique générale*. Paris: Gallimard, 1966, esp. pp. 225-66.
———. "L'Appareil formel de l'énonciation." *Langages*, 17 (1970), 12-18; rpt. in *Problèmes de linguistique générale*, II. Paris: Gallimard, 1974.
Bruss, Elizabeth. *Autobiographical Acts*. Baltimore: Johns Hopkins Univ. Press, 1976, esp. pp. 1-31.
Bonnet, Paul. "Les Diverses Manières d'appeler Néron dans *Britannicus*." *Bulletin de Liaison Racinienne*, 6 (1958), 16-18.
Booth, Wayne C. *The Rhetoric of Fiction*. Chicago: Univ. of Chicago Press, 1961.
Bremond, Claude. *Logique du récit*. Paris: Seuil, 1973.
Butor, Michel. "L'Usage des pronoms personnels dans le roman." In *Répertoire II*. Paris: Editions de Minuit, 1959, esp. pp. 61-72.
Chatman, Seymour. "On the Formalist-Structuralist Theory of Character." *Journal of Literary Semantics*, 1 (1972), 57-79.
———. *Story and Discourse*. Ithaca: Cornell Univ. Press, 1978, esp. ch. 3.
Cixous, Hélène. "The Character of 'Character.'" *NLH*, 5 (1974), 383-402.
Compagnon, Antoine. *Nous, Michel de Montaigne*. Paris: Seuil, 1980.
Cook, Albert. "Person." In *Prisms*. Bloomington: Indiana Univ. Press, 1967, pp. 148-87.
Culler, Jonathan. *Structuralist Poetics*. Ithaca: Cornell Univ. Press, 1975, esp. pp. 230-38.
Démoris, René. "La Symbolique du nom de personne dans 'les Liaisons dangereuses.'" *Littérature*, 36 (December 1979), 104-19.
Ducrot, Oswald. "Les Indéfinis et l'énonciation." *Langages*, 17 (March 1970), 91-111.
Epstein, E.L. *Language and Style*. London: Methuen, 1978, esp. ch. 4.
Ferrara, Fernando. "Theory and Model for the Structural Analysis of Fiction." *NLH*, 5 (1974), 244-68.
Fish, Stanley E. "Literature in the Reader: Affective Stylistics." In *Self-Consuming Artifacts*. Berkeley: Univ. of California Press, 1972, pp. 383-427.

Fowler, Roger. *Linguistics and the Novel*. London: Methuen, 1977, esp. pp. 26-38.
Gass, William H. "The Concept of Character in Fiction." In *Fiction and the Figures of Life*. New York: Knopf, 1970, pp. 34-54.
Genette, Gérard. *Figures III*. Paris: Seuil, 1972, esp. pp. 251-67.
Gillie, Christopher. *Character in English Literature*. London: Chatto & Windus, 1967.
Greimas, A.J. "Les Actants, les acteurs et les figures." In *Sémiotique narrative et textuelle*. Eds. Claude Chabrol, et al. Paris: Larousse, 1973, pp. 161-76.
Hamon, Philippe. "Pour un statut sémiologique du personnage." *Littérature*, 6 (1972), 86-110; revised version in *Poétique du récit*. Eds. Roland Barthes, et al. Paris: Seuil, 1977, pp. 115-80.
Harvey, W.J. *Character and the Novel*. Ithaca: Cornell Univ. Press, 1965.
Héroïsme et création littéraire sous les règnes d'Henri IV et de Louis XIII. Paris: Klincksieck, 1974.
Holland, Norman. "Character and Identification." In *The Dynamics of Literary Response*. New York: Oxford Univ. Press, 1968, pp. 262-80.
———. "UNITY IDENTITY TEXT SELF." *PMLA*, 90 (1975), 813-22. Also discussion, *PMLA*, 91 (1976), 293-95, 920-22.
Iser, Wolfgang. *The Implied Reader: Patterns of Communication in Prose Fiction from Bunyan to Beckett*. Baltimore: Johns Hopkins Univ. Press, 1974.
Jakobson, Roman. "Les Embrayeurs, les catégories verbales et le verbe russe." In *Essais de linguistique générale*. Paris: Editions de Minuit, 1963, pp. 176-96. Original English version: "Shifters, Verbal Categories and the Russian Verb." Russian Language Project, Dept. of Slavic Languages and Literatures, Harvard Univ., 1957.
Jost, François. "Le *Je* à la recherche de son identité." *Poétique*, 24 (1975), 479-87.
Kempf, Roger. *Sur le corps romanesque*. Paris: Seuil, 1968.
Krailsheimer, A.J. *Studies in Self-Interest*. Oxford: Clarendon Press, 1962.
Langbaum, Robert. "Character versus Action in Shakespeare." In *The Poetry of Experience*. New York: Norton, 1957, pp. 160-81.
———. *The Mysteries of Identity*. New York: Oxford Univ. Press, 1977, esp. pp. 1-21.
Lecointre, Simone, and Jean Le Galliot. "L'Appareil formel de l'énonciation dans *Jacques le Fataliste*." *Le Français Moderne*, 40 (1972), 221-31.
———. "Le Je(u) de l'énonciation." *Langages*, 31 (1973), 64-79.
Le Huenen, Roland, and Paul Perron. "Le Signifiant du personnage dans 'Eugénie Grandet.'" *Littérature*, 14 (1974), 36-48.

Lejeune, Philippe. *Le Pacte autobiographique*. Paris: Seuil, 1975.
———. *Je est un autre*. Paris: Seuil, 1980.
Léonard, Martine. "Construction de 'l'effet-personnage' dans *La Femme de trente ans*." In *Le Roman de Balzac*. Eds. Roland Le Huenen and Paul Perron. Montreal: Didier, 1980, pp. 41-50.
Lotman, Iouri. "Le Concept de personnage." In *La Structure du texte artistique*. Paris: Gallimard, 1973 (1970), pp. 334-41.
Lyons, John D. "The Cartesian Reader and the Methodic Subject." *L'Esprit Créateur*, 21 (1981), 37-47.
Meyerson, Ignace, ed. *Problèmes de la personne*. The Hague: Mouton, 1973.
Mitterand, Henri. "Corrélations lexicales et organisations du récit: Le vocabulaire du visage, dans *Thérèse Raquin*." In *Linguistique et littérature*. Paris: Nouvelle Critique, 1968, pp. 21-28.
Nelson, Lowry, Jr. "The Fictive Reader and Literary Self-Reflexiveness." In *The Disciplines of Criticism*. Eds. Peter Demetz, *et al*. New Haven: Yale Univ. Press, 1968, pp. 173-91.
Perret, Delphine. "Les Appellatifs: Analyse lexicale et actes de parole." *Langages*, 17 (March 1970), 112-18.
Peytard, Jean. "Signes d'encre ou le personnage-texte." In *Syntagmes*. Paris: Les Belles Lettres, 1971, pp. 115-51.
———. "Approches du personnage." In *Syntagmes*, II. Paris: Les Belles Lettres, 1979, pp. 133-69.
Poulet, Georges. "Phenomenology of Reading." *NLH*, 1 (1969), 53-68.
———. *Entre moi et moi: Essais critiques sur la conscience du moi*. Paris: Corti, 1977, esp. pp. 9-29.
Price, Martin. "The Other Self: Thoughts about Character in the Novel." In *Imagined Worlds: Essays on Some English Novels and Novelists in Honour of John Butt*. Ed. Maynard Mack. London: Methuen, 1968, pp. 279-98.
Prince, Gerald. "Introduction à l'étude du narrataire." *Poétique*, 14 (1973), 178-96.
Proust, Jacques. "Le Corps de Manon." *Littérature*, 4 (December 1971), 5-21.
Rastier, François. *Essais de sémiotique discursive*. Tours: Mame, 1973, pp. 185-221.
Ray, William. "Recognizing Recognition: The Intra-Textual and Extra-Textual Critical Persona." *Diacritics*, 7 (December 1977), 20-33.
Resch, Yannick. *Corps féminin, corps textuel: Essai sur le personnage féminin dans l'œuvre de Colette*. Paris: Klincksieck, 1973.
Richard, Jean-Pierre. "Portrait du personnage." In *Micro-lectures*. Paris: Seuil, 1979, pp. 25-41.

Rousset, Jean. *Forme et signification*. Paris: Corti, 1964.
———. *Narcisse romancier*. Paris: Corti, 1973.
Scholes, Robert, and Robert Kellogg. "Character in Narrative." In *The Nature of Narrative*. New York: Oxford Univ. Press, 1966, pp. 160-206.
Simpson, David. "Putting One's House in Order: The Career of the Self in Descartes' Method." *NLH*, 9 (1977), 83-101.
Slatoff, Walter. *With Respect to Readers*. Ithaca: Cornell Univ. Press, 1970.
Spacks, Patricia Meyer. *Imagining a Self: Autobiography and Novel in Eighteenth-Century England*. Cambridge: Harvard Univ. Press, 1976.
Spitzer, Leo. "The Style of Diderot." In *Linguistics and Literary History*. Princeton: Princeton Univ. Press, 1948, pp. 135-91.
Starobinski, Jean. "Montaigne en mouvement." *Nouvelle Revue Française*, 85-86 (January-February 1960), 16-22, 254-66.
———. "Le Style de l'autobiographie." *Poétique*, 3 (1970), 257-65; also in his *La Relation critique*. Paris: Gallimard, 1971, pp. 83-98. English version in *Literary Style: A Symposium*. Ed. Seymour Chatman. Oxford: Oxford Univ. Press, 1971, pp. 285-96.
Sumi, Yochio. "Autour de l'image du jeu d'échecs chez l'auteur du *Neveu de Rameau*." In *Recherches nouvelles sur quelques écrivains des lumières*. Ed. J. Proust. Geneva: Droz, 1972, pp. 341-63.
Todorov, Tzvetan. *Littérature et signification*. Paris: Larousse, 1967.
———. "La Grammaire du récit." *Langages*, 12 (1968), 94-102.
———. *Grammaire du Décaméron*. The Hague: Mouton, 1969.
———. "Les Hommes-récits." In *Poétique de la prose*. Paris: Seuil, 1971, pp. 78-91.
———. "Personnage." In *Dictionnaire encyclopédique des sciences du langage*. Eds. Oswald Ducrot and Tzvetan Todorov. Paris: Seuil, 1972, pp. 286-92.
Tomachevski, B. "Thématique." In *Théorie de la littérature*. Ed. T. Todorov. Paris: Seuil, 1965, pp. 263-308.
Ubersfeld, Anne. *Lire le théâtre*. Paris: Editions Sociales, 1978, chs. 2, 3, 6.
Vance, Christie. "Rousseau's Autobiographical Venture: A Process of Negation." *Genre*, 6 (March 1973), 98-113.
Vance, Eugene. "Augustine's *Confessions* and the Grammar of Selfhood." *Genre*, 6 (March 1973), 1-28. French version in *Poétique*, 14 (1973), 163-77.
Vannier, Bernard. *L'Inscription du corps: Pour une sémiotique du portrait balzacien*. Paris: Klincksieck, 1972.
Vitz, Evelyn Birge. "Type et individu dans 'l'autobiographie' médiévale." *Poétique*, 24 (1975), 426-45.

Lejeune, Philippe. *Le Pacte autobiographique*. Paris: Seuil, 1975.
———. *Je est un autre*. Paris: Seuil, 1980.
Léonard, Martine. "Construction de 'l'effet-personnage' dans *La Femme de trente ans*." In *Le Roman de Balzac*. Eds. Roland Le Huenen and Paul Perron. Montreal: Didier, 1980, pp. 41-50.
Lotman, Iouri. "Le Concept de personnage." In *La Structure du texte artistique*. Paris: Gallimard, 1973 (1970), pp. 334-41.
Lyons, John D. "The Cartesian Reader and the Methodic Subject." *L'Esprit Créateur*, 21 (1981), 37-47.
Meyerson, Ignace, ed. *Problèmes de la personne*. The Hague: Mouton, 1973.
Mitterand, Henri. "Corrélations lexicales et organisations du récit: Le vocabulaire du visage, dans *Thérèse Raquin*." In *Linguistique et littérature*. Paris: Nouvelle Critique, 1968, pp. 21-28.
Nelson, Lowry, Jr. "The Fictive Reader and Literary Self-Reflexiveness." In *The Disciplines of Criticism*. Eds. Peter Demetz, *et al*. New Haven: Yale Univ. Press, 1968, pp. 173-91.
Perret, Delphine. "Les Appellatifs: Analyse lexicale et actes de parole." *Langages*, 17 (March 1970), 112-18.
Peytard, Jean. "Signes d'encre ou le personnage-texte." In *Syntagmes*. Paris: Les Belles Lettres, 1971, pp. 115-51.
———. "Approches du personnage." In *Syntagmes*, II. Paris: Les Belles Lettres, 1979, pp. 133-69.
Poulet, Georges. "Phenomenology of Reading." *NLH*, 1 (1969), 53-68.
———. *Entre moi et moi: Essais critiques sur la conscience du moi*. Paris: Corti, 1977, esp. pp. 9-29.
Price, Martin. "The Other Self: Thoughts about Character in the Novel." In *Imagined Worlds: Essays on Some English Novels and Novelists in Honour of John Butt*. Ed. Maynard Mack. London: Methuen, 1968, pp. 279-98.
Prince, Gerald. "Introduction à l'étude du narrataire." *Poétique*, 14 (1973), 178-96.
Proust, Jacques. "Le Corps de Manon." *Littérature*, 4 (December 1971), 5-21.
Rastier, François. *Essais de sémiotique discursive*. Tours: Mame, 1973, pp. 185-221.
Ray, William. "Recognizing Recognition: The Intra-Textual and Extra-Textual Critical Persona." *Diacritics*, 7 (December 1977), 20-33.
Resch, Yannick. *Corps féminin, corps textuel: Essai sur le personnage féminin dans l'œuvre de Colette*. Paris: Klincksieck, 1973.
Richard, Jean-Pierre. "Portrait du personnage." In *Micro-lectures*. Paris: Seuil, 1979, pp. 25-41.

Rousset, Jean. *Forme et signification*. Paris: Corti, 1964.
———. *Narcisse romancier*. Paris: Corti, 1973.
Scholes, Robert, and Robert Kellogg. "Character in Narrative." In *The Nature of Narrative*. New York: Oxford Univ. Press, 1966, pp. 160-206.
Simpson, David. "Putting One's House in Order: The Career of the Self in Descartes' Method." *NLH*, 9 (1977), 83-101.
Slatoff, Walter. *With Respect to Readers*. Ithaca: Cornell Univ. Press, 1970.
Spacks, Patricia Meyer. *Imagining a Self: Autobiography and Novel in Eighteenth-Century England*. Cambridge: Harvard Univ. Press, 1976.
Spitzer, Leo. "The Style of Diderot." In *Linguistics and Literary History*. Princeton: Princeton Univ. Press, 1948, pp. 135-91.
Starobinski, Jean. "Montaigne en mouvement." *Nouvelle Revue Française*, 85-86 (January-February 1960), 16-22, 254-66.
———. "Le Style de l'autobiographie." *Poétique*, 3 (1970), 257-65; also in his *La Relation critique*. Paris: Gallimard, 1971, pp. 83-98. English version in *Literary Style: A Symposium*. Ed. Seymour Chatman. Oxford: Oxford Univ. Press, 1971, pp. 285-96.
Sumi, Yochio. "Autour de l'image du jeu d'échecs chez l'auteur du *Neveu de Rameau*." In *Recherches nouvelles sur quelques écrivains des lumières*. Ed. J. Proust. Geneva: Droz, 1972, pp. 341-63.
Todorov, Tzvetan. *Littérature et signification*. Paris: Larousse, 1967.
———. "La Grammaire du récit." *Langages*, 12 (1968), 94-102.
———. *Grammaire du Décaméron*. The Hague: Mouton, 1969.
———. "Les Hommes-récits." In *Poétique de la prose*. Paris: Seuil, 1971, pp. 78-91.
———. "Personnage." In *Dictionnaire encyclopédique des sciences du langage*. Eds. Oswald Ducrot and Tzvetan Todorov. Paris: Seuil, 1972, pp. 286-92.
Tomachevski, B. "Thématique." In *Théorie de la littérature*. Ed. T. Todorov. Paris: Seuil, 1965, pp. 263-308.
Ubersfeld, Anne. *Lire le théâtre*. Paris: Editions Sociales, 1978, chs. 2, 3, 6.
Vance, Christie. "Rousseau's Autobiographical Venture: A Process of Negation." *Genre*, 6 (March 1973), 98-113.
Vance, Eugene. "Augustine's *Confessions* and the Grammar of Selfhood." *Genre*, 6 (March 1973), 1-28. French version in *Poétique*, 14 (1973), 163-77.
Vannier, Bernard. *L'Inscription du corps: Pour une sémiotique du portrait balzacien*. Paris: Klincksieck, 1972.
Vitz, Evelyn Birge. "Type et individu dans 'l'autobiographie' médiévale." *Poétique*, 24 (1975), 426-45.

Webber, Joan. *The Eloquent "I": Studies in Style and Self*. Madison: Univ. of Wisconsin Press, 1968.
Wilson, Rawdon. "The Bright Chimera: Character as a Literary Term." *Critical Inquiry*, 5 (1979), 725-49.
Zéraffa, Michel. *Personne et personnage*. Paris: Klincksieck, 1969.

FRENCH FORUM MONOGRAPHS

1. Karolyn Waterson. *Molière et l'autorité: Structures sociales, structures comiques.* 1976.
2. Donna Kuizenga. *Narrative Strategies in* La Princesse de Clèves. 1976.
3. Ian J. Winter. *Montaigne's Self-Portrait and Its Influence in France, 1580-1630.* 1976.
4. Judith G. Miller. *Theater and Revolution in France since 1968.* 1977.
5. Raymond C. La Charité, ed. *O un amy! Essays on Montaigne in Honor of Donald M. Frame.* 1977.
6. Rupert T. Pickens. *The Welsh Knight: Paradoxicality in Chrétien's* Conte del Graal. 1977.
7. Carol Clark. *The Web of Metaphor: Studies in the Imagery of Montaigne's Essais.* 1978.
8. Donald Maddox. *Structure and Sacring: The Systematic Kingdom in Chrétien's* Erec et Enide. 1978.
9. Betty J. Davis. *The Storytellers in Marguerite de Navarre's* Heptaméron. 1978.
10. Laurence M. Porter. *The Renaissance of the Lyric in French Romanticism: Elegy, "Poëme" and Ode.* 1978.
11. Bruce R. Leslie. *Ronsard's Successful Epic Venture: The Epyllion.* 1979.
12. Michelle A. Freeman. *The Poetics of* Translatio Studii *and* Conjointure: *Chrétien de Troyes's* Cligés. 1979.
13. Robert T. Corum, Jr. *Other Worlds and Other Seas: Art and Vision in Saint-Amant's Nature Poetry.* 1979.
14. Marcel Muller. *Préfiguration et structure romanesque dans* A la recherche du temps perdu *(avec un inédit de Marcel Proust).* 1979.
15. Ross Chambers. *Meaning and Meaningfulness: Studies in the Analysis and Interpretation of Texts.* 1979.
16. Lois Oppenheim. *Intentionality and Intersubjectivity: A Phenomenological Study of Butor's* La Modification. 1980.
17. Matilda T. Bruckner. *Narrative Invention in Twelfth-Century French Romance: The Convention of Hospitality (1160-1200).* 1980.
18. Gérard Defaux. *Molière, ou les métamorphoses du comique: De la comédie morale au triomphe de la folie.* 1980.
19. Raymond C. La Charité. *Recreation, Reflection and Re-Creation: Perspectives on Rabelais's* Pantagruel. 1980.
20. Jules Brody. *Du style à la pensée: Trois études sur les* Caractères *de La Bruyère.* 1980.
21. Lawrence D. Kritzman. *Destruction/Découverte: Le Fonctionnement de la rhétorique dans les* Essais de Montaigne. 1980.
22. Minnette Grunmann-Gaudet and Robin F. Jones, eds. *The Nature of Medieval Narrative.* 1980.
23. J.A. Hiddleston. *Essai sur Laforgue et les* Derniers Vers *suivi de Laforgue et Baudelaire.* 1980.
24. Michael S. Koppisch. *The Dissolution of Character: Changing Perspectives in La Bruyère's* Caractères. 1981.
25. Hope H. Glidden. *The Storyteller as Humanist: The* Serées *of Guillaume Bouchet.* 1981.
26. Mary B. McKinley. *Words in a Corner: Studies in Montaigne's Latin Quotations.* 1981.

27. Donald M. Frame and Mary B. McKinley, eds. *Columbia Montaigne Conference Papers*. 1981.
28. Jean-Pierre Dens. *L'Honnête Homme et la critique du goût: Esthétique et société au XVIIe siècle*. 1981.
29. Vivian Kogan. *The Flowers of Fiction: Time and Space in Raymond Queneau's Les Fleurs bleues*. 1982.
30. Michael Issacharoff et Jean-Claude Vilquin, éds. *Sartre et la mise en signe*. 1982.
31. James W. Mileham. *The Conspiracy Novel: Structure and Metaphor in Balzac's Comédie humaine*. 1982.
32. Andrew G. Suozzo, Jr. *The Comic Novels of Charles Sorel: A Study of Structure, Characterization and Disguise*. 1982.
33. Margaret Whitford. *Merleau-Ponty's Critique of Sartre's Philosophy*. 1982.
34. Gérard Defaux. *Le Curieux, le glorieux et la sagesse du monde dans la première moitié du XVIe siècle: L'exemple de Panurge (Ulysse, Démosthène, Empédocle)*. 1982.
35. Doranne Fenoaltea. *"Si haulte Architecture." The Design of Scève's Délie*. 1982.
36. Peter Bayley and Dorothy Gabe Coleman, eds. *The Equilibrium of Wit: Essays for Odette de Mourgues*. 1982.
37. Carol J. Murphy. *Alienation and Absence in the Novels of Marguerite Duras*. 1982.
38. Mary Ellen Birkett. *Lamartine and the Poetics of Landscape*. 1982.
39. Jules Brody. *Lectures de Montaigne*. 1982.
40. John D. Lyons. *The Listening Voice: An Essay on the Rhetoric of Saint-Amant*. 1982.
41. Edward C. Knox. *Patterns of Person: Studies in Style and Form from Corneille to Laclos*. 1983.

French Forum, Publishers, Inc.
P.O. Box 5108, Lexington, Kentucky 40505

Publishers of *French Forum*, a journal of literary criticism